The People of a Suffolk Town

Halesworth 1100 - 1900

Michael and Sheila Gooch

First published 1999
Copyright © 1999 Michael and Sheila Gooch
ISBN 0 9523245 1 2

Published by   Michael and Sheila Gooch
                  2 London Road
                  Halesworth
                  Suffolk IP19 8LH

Designed by   Simon Gooch

Printed by   Technographic Design & Print Ltd
                  Colchester, Essex CO7 0SX and
                  Halesworth, Suffolk IP19 8TS

Cover Picture: The Saltonstall Family 1636-7 by David Des Granges
                  The Tate Gallery, London 1999

Contents

Introduction and Abbreviations   5

Part One - 12th to 17th Centuries

Argentein Family, *Lords of the Manor* c.1130 to 1424   8
Payn, Adam *Cleric* fl.1361   10
Garveys, Robert *Extortioner* fl.1364-8   11
Allington Family *Lords of the Manor* 1424 to 1706   12
Clement, Thomas *Benefactor* died 1438   14
Norton Family c.1460 to 1673   15
Annable, Walter *Rector* died 1465   18
Everard, John died 1476   19
Popson, Thomas *Schoolmaster* 1532-?96   20
Argall, John *Rector* c.1542-c.1609   21
Moore, Phillip *Physician* fl.1565   23
Browne, John *Progenitor* died 1581   23
Feltham, Thomas *Man of Property* died 1591   24
Assheton, James *Rector* 1573-?1644   25
Ingham Family 1580 to 1776   27
Saltonstall and Base Families 1596 to 1688   29
Fawether, Samuel *Justice* c.1620-56   31
Cary, William *Benefactor* 1622-86   32
Bedingfield Family 1638 to 1705   34
Betts, William *Lord of the Manor* 1650-1709   37
Lone, Roger *Petitioner* fl.1675   39
Pullyn, Peter *Attorney* 1688-1753   39
Kirby, John *Surveyor* c.1690-1753   41
Badeley Family 1693 to 1899   45

Part Two - 18th Century

Anguish, Thomas *Rector* 1700-63   48
Jermyn Family 1708 to 1857   49
Forster, Thomas *Rector* c.1710-85   53
Norford, William *Surgeon* ?1715-93   55
Plumer Family *Lords of the Manor* 1739 to 1833   57
Dresser and Day Families 1746 to 1855   58
Suggate, George *Watchmaker etc* 1751-1844   60
Woodcock, John *Banker* 1751-1801   61
Langslow, Richard *Physician* 1752-1812   65
Robinson, Francis *Man of Property* 1756-1843   69
Tanqueray, Thomas *Schoolmaster and Clergyman* 1763-1841   71
Cufaude, John *Attorney* 1765-1837   73
Dennant, John *Minister* 1766-1851   74

White, Robert Gostlin *Attorney* 1767-1828   77
Hugman, John *Poet and Tanner* 1770-1846   80
Tuthill, Sir George Leman *Physician* 1772-1835   82
Crabtree, Robert 1772-1840 and John 1806-70 *Attorneys*   84
D'Urban, Sir Benjamin *Soldier* 1777-1849   88
Easterson, Thomas *Ironfounder* 1777-1858   93
Baas, Robert *Gentleman* 1778-1875   95
Tippell, Thomas *Printer* 1780-1855   96
Packard, Harrison *Cleric* 1783-1860   98
Hooker, Sir William Jackson 1785-1865
    and Sir Joseph Dalton 1817-1911 *Botanists*   101
Wilkinson, John Brewster *Cleric* 1785-1862   104
Turner, James *Banker* 1786-1820   106
Stead, Patrick *Maltster* 1787-1869   109
Whately, Richard *Rector and Archbishop* 1787-1863   113
Appleton, Robert *Architect* 1790-1859   116
Pedgrift Family 1790 to 1896   118
Canova, Peter *Jeweller* 1796-1882   120
Harvey, Joseph *Schoolmaster* 1797-1861   122
Hankinson, Robert Edwards *Rector* 1798-1868   124
Johnston, Andrew *Banker* 1798-1862   127

Part Three - 19th Century
Turner, Samuel Blois *Cleric and Antiquary* 1805-82   134
Gilbert, Wilkinson John *Artist* born 1805   136
George, Thompson *Maltster* 1806-74   139
Phipps, Augustus Frederick *Rector* 1809-96   141
Burleigh, Robert William *Maltster* 1815-83   142
Cross, Frederick *Solicitor* 1818-92   143
Babington, Francis Evans *Banker* 1830-1920   144
Upcher, Abbott Roland *Rector* 1849-1929   145
Lansbury, George *Politician* 1859-1940   146
Dennington, Ernest Edward *Manufacturer* 1862-1927   149
Rugby, Lord *Colonial Governor* 1877-1969   152

Appendix I. Lords of the Manor of Halesworth   155
Appendix II. The Argentein manors and holdings   156
Appendix III. List of Rectors of Halesworth   157

Index of Names   158

Introduction

In 1994 we published *The Story of a Suffolk House*, an account of what is now known as Gothic House, Halesworth, over some five hundred years. This was the fruit of four years' research, in the course of which we came to realise that an apparently rather ordinary market town had a complex history full of interesting families and characters. This immediately set the theme for another book, and five years later here it is.

Halesworth's reputation as "a town without any history", compared to such neighbours as Bungay, Beccles and Southwold, was not helped by Sir Nikolaus Pevsner having a bad day there in 1961 and writing "there is nothing of special architectural interest in Halesworth". This by-passing of the town by historians means that the Halesworth researcher is working in an almost virgin field, and exciting discoveries may be made at any time.

Now for the form of this book: after much pruning we have sixty-eight brief biographies, some covering one individual and others a family. These are arranged chronologically by date of birth, or first appearance, in three sections: the first up to 1699, the second to 1799, and the third to 1899. We have gone back to primary sources wherever possible, and these are listed at the end of each item. With persons who achieved wider fame - usually those included in the *Dictionary of National Biography* - we have generally accepted the descriptions of their later careers, but have carefully checked, and in some cases revised, their local connections. Where we do not know we have said so, and we hope some of our readers may be able to fill the gaps. **Bold type** is used in the text to assist in cross-referencing to other biographies.

Finally a few words of thanks. Anyone writing about the people of this corner of Suffolk owes a tremendous debt to Rachel Lawrence, author of *Southwold River* (1990, 1997). Despite its title her book is equally concerned with Halesworth people of the 18th and 19th centuries, and her painstaking researches form a solid basis for any further enquiry. Another author, whom we cannot thank in person, is the late James Newby, whose pioneering books on Independency (1936) and Patrick Stead (1964) cover much more than their titles suggest.

For reading through and commenting on our drafts we have to thank Dr Anthony Batty Shaw on D'Urban and Gooch; Dr John Blatchly on Kirby and Jermyn; Tony Copsey on publications; and Professor Colin Richmond on our Medieval characters. Many other friends have given encouragement and advice. Numerous libraries and record offices have been visited, but we are particularly grateful to the staff of the Suffolk Record Office, especially the Lowestoft branch; the Norfolk Record Office and the Norfolk Studies Library; and Halesworth Library for obtaining so many obscure books. Illustrations have come from many sources, and these are acknowledged individually in the text, but we must thank the Halesworth Team Ministry and Parochial Church Council for permission to reproduce documents in the parish collection held at Lowestoft Record Office; Cross, Ram, solicitors of Halesworth; Rodwell & Co., solicitors of Halesworth; and finally Peter Punchard for allowing us to reproduce items from his unrivalled collection of early Halesworth photographs.

Abbreviations

Alumni Cantab.: Venn, J. *Alumni Cantabrigensis* (1922)
Alumni Oxon.: Foster, J. *Alumni Oxoniensis* (1891)
Blomefield: Blomefield, F. *History of Norfolk*
Brown, Haward & Kindred: *Dictionary of Architects of Suffolk Buildings* (1991)
C.A.P.C.: Calendar of Acts of the Privy Council
C.C.R.: Calendar of Close Rolls
C.I.P.M.: Calendar of Inquisitions Post Mortem
C.P.R.: Calendar of Patent Rolls
C.R.S.: Catholic Records Society
C.S.P.: Calendar of State Papers
Copinger: Copinger, W.A. *The Manors of Suffolk* (1905)
Copsey: Copsey, A.T. *Book Distribution and Printing in Suffolk* (1994)
D.N.B.: Dictionary of National Biography
Farrer: Farrer, A. *Heraldry in Norfolk Churches*
Gooch, M & S: *The Story of a Suffolk House* (1994)
H.M.C.R.: Halesworth Manor Court Rolls
H.P.R.: Halesworth Parish Registers (SROL)
H.R.M.C.R.: Halesworth Rectory Manor Court Rolls (SROL)
I.G.I.: International Genealogical Index
Lawrence, R. (1986): *An Early 19th Century Malting Business*, P.S.I.A. XXXVI
Lawrence, R. (1990): *Southwold River*
Munk's Roll: Roll of the College of Physicians
Muskett: *Suffolk Armorial Families*
Newby (1936): *History of Independency in Halesworth and District*
Newby (1964): *The Patrick Stead Hospital*
Palmer: Palmer, C.J. *The Perlustration of Great Yarmouth*
P.C.C.: Prerogative Court of Canterbury
P.R.O.: Public Record Office
P.S.I.A.: Proceedings of the Suffolk Institute of Archaeology
Suckling: Suckling, A. *History and Antiquities of Suffolk* (1846)
S.R.O.B.: Suffolk Record Office, Bury St Edmund's
S.R.O.I.: Suffolk Record Office, Ipswich
S.R.O.L.: Suffolk Record Office, Lowestoft
T.S.N.S.: Transactions of Suffolk Naturalists' Society
Van Zwanenburg: M.S. notes on Suffolk doctors - SROI
V.C.H.: Victoria County Histories
W.E.A.: Workers' Educational Association

Part One

12th to 17th Centuries

Argentein Family *Lords of the Manor* c.1130 to 1424

Argenteins held the Manors of Halesworth and Dame Margery's in Halesworth for about three centuries. As so often happened, these manors came into the family by a marriage - Sir Reginald Argentein to Rose, heiress of Thomas de Halesworth, before 1130. By about 1420 the last male Argentein had died out and the line was extinct, the property passing, again by marriage, to the **Allingtons**.

For three hundred years the Argenteins ruled their manors, not only in Halesworth and other parts of Suffolk, but in no less than eleven counties in the South of England; they also held many important offices from the Crown. In spite of this there is no great house to remind us of past glories, indeed the Manor House at Halesworth was reported, in *The Chorography of Suffolk*, as "ruinated" and its park "disparked" as early as 1602.

The main manors and presumably the Argenteins' main residence were at Great and Little Wymondley in Hertfordshire, which they held as of the right of Cup Bearer to the King at his coronation; however, they must have also held an important post in Suffolk as at least two holders of the title chose to be buried in Halesworth church. A curious story is told of the obsequies of Sir John Argentein, who died in 1383 and wished to be buried in the town. His ancestor Sir Richard had founded a priory at Little Wymondley, part of which still exists, whose Prior had been entrusted with the deeds of Sir John's properties. The Prior was on his way to Halesworth for the funeral when he and his companions were waylaid on Newmarket Heath and compelled to return to Little Wymondley, then bring the deeds in a chest to be handed over to William, Sir John's illegitimate son. Not only that, but Sir John's daughter Margaret (or Matilda) and her husband Ivo FitzWaryn and their companions were assaulted at Halesworth by William's faction, and claimed they could not therefore carry out a decent burial.

Where the organ now stands in the church was the entry to the Argentein chapel, but it is not clear whether this existed before the disastrous funeral or was built as a face-saver afterwards by Sir William. His slab, the brass having been removed, now lies in the Chancel South chapel where it was moved at a later date.

The Chorography of Suffolk tells us: "In the Chauncell there layeth under a marble stone buryed Sir William Argentein over his head this superscription in brasse

'Hic jacet Gulielmus Argentein miles D'nus de Halesworth qui obiit 15
die mensis Februar' A'o D'ni 1418 cuius a'i'e. p'pit. Deus'
He layeth pictured in brasse in complet Armour treading upon a lyon about his neck a coller of SS. On it were 2 escutcheons on eyther side of him but are both taken away". It is possible to see the indents of the brasses and to imagine the tomb complete.

The stained glass shields in the Chancel's South window, showing Argentein three cups, Allington six billets and the combined arms must date from after the marriages of Sir William's granddaughters, after 1400. The full line of descent can be read in Suckling's *History and Antiquities of Suffolk* and Copinger's *Manors of*

Suffolk, but some details will serve to give an idea of the importance of this family.

Reginald de Argentein, who died about 1223, was Sheriff of Hertford-shire and Essex, and a King's Justice in 1198. His son Richard, who died in 1246, was also Sheriff, as well as Custodian of Hertford Castle, Steward of Henry III's Household and a Justice in Normandy. It was this Richard who obtained the grant of a market at Newmarket in 1227 and at Halesworth in 1229. He took part in more than one Crusade, and Matthew Paris lists him as amongst the nobles who died in England in 1246 and whose death was consid-ered a great loss to the kingdom. Paris describes him as "a brave knight who had long fought faithful-ly for God in the Holy Land". Richard founded the Priory at Wymondley mentioned above and also the Hospice of St John and St James and the Leper Hospital of St Nicholas, both in Royston, Hertfordshire.

Richard's son Sir Giles Argentein, who died in 1283, played an equally important national role, and must have led a very busy life. In 1231 he fought and was imprisoned in Wales; in 1241 he was in Gascony; he was Governor of Windsor Castle in 1262 and fought in the Battle of Lewes in 1265 with Simon de Montfort. He was also a Member of Parliament in 1258. His wife was Matilda, daughter of Sir Robert de Aiguillon who held lands at Flitcham, Norfolk. Sir Giles was her sec-ond husband.

Their son Reginald, born 1242, made a very good match by marrying Lora, sister of Robert de Vere, 5th Earl of Oxford, who held Castle Hedingham in Essex, and was Hereditary Chamberlain to the King. This linked rather neatly with the

9

Argenteins' royal service as Butler. At Henry III's coronation, Hugh de Vere served the King with water, basins and towels and Reginald de Argentein served the King with wine in a silver gilt cup. Both Stewards were allowed to retain these items in their families.

Sir Reginald and Lora's son John married twice: firstly Joan Bryan of Hatley, Bedfordshire, then Agnes de Bereford, daughter of William de Bereford of Ketteringham and Melton, Norfolk. When this John died in 1318 his son and heir, also John, was less than a year old. His mother Agnes thus held all the estates, and John did not finally inherit them until 1375, after his mother's death. He had married Margaret, daughter of Robert D'Arcy of the D'Arcy family of Great Sturton, Lincolnshire and Danbury, Essex; it was at John's death that the great wrangle arose with William, the illegitimate son, as Margaret had produced three daughters - Matilda (Maud), Elizabeth and Joan - but no sons.

As has been previously described, Sir William successfully claimed the properties, by fair means or foul. His first wife was Isabel, daughter of Sir William Kerdiston of Little Melton, Norfolk; he later married twice more. In his will of 1417, written at Halesworth and proved 1419, he bequeathed 20 shillings to the high altar of Halesworth church and £5 for repairs to the fabric. At the premature death of his grandson John, his heir, in 1423, everything went to John's sisters Joan and Elizabeth, who had married the Allington brothers - Robert and William, of Horseheath, Cambridgeshire. Thus the Halesworth Manor finally passed from the Argentein family.

There are no portraits of the Argenteins so far discovered, but there is a memorial brass dated 1427 to Sir William's third wife, Lady Margaret (Hervey) at Elstow Priory, near Bedford; it is illustrated in Pevsner's *Bedfordshire*, The Buildings of England (1974), p85. The British Library (Sloane 1301 f.146v), has drawings of Argentein tomb slabs from the Priory, and one now in Baldock church.

Sources

Gooch, M & S / D.N.B. / Suckling Vol II / Blois, Sir I. 'Genealogy of a Suffolk Family', Add. MSS, British Library / Copinger / Blomefield *History of Norfolk* Vol 5 / V.C.H. Bedfordshire and Hertfordshire / Hore, J.P. *The History of Newmarket* Vol I (1885) / Testa de Nevill / Foss's Judges / Black Prince's Register / State Papers, various / Anderson, Verily *The De Veres of Castle Hedingham*, T.Dalton (1993) / Middleton-Stewart, Dr J. / *History of Parliament* Vol II (1992)

Payn, Adam *Cleric* fl. 1361

A Clerk in Holy Orders, Adam Payn's name appears in connection with the Halesworth Manor, in an Inquisition Post Mortem of 1382/3, after the death of **Sir John Argentein**, as holding the Manor on behalf of Margaret, the wife of Sir John. According to Suckling's *History of Suffolk*, Adam was Rector of Brampton, near Halesworth, from 1361 to 1405. In a Close Roll of 24th September 1334, Geoffrey Payn is described as "of Halesworth", and in 1346 was attorney to Sir Robert de Ufford, Earl of Suffolk. It seems fair to assume that Adam was a son of Geoffrey. In 1347 a Sir Geoffrey Payn was killed at the Siege of Calais, together with Sir John Payn.

William Payn was an executor of Ivo Fitz Waryn in June 1391; he may not be connected to Adam, but Ivo Fitz Waryn was the husband of Matilda, daughter of Sir John Argentein.

John Payn and Roger Payn both figure in an account roll of Halesworth Rectory Manor, 1377-99.

Adam Payn held not only Halesworth Manor but also Ketteringham and Little Melton, Norfolk - both Argentein holdings.

Sources

Suckling / I.P.M. Vol XV 1-7 Richard II (1377-1383) / Close Rolls: Edward III 1333-1337; 14 Richard II June 1391, also 27 August, 1346

Garveys, Robert *Extortioner* fl 1364-8

Robert Garveys was a local villain whose villainy was sufficiently annoying to have ensured him a sort of immortality in the Public Record Office. This document tells all we know about him:-

"13. On the Tuesday after the nativity of St John the Baptist 41 Edward III (1367-8) Robert Garveys came to Alan Bolt at Halesworth and charged him with trespass against him and his, threatening him in life and limb, for fear of which he made a fine of half a mark with the said Robert who is a common threatener of people.

14. On Whit Monday 38 Edward III (1364-5) the said Robert came to James Shoute of Halesworth and threatened to beat him, for fear of which he made a fine of 40d. with the said Robert against his will and by extortion and the said Robert is a common extortioner.

15. On Michaelmas Day 41 Edward III the said Robert came and assaulted Thomas Ulf at Rumburgh and beat and ill-treated him so that his life was despaired of, and the said Robert is a common insulter.

Duplicated and sent before the King".

Source

Inquisitiones Misc. (Chancery) vol III p699

Allington Family *Lords of the Manor* 1424 to 1706

After the long tenure of the **Argentein** family, the Manor of Halesworth and the lesser Manor of Dame Margery's passed by marriage to the Cambridgeshire family of Allington. The male line of Argenteins came to an end with Sir John, who died in 1423-4 leaving as co-heiresses his two sisters. They married two Allington brothers - Elizabeth to William and Joan to Robert, and the elder, William, inherited the widespread Argentein estates, including the Manor and Advowson of Halesworth.

The Allington family had been seated for at least one generation at Horseheath, a few miles South of Newmarket, which was one of the Argenteins' principal manors, so this proximity may explain the double marriage. With the Argenteins' property at Wymondley in Hertfordshire the Allingtons also acquired the honour of being Cup-Bearer at all coronations. William died in 1459 and like all the family was buried at Horseheath. He was succeeded by John, who was recorded as holding manors in Buckinghamshire, Bedfordshire, Suffolk, Hertfordshire, Essex, and no less than six in Cambridgeshire.

John's son William succeeded in 1480 but backed the wrong side at Bosworth Field, 1485, and died in battle aged only thirty-five. His heir was twelve-year old Giles who later bore the cup at the coronation of Henry VIII, and attended the Field of the Cloth of Gold, but died aged just thirty-two.

Another Giles succeeded him, aged twenty, and - unusually for the Allingtons - lived into his eighties. He was Sheriff of Cambridgeshire and Huntingdon, was present at the Siege of Boulogne in 1544, and married three times, his last wife being Margaret, mother of **John Argall**, a notable Rector of Halesworth. Sir Giles lived long enough to have the expensive honour of entertaining Queen Elizabeth and her retinue at Horseheath during the Royal Progress of 1578. The royal party arrived from nearby Kirtling Hall, the seat of Lord North, on the 3rd of September and probably stayed four days, during which the Privy Council met twice to consider various weighty matters.

Sir Giles died in 1586, but Margaret lived a further five years. Her will, proved on 30th September 1592, shows that she returned for burial to her London origins - "to be buried in the parish church of St Faith's under Powles, late called the Jesus Chapel, in the tombe where my late husband Thomas Argall Esq. deceased, lyeth buried". This was a small church literally under Old St Paul's. It and its monuments disappeared under the crypt of Wren's great cathedral. The will is entirely concerned with her Argall relations, including her son John, of Halesworth, and his daughter Mary, who is to get £100 for her marriage portion.

Two generations of heirs had died during Sir Giles's long life, and he was succeeded by his great-grandson, another Giles, in 1586, then aged fourteen, who later got into trouble for marrying, as his second wife, his niece Dorothy Dalton, for which he was fined heavily. He died in 1638 and was succeeded by his son William who became the first Baron Allington, the Irish title being granted in 1642, but died young in 1648. His son, another William, became MP for Cambridgeshire and Lord Lieutenant, and in 1682 was raised to the English peerage as Baron Allington of Wymondley. He embarked in 1663 on an ambitious rebuilding of Horseheath Hall, the architect being Sir Roger Pratt of Ryston in West Norfolk. John Evelyn visited the house in 1670 and believed it had cost "little less than 20,000 pounds". A less flattering glimpse comes from Samuel Pepys, who was in 1667 discussing the vacant Governorship of Tangier with Sir H. Cholmly who "showed me a young silly Lord (one Lord Allington) who hath offered a great sum of money to go... he having a fine Lady, and a great man would be glad to have him out of the way".

As so often pride went before a dramatic fall. William had no male heirs and of his two brothers Argentine was killed in action with the Navy and Hildebrand never married. In 1684 Hildebrand succeeded, but in 1700 sold the Hall and most of the estate to John Bromley, a Barbados planter, for £42,000. Involved in the sale was **William Betts**, a lawyer of London and Yoxford, and in 1706 the Manor of Halesworth was sold to him. Hildebrand, Lord Allington, died in 1722, and the title died with him. Horseheath Hall fared little better, being completely demolished in 1777, and all that survives are two splendid pairs of wrought iron gates on Queen's Road, Cambridge, one opening into the grounds of Trinity College and the other to St John's.

Looking now at the Allingtons' Halesworth connection, it is evident that in their earlier years they maintained a house in the town - John Paston III called there on the 2nd June 1464 in order to get support in his lawsuit with the Jenney family, and wrote thence to his father "Ther are no more at home bot John Alyngton, and I shewyd hym the byll of the names of the inquest... and to all of them A. sent a man of hys... Wretyn in hast at Hallysworthe the Saterday next after Trinite Sonday, your sone and lowly servant John P. he yongest".

There are other signs of the Allington family's close interest in Halesworth at this period. The Rector, **Walter Annable**, was godfather to John Allington's daughter Mary, and in his will of 1465 named John as principal executor, while Elizabeth Morell, who died at Halesworth in 1469, described John Allington as her master, but had been godmother to Mary and her sister Elizabeth.

By the 17th century things were very different and the Allingtons were absentee Lords. *The Chorography of Suffolk*, in 1602, says "In this towne was a parke and in it a goodly house, the one now ruinated and the other disparked; the parke was let out by Coppye by old Sir Giles Allington Knight when he left Suffolke to dwell at Horseheath Hall in Cambridgeshire, who was great grandfather to Giles Allington Esq. who is now possessed thereof".

"Old Sir Giles" had been Lord from 1522 to 1586 and it is likely that the Hall in Halesworth had been vacated by 1577 when a detailed survey of the Manor mentions "the site of the Manor, in tenure of Richard Sone". The wording of the survey however suggests that this was quite recent as it also mentions "the way leading towards the Park", "the great garden of the Lord", and "the Lord's way". The site of the Manor is now Church Farm, but names persist and on the 1839 tithe map a ten acre field by Church Farm was still known as "Great Park".

Sources

Suckling II / Parsons, C. *Horseheath Hall and its Owners* / Davis, N. *Paston Letters and papers of the 15th Century* (1971) / MacCulloch, D. *The Chorography of Suffolk,*

S.R.S. (1976) / Richmond, C. *Halesworth Church and its 15th Century Benefactors* (1996) / Dovey, Z. *An Elizabethan Progress* (1996) / Halesworth W.E.A. *Towards a Local History* / Will of Margaret - PROB.11.80f.72Harrington

Clement, Thomas *Benefactor* died 1438

One of the finest interior features of Halesworth church is the door from the chancel into the vestry [see illustration]. It has been rather heavily restored, like much in this church, but enough original work survives to show its quality. Above the label is an inscription, flanked by two angels holding shields, in black letter, reading "Orate p. aiabus Thome Clement et Margarete cosortis sue qui istud vestiarum fieri fecunt" [Pray for the souls of Thomas Clement and Margaret his consort who caused this vestry to be made]. Oddly, the letterer ran out of space and the last two words are on the shield of the right-hand angel.

Thomas Clement died in 1438, his will being written in September and proved the following month. Margaret is the first named of the five executors and the later Rector **Walter Annable** is a witness. Thomas asks to be buried in the churchyard and leaves twenty shillings for church repairs. Apart from this small sums go to the chaplain John Sharpe and the parish clerk, and one shilling each to his sons and daughters, who are not named. There is no mention of the vestry, so it must have been complete by the date of his death, apart from the inscription.

Other documents throw slightly more light on Thomas. In the Calendar of Patent Rolls, dated November 1429, is a pardon to Robert Fitz Rauf of Keteryngham, Norfolk, for not appearing before the Justices to answer John Reve, late chaplain of Halesworth, and Thomas Clement of Halesworth touching a debt of five marks. In the Iveagh manuscripts at Ipswich Record Office is a feoffment dated September 1433 regarding properties in Halesworth, Holton and Mells owned by Roger Barker, in which Walter Annable, clerk, is one of the feoffees and Thomas

Entry to the Clement vestry in Halesworth church

14

Clement one of the witnesses. Finally, again in the Patent Rolls, there is a dispute over Thomas's will in February 1462 in which Thomas Barker late of Halesworth, husbandman, failed to appear before Justices in the late reign (ie before March 1461) touching a plea that he render forty shillings to John Cobbe, chaplain, Robert Borell, Nicholas Stampard and William Elmy, executors of the will of Thomas Clement, late of Halesworth.

Sources

Richmond, C *Halesworth Church and Fifteenth Century Benefactors* (1996) / C.P.R: Henry VI 10.11.1429 & Edward IV 6.2.1462 / Iveagh MS: SROI. ref 1538/245/5

The Norton Family c.1460 to 1673

The first member of the Norton family to be firmly placed in Halesworth was Walter, son of Andrew, who was descended from a long line of North Country Nortons and Conyers. These families were described in *The Story of a Suffolk House* (M&S Gooch, 1994). Walter Norton was a wealthy merchant; he married twice and by his first wife Joan had a son, Robert, born 1500.

It was Robert who established the Norton presence in Halesworth by building Gothic House, opposite the church. In erecting this prominent building he joined together two holdings (Baxter's and Bunting's). Baxter's we assume to be the South end of the block (now part of Dairy Farm), and as the building appears today it can clearly be seen as the lower end, with half-timbering exposed, and a rather odd roofline. It is now believed that originally this end showed a gable to the road, and extended towards Gothic House. When the new frontage was built by Robert Norton it terminated with a gable to match the North end, but this formed a valley gutter between the two premises which was covered by extending the main roof not long after. This has been proved by the discovery of a blocked mullion window in the roof space of Dairy Farm.

Robert was middle-aged when his father died, and he had already a family of seven children by his wife Mary Copcot of Hertfordshire. He held extensive lands and manors in the vicinity of Halesworth, Wissett and Holton and the surrounding area. He also supplied large quantities of Suffolk cheese and butter to the English garrisons in France, probably through the influence of his fellow-Catholic the Duke of Norfolk, from 1546 to 1553.

His will, dated 4th August 1561, lists his possessions as well as his lands: "a great round silver salt; twelve silver spoons, one silver pot, a goblet parcel gilt... a silver salt; six silver spoons; a featherbed; six silver spoons; a silver pot; a featherbed... a flat piece of silver parcel gilt; the least silver gilt salt" - all to be divided between his children. It is astonishing to think of such a princely quantity of silverware in a Halesworth house. He also left 20 shillings to repair the highway to Beccles; 40 shillings to the repair of Halesworth church; 43s 4d to those attending the funeral (presumably to ensure a good attendance!) and a handsome

Gothic House and Dairy Farm, formerly the Norton residence, Halesworth. From a water-colour by A.A.Eisenhofer, 1885

bequest to the poor of the town for the next five years - penny loaves and red her-rings, as well as money. His cash bequests exceeded £1,500.

His widow Mary moved to Chediston - Gothic House was left to their son Walter - at a time when Catholic families were beginning to be in difficulties for their recusancy. Nevertheless when she died in 1584 she was buried in Halesworth church "in the chapel where my husband now lieth".

Walter II was in his late twenties when Robert, his father, died. He became a lawyer at Gray's Inn after three years at Gonville Hall, Cambridge. He married well, to Katherine (or Ruth), daughter of Sir Henry Bedingfield of Oxburgh and his wife Katherine. In the *Herald's Visitation* of 1561 were recorded their heraldic arms: Walter displayed four quarterings, while Katherine showed twelve - show-ing her superior family connections. He had inherited his father's lands, and had extended them, going as far as Lincolnshire; he was obviously considered reli-able, being appointed a Commissioner in Suffolk in 1569 to enquire into prohib-ited exports.

Walter's spiritual principles would not allow him to compromise with the reformed religion and he stoutly clung to the Catholic faith, for which he paid a heavy price. In 1577 he was ejected from Gray's Inn; in 1588 he was imprisoned in Norwich Castle and then moved to Wisbech Castle. He pleaded for release because of "his distressed state" in 1591, so that he could look after his affairs; and by 1593 he died, apparently leaving no will.

Walter had sold Gothic House in 1582, but his eldest son Henry managed to succeed to most of his lands. Henry had married Anne, daughter of Edward Sulyard of Haughley Park, Suffolk, another prominent Catholic recusant. They were pursued constantly. The *Bishop's Visitation* of 1606 to Chediston (where they now lived) recorded: "Henry Norton Esq, he is a Popish Recusant and refuseth to repair to church to hear Divine Service. Anne Norton his wife for the same. Catherine Norton, widow [his mother], for the same. Henry Norton, he refuseth to have his children [twelve of them] baptised in the same church. Edmund Norton gent [his brother], he refuseth to receive the communion".

When Henry died in 1638, at Chediston, he managed to leave something to the children of his wife's jointure lands (given on their marriage). He also left a house in Bracondale, Norwich, which he bought in the name of one of his sons (as a way of avoiding fining or forfeiture because of his recusancy). There is a surviving Inventory of the contents of this house - which sounds very comfortable - including descriptions such as "bed hangings of yellow taffety... 30 pairs of sheets..." etc. It seems that despite their ordeals the family were not entirely impoverished.

A change of fortune - under King Charles I - was already apparent: Henry's eldest son, Walter III, born about 1600, had become a baronet in 1635, as well as High Sheriff of Lincolnshire, with the grant of 1,600 acres in Nova Scotia. He married twice - firstly Mary, daughter of Edward, 10th Lord Stourton, of Wiltshire; the second was Mary Daniell of Acton, near Sudbury. By the first Mary he had four children. Sir Walter still held lands and manors in the Halesworth area, but increasingly gravitated towards Lincolnshire, where large land holdings were being reclaimed from the Wash - 1,200 acres at Tydd St Mary's marsh, for example. Fen drainage was unpopular and riotous assemblies gathered to throw down the banks, and Sir Walter was in one instance threatened with prosecution in Star Chamber.

He seems to have compromised on the religious question, and even attended church and received the sacrament at Bramfield in 1640 (he held lands at Mells, nearby). When he died in June 1647 he was intestate, but an Administration was issued eight years later because of a complicated land transaction with the Marquess of Argyll and other titled gentlemen.

His eldest son Edward inherited the baronetcy. Sir Edward had been born in London and seems to have always lived there. He never married and his will, proved in 1673, left all his property to a "Mr Daniel Norton of London, merchant". Unfortunately the property he inherited from his father was so encumbered with debts that the executors decided it was not worth having.

Sources

Gooch, M & S / H.M.C.R. 1577 Extent; 1582 Rental / P.C.C. Loftes D.30 / CRS Vol XXII / A.P.C. 16.10.1588 & 1591 / N.C.C. Will. NRO INV. 46/72 / L.R.O. HD/45/16/5 / C.S.P. 18.8.1636 / P.R.O. Prob. 6/32 - 22.2.1655 / P.R.O. Prob 11/342

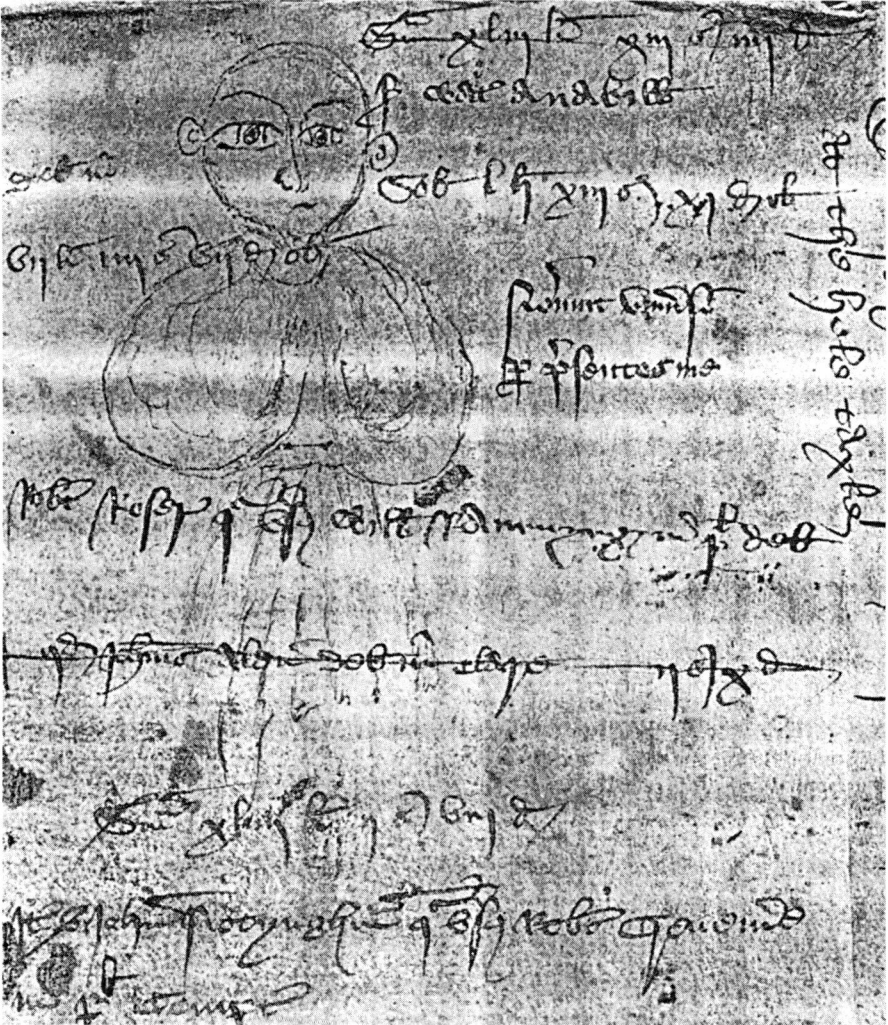

'Walt.Annabill', from Nicholas Greenhagh's account book.

Annable, Walter *Rector* died 1465

Suckling does not mention Annable in his list of Rectors of Halesworth, going straight from William Hardy, installed in 1408, to Edward Lohton, 1465. We owe the discovery of Annable to Professor Colin Richmond, who has kindly allowed us to quote from his two articles listed under Sources. It is especially interesting that he has identified the "doodle" [see illustration], as this is by far the earliest portrait of a Halesworth resident.

The portrait appears in the account book of Nicholas Greenhagh, Bailiff of Blythburgh, which spans the years 1444-56. It is opposite the page covering the year 1450-1, so it may coincide with Walter's appointment as Rector of Spexhall. He had however been in or near Halesworth for some time before that, as he witnessed the will of **Thomas Clement** in 1438, and was obviously in demand as a feoffee, as he appears in two deeds in the Iveagh manuscripts for properties in Halesworth and Mells in 1433 and 1442. It was only after twelve years at Spexhall that he became Rector of Halesworth for the last two years of his life, 1463-5.

Walter's will reveals that he was closely connected with the **Allington** family, Lords and patrons of Halesworth, as John Allington was his chief executor and John's daughter Mary was his godchild. On a lighter note, he left two large spits, one to each of the gilds of Halesworth church, for use at their annual feasts.

Sources

Richmond, C. *A Fifteenth Century Rector of Halesworth*, P.S.I.A.H. XXXVIII (1996) / Richmond, C. *Halesworth Church and Fifteenth Century Benefactors* (1996)

Everard, John died 1476

Mounted on the West wall of Halesworth church is one of the building's few surviving brasses, the demi-figure of a civilian (ie not priest or knight) with the inscription - "Orate p. aia Johis Everard qui obiit quindecmo die mensis Octobr anno dm MCCCCLXXVI cui ane propic de Amen" [Pray for the soul of John Everard who died the fifteenth day of the month of October AD 1476 on whose soul may God have mercy]. This brass would originally have been set in a floor slab which had been boarded over. It was rediscovered in 1858, when the Georgian box-pews were replaced by the present benches, and re-set on the wall.

The Everards were an old-established family at Linstead Magna who nevertheless tended not to be buried there. John's father, also John, was buried at Metfield in 1432. John II - died 1476, subject of the church memorial - and also of Linstead Magna, left an annuity of ten marks to his son John III, a chaplain, to pray for his soul, a pair of brass candlesticks for the high altar at Halesworth, and a bequest to Metfield church where his father was buried. The 1561 *Herald's Visitation* shows him as having been married to Margaret Dale of Shenfield, and having as son and heir Henry of Linstead and Chediston who died in 1498. John III entered the church and was chaplain at Halesworth, but died at Wrentham in 1502 and willed to be buried there beside his sister Margaret.

The Linstead line appears to have been continued by Henry and his descendants, mostly called Henry. After the Reformation they remained loyal to the old religion,and were allied by marriage to two leading recusant families - the Gawdys of Redenhall and the De Greys of Merton. When Queen Elizabeth made her Progress through East Anglia in 1578, sweeping up recusants on the way, the Henry Everard of the day was summoned before the Privy Council, meeting at

Norwich on the 22nd August, together with Edmund Bedingfield, William Hare and Thomas Sulyard. They were ordered "to remain in such houses in Bury as the Bishop shall appoint till Michaelmas next", there to receive corrective instruction. However he was lucky compared to **Walter Norton**, who spent the last twelve years of his life in jail. Henry was released early on the plea of his kinsman Bassingbourne Gawdy, who put up £200 surety. The recusancy persisted, as Will Dowsing, visiting Linstead Magna in 1644, mentions the "drunkard Francis Evered" as a recusant and in November 1648 he was having his properties sequestered by the victorious Parliamentarians. The family survived, however, as in 1675 Thomas Everard and Sarah his wife were buying a newly-built tenement in Halesworth.

Sources

Halesworth Times 24.8.1858 / Richmond, C. *Halesworth Church and Fifteenth Century Benefactors* (Aberystwyth 1996) / C.A.P.C. / Copinger / Dovey, Z. *An Elizabethan Progress* (1996) / H.R.M.C.R.

Popson, Thomas *Schoolmaster* 1532 - ?96

Information about the early days of education in Halesworth is scanty. The first record known is the **Rev. John Argall's** Communion Book of 1580 onwards, where entries on 2nd February 1580 include Mr Henry Cocke, Schoolmaster. He figures again in 1582. It is likely that he instructed Edmund Barker of Sibton, who attended schools at Halesworth and Dalling, Norfolk, before being admitted to Gonville and Caius College, Cambridge, in 1579. He may also have taught Edmund and Anthony Bedingfield, sons of Edmund Bedingfield Esq., who were born at Debenham, went to Halesworth School and on to Gonville and Caius in 1584.

By 1586 Reynolds Rabett, son of Reynold Rabett, born at Bramfield, was admitted to the same college after schooling at Wenhaston and Halesworth "under Messrs Cox and Ablesonn". In 1587 Gonville and Caius took John Browne, son of John Browne, gentleman, and born at Spexhall. His school was Halesworth under Mr Popson. It looks as if this may be the year that he took over the school.

Thomas Popson (or Popeson) had a good education himself. Born at Denham, Buckinghamshire, about 1532, he was admitted to King's College, Cambridge, as a scholar from Eton in 1550. He became BA, then MA in 1558, and was a Fellow 1553-9. The years between 1559 and his arrival in Halesworth in 1587 form a considerable interval; he would by then have been about fifty-five years of age and must have gathered extensive experience, either in teaching or in the Church. It is believed he taught at Eye during this period.

By 1591 he had moved up the road to Bungay Grammar School, as on 1st March that year he had laid down "Ordinances and Rules concerning the

Grammar Schole at Bungay... and to be observed by the Master, Scholars and co-feffyes for the continuall maintenance of the Schole... " - these rules were based on Eton practices. The Rev. Simon Barfellow, in his will of 1593, refers to his "well-beloved friend" Thomas Popson, master of the Grammar School, to whom he had lent £10 towards building a free school.

In Thomas Popson's will of 1596 he left properties to his wife for her life and after to help support the schoolmaster and scholars. He left lands in Bungay and Hempnall to provide ten scholarships for local boys at Emmanuel College, Cambridge, to help with their living expenses - the College allowed them to eat the leftovers from the High Table. By 1869 these allowances had lapsed.

By 1597 George Kinge had taken over in Halesworth. Bishop Redman's *Visitation* states "He teacheth a schole". He moved on in 1607 to become Rector of Holton. From the Norwich Subscription Books, which list teachers and medical men who had sworn oaths to the Bishop, scholastic licences were issued to teachers at Halesworth from 1670 onwards:-

28 May 1670 - Anton Frank BA
17 June 1678 - Thomas Richardson
12 August 1662? - Thomas Armstrong
12 November 1760 - Jas. Flower
20 October 1740 - Fran. Robinson
27 June 1786 - Jo. Bird
19 June 1801 - **Tho. Tanqueray**

Apparently Halesworth never had a grammar school - presumably because no-one founded one - and Bungay was not far away.

One other name occurs in connection with the teaching profession. In the vestry of Halesworth church is a very worn memorial slab to Henry Kifford, clerk, late Rector of Dennington, and Prudence his wife, with dates 1752 and 1719. The *East Anglian Miscellany* quotes from the Licence Register (an item not found subsequently by us): "April 17th 1704 - Henry Kifford AB [that is, BA] of Halesworth granted permission to teach boys the arts of reading, writing and the rudiments of grammar, within the Archdeaconry of Suffolk".

Sources

N.R.O. / S.R.O.L. / E.A.N & Q / Alumni Cantab. / Houghton, R.R. *Bungay Grammar School* (1965) / Essay by Evans, N. *Essays on East Anglian History* p137 The Centre of East Anglian Studies (1996) / Diocesan Records

Argall, John *Rector c.1542-c.1609*

One of the most notable Rectors of Halesworth, and one of whom we have more personal information than most, thanks to the survival of his record of Communions celebrated from 1580 to 1609, was John Argall.

He was born in London, the third son of Thomas Argall and his wife Margaret

Talkarne. In 1560 they acquired Low Hall Manor at Walthamstow, but Thomas died in 1562 and Margaret later married **Sir Giles Allington** of Horseheath, Cambridgeshire, a connection which would later be of importance to John. He entered Christchurch College, Oxford, and took BA in 1562, MA in 1565 and BD in 1582, becoming Vicar of Chalgrove, Oxfordshire, and Rector of Cadleigh, Devon, before moving to Halesworth in 1580, thanks no doubt to the patron there being his stepfather Sir Giles. He later added the nearby Rectories of Holton in 1585 and Heveningham in 1590. His mother died the following year [her will is summarised in our Allington family article]. John probably belonged to the Puritan wing of the Church, as the will of one of his parishioners, Thomas Shipdam, proved in 1590, names him first in a list of preachers who are to "contenew the place of exercise at Halesworthe as yt hath been used heretofore", meaning probably a regular weekday sermon in the Market Place, for which each preacher would get sixpence for his dinner.

John Argall appears in numerous publications, but they all seem to derive their information from Wood's *Athenae Oxoniensis*, which claims that he was "esteemed a noted disputant during his stay in the University: was a great actor in plays at Christchurch, particularly when the Queen was entertained there in 1566, and when at ripe years a tolerable theologist and preacher", also that "being so much devoted to his studies that he was unmindful of his worldly concerns, he lived and died poor, on which he used to make this pious reflection that whereas the Great God had raised many of his cronies and contemporaries to high dignities in the church... he was detained in the chains of poverty by his great sins". His published works are *De Vera Penitentia*, London 1604, and *Introductio ad Artem Dialecticam*, London 1605.

The Halesworth Communion Book opens "John Argall Rector de Halsworth in com. de Suff. This book was bought 1580... Luke Taylor was pson. before and dyed on Mayday after the great earthquake 1580". John carefully records the names of all persons receiving communion, but this only took place at the main festivals of the year, for instance in 1582 only on Palm Sunday, Easter Day, Midsummer Day and Christmas Day.

Numbers varied widely: for instance 161 communicants on the Sunday after Easter 1605, whereas on Easter Day 1581 only twenty-seven attended, and "for the poor nothing, because all the communicants almost were poor them selves". Fair quantities of wine were consumed, as on Trinity Sunday 1605 - three quarts sack and four quarts claret for 133 communicants. In 1594 "there was a Communion upon the Feast of the Nativitie of Christ commonly called Christmas Day, but the weather was so cold that I could not thaw my ink to wright down ye names of ye communicants".

The book gives the impression of a painstaking resident Rector, totally at variance with Bishop Redman's visitation of 1597, held in Snape church, when he was told "Halesworth: Argall Rector here. He is not resident. Neyther he nor the parishioners have gone the perambulation for VI yeares". Another conflict of evidence concerns the date of his death: all the printed sources say that he died at a feast at Chediston and was buried in Halesworth church on the 8th October 1606, but the Communion Book continues in the same careful handwriting till the Sunday after Easter, 1609.

Communicants List: SROL (124/C.10/1) / V.C.H. Essex 1612 / Alumni Oxon /
D.N.B. / Bishop Redman's visitation 1597: N.R.S. vol XVIII

Moore, Phillip *Physician* fl. 1656

A physician and surgeon, Phillip Moore is reputed to have practised in
Halesworth, but no proof of this has so far been found.

He is known principally for compiling *Old Moore's Almanac*, the original being
published in London in 1573, the full title being *An almanack and prognostication
for XXXIIII (34) yeares etc.*

Previously he wrote a book of medical advice,*The Hope of Health*, "wherein is
conteined a goodlie regiment of life: as medicine, good diet, and the goodlie
vertues of sondrie herbes", with "a table for XXX yeres to come". This was also
printed in London, in November 1565, and was dedicated to Sir Owen Hopton.
At this date Sir Owen was Sheriff of Norfolk and Suffolk, residing at Cockfield
Hall, Yoxford. Later he was Lieutenant of the Tower of London (1570-90) and
Member of Parliament for Suffolk in 1591. He would obviously be a very influ-
ential patron, and points towards Moore being in the locality.

This first book includes verses written by his friend William Bullein, also a
physician and a native of Ely; he published *An almanack and prognostication of
Master Bullein* in 1569, so they seem to have been a popular type of book.
However, there is a later rival to Phillip: *Old Moore's Almanac* as published nowa-
days claims direct descent from Dr Francis Moore's *Original Old Moore's Almanac*
for 1778.

D.N.B. / Visitations of Suffolk, 1561 / Van Zwanenburg

Browne, John *Progenitor* died 1581

One of the few surviving brasses in Halesworth church reads - "Here lieth John
Browne of Hallesworth who lived a quiet life and died the 23 of August in the
year 1581, of the age of LXXX years and XXV weeks. He had by his onely wyfe
with whom he lived 54 years and 5 months 6 sons and 10 daughters. He had also
65 grandchildren of whom 54 were living at the daye of his decease".

John Browne appears in the 1577 survey of Halesworth Manor as holding a
freehold messuage in Thoroughfare, probably where Cross Ram's office now
stands, together with various small parcels of land, and one larger - three acres

in Bunting's Fen - his total rentals being fifteen shillings and three pence.

The brass has an interesting history, recorded on an adjoining tablet - "These brasses were dragged out of the River Waveney in the year 1825 at a spot called the 'roaring arch' at the second bridge on Earsham Dam, and fell into the hands of Revd. S. Blois Turner, by whom they have been restored". **Turner** had spotted that they fitted the matrices in a stone slab uncovered during the restoration of the church, and had the slab and brasses mounted on the wall. The Browne brass is a palimpsest, ie an older brass reversed and cut down in size, and is hinged so that both sides can be seen. Turner was able to show the restored brasses to the members of the Suffolk Institute of Archaeology, meeting in Halesworth on the 11th August 1870.

Sources

P.S.I.A. vol IV p444 / Halesworth W.E.A. *Towards a Local History*

Feltham, Thomas *Man of Property* died 1591

The Feltham family were based in Westhall from at least the early 15th century, with family wills dated 1473, 1535 and 1559, and an inscription on the rood screen in the church (c.1512) inviting prayers for the souls of Thomas Felton and his wife Margaret. By the mid-16th century John Feltham had settled in Halesworth and married a daughter of the Smythe family of the town. Their eldest son was Thomas, who married Margaret Jackson, from Derbyshire, and soon started amassing properties in Halesworth. By the time of the 1577 survey of Halesworth Manor, Thomas held the capital messuage Walpoles, later the Three Tuns (and now the Social Club), and the adjacent property Towers - now the pet shop - together with Shouldhams in Steeple End, as well as Hunts ("now waste") between Towers and Walpoles, and Palmers "lying next to the Church Grate" for which he paid per annum one gilly flower. He also held various gardens and meadows totalling about fifty-eight acres, but the core of his property was the block of buildings around Walpoles, dominating the West end of the Market Place. By the time he wrote his will, in February 1590, Thomas had also acquired the capital messuage now Gothic House and Dairy Farm, opposite the church, "purchased of Mr **Norton**", together with lands that made up thirty-two acres. He thus held the two most important private houses in town, which also show such similarities in interior details and mouldings as to suggest the same carpenter-designer's hand. Outside Halesworth he held properties in Wenhaston, Mutford, Wissett, Mells, Bramfield, Thorington, Rushmere, Ellough, Henstead, Westwood, Yoxford, Wangford, Reydon, and the Manor of Westhall Hall.

His will, proved in April 1591, leaves the former Norton messuage to his second wife Winifrede and son Thomas, not yet of age. Thomas, at twenty-one, is to have all lands in Halesworth, Wissett, Mells and Bramfield. Son John gets lands in Wenhaston and the Manor of Thorington, and son Owen has all lands in Mutford, Rushmere, Ellough and Henstead plus - among other things - "my ring called the spread eagle". His daughters Frances, Elizabeth, Tabitha, Philipp and Prudence are to have £200 each at twenty-one, as is "the child my wife is with, if female" (if male, he adds later, the child is to get Lymbalds, now leased to Mr Hopton). After various small bequests he instructs his executors to take all outstanding profits from the Clerkship of the Peace of the Hundred of Blything and other debts. His bequests to the poor are all expressed in terms of sheep - ten to Halesworth, six to Beccles, five to Mutford, three each to Bliborough, Walberswick, Wissett, Holton and Bramfield, two each to Rumburgh and Spexhall, and finally ten sheep to the school at Wenhaston. The executors are to be his brother Robert, brother [-in-law] George Downing, and son Thomas.

Sources

Visitation of Suffolk, 1612 / Halesworth WEA *Towards a Local History* (survey of 1577) / Will: P.C.C. PROB.11/777.f.185

Assheton, James *Rector* 1573 -?1644

In the chancel of Halesworth church hangs a most unusual monument in the form of a painted oak panel. Beneath three coats of arms is the inscription - "Richard Assheton borne 26 July 1622 son and heir of Ralphe Assheton of Kirkby in the countie of Yorke sonne of Sr Richard Assheton of Middleton in ye county of Lancaster Kt. & Katheren wife to the said Ralphe (daughter to William Brereton of Ashley in the county of Chester esq). Lately fellowe comoner in the pious & learned Society of Sydney Sussex Colledge in Cambridge, where his course of life was such that it gained ye love of all & deserved ye imitation of the best; rendred up his Soule to the almighty at ye house of his worthy loving kinsman James Assheton Bachelor of Divinity & Rector of this church May the 28 1641 & his body to be intered under his Tombe stone in this Chancell in hope of a joyfull resurrection."

So the monument is not to our Rector but to his great-nephew, no doubt spending his long vacation at Halesworth rather than at his own home in Yorkshire. The first two shields are of Ashton quartering Barton and the third has the impressive twenty-four quarterings of Brereton, for Richard's mother.

The Asshetons were a family established since 1439 at Middleton, now a northern suburb of Manchester, but originating in adjacent Ashton-under-Lyne. Middleton church was largely rebuilt by the family, including the Ashton Chapel which bears the date 1523. The Sir Richard referred to on the tablet was knighted in 1603 and his younger brother was James, the Rector. Sir Richard's second son was Ralph, and his son was Richard the Cambridge scholar.

Venn says that James entered St John's College in 1591, took MA in 1598, BD in 1606, became a Fellow in 1603, Rector of Halesworth in 1616, and possibly

Wooden tablet to Richard Assheton, died 1641, in Halesworth church

Vicar of Hemel Hempstead in 1644. This last move seems unlikely at the age of seventy-one, though Cussans in his history of Hertfordshire lists a James Ashton being appointed Minister there on 18th May 1644, Parliament being the patron. He was succeeded by George Kendall, then by John Warren in July 1646, so his tenure, if any, must have been very brief. In fact James was not the first of his family in Halesworth, as he had taken over the living from his second cousin Abdias (1563-1633) who was Rector from 1606 to 1616 and then went on to the family living of Middleton, which he held until his death. It remains unclear how

Abdias obtained the Halesworth living, whose patrons were then the **Allington** family.

The main branch of the family went on to produce another Ralph Ashton (1606-1650) who led the Parliamentary armies in Lancashire through the Civil War, captured Wigan and Liverpool and relieved the siege of Nantwich. His son, another Ralph, no doubt by some nimble footwork gained a Baronetcy in 1660, but the title expired in 1765 for want of a male heir, and the Middleton estate passed by marriage to the Lords Suffield. Middleton Hall was demolished in 1845 to make way for a cotton mill.

Sources

Heraldry of Suffolk Churches, no.27 / V.C.H. Lancashire / Alumni Cantab. / Burke: *Extinct Baronetcies*

The Ingham Family 1580 to 1776

In 1712, on 6th March, Martha, daughter of William and Martha Ingham, was baptised in Halesworth. Her father is described as "attorney-at-law". This is the first definite date we have placing Inghams in Halesworth. William came from a Theberton family, and the first Ingham named in Theberton Parish Register is Francis, who flourished 1580-1630. The Inghams of Theberton used a coat of arms also used by the Inghams of Ingham, Norfolk, although they in turn are mentioned as being of Weybread in Suffolk. Copinger, in Volume IV, states that Weybread was held by Sir Oliver de Ingham in 1281, then it went to his son, also Oliver, in 1308. From him it passed to his daughter Joan who married Sir Miles Stapleton.

Ingham church had a brass memorial to Sir Miles de Stapleton, died 1364, and his wife Joan Ingham; it has now disappeared. There is still a tomb chest and effigy of Sir Oliver de Ingham, who died 1344, presumably father of Joan. Copinger also quotes an Olivia de Ingham at Withersdale, near to Weybread, in 1316. Both Joan Corder and Reynolds and MacLachlan quote later Inghams as using the earlier heraldic arms - whether by right or by wishful thinking we do not know.

Francis Ingham of Theberton's son Thomas in turn had a son Thomas II, born 1652 at Theberton. He married Melicent and their memorial is in Theberton church; she died in 1708 in her 56th year, he died 1720/1. They had an extensive family: Thomas III, who died in 1707 and describes himself as maltster in his will; Robert, baptised in 1682, who went to Cambridge and became a Fellow at Caius College, but died young in 1705; John, a draper and tobacconist at Yoxford, who died in 1712 and left a will and an inventory. William, Peter and Charles all survived their father; there were also four daughters - Mary, Elizabeth, Margaret and Melicent.

Thomas II's will of 1718, proved in 1721, comprehensively describes the whole family. He is described as "of Theberton in the County of Suffolk, yeoman". His "messuage wherein I now do dwell" in Theberton, with all its lands etc are bequeathed to his grandson Thomas, son of his deceased son Thomas of Leiston. This fourth Thomas was later recorded as "of Doncaster" when marrying Ann Eastland, widow, of Bury St Edmund's on 26th June 1740. A very long list of other properties are left to Thomas II's other grandchildren, both the sons and daughters of Thomas III and of John of Yoxford, both deceased. All these grandchildren were under the age of twenty-one in 1718. His sole executor was his son William, the Halesworth attorney who commenced this story. An interesting sidelight is Thomas's jaundiced view of his son-in-law the Rev. Thomas Ross, who had married Melicent, and who was obviously untrustworthy; Melicent's inheritance is clearly stated not to be subject to the principle of "coverture", the idea that a married woman's property is the property of her husband.

William Ingham's attorney's practice was very successful, as by the time of his death in 1734 he bequeathed not only the Stewardship of the Blois family of Yoxford and the **Plumer family** of Halesworth, but also the ownership of the Rookery estate at Yoxford. These passed to his nephew John, son of his brother John of Yoxford, for lack of heirs of his own blood, both Martha his wife and Martha his daughter having died.

John Ingham junior's career is fully described in Rachel Lawrence's book *Southwold River*; suffice it to say that he carried on his uncle's responsibilities and added further ones by becoming a Commissioner at the meeting held subsequent to the Act passed 1st April 1757 to establish the Navigation on the River Blyth from Halesworth Bridge to Southwold Haven. He acted in this capacity until 1771. In 1764 he became a Guardian of the House of Industry at Bulcamp at a meeting held at the Angel Inn, Halesworth, on 3rd December. As Steward to the Blois estate he was fully occupied, often in raising money to send Sir John Blois on his continental tours; sometimes this had to be raised from William Plumer, Lord of the Manor of Halesworth. Eventually the Blois estate was put into the hands of Trustees, of whom John junior was one, in 1772 when in his seventies. His partner in Yoxford was Richard Crowfoot; his Clerk was John Barmby.

As well as inheriting the Rookery estate at Yoxford, John junior had purchased the Theberton manor from William Bradley before 1750. Copinger states that before 1778 it was sold to George Doughty of Leiston, either by John himself before his death in 1776 or by his partner Richard Crowfoot. John Ingham's will, proved in April 1776 at London, instructs Crowfoot as sole executor to dispose of all properties in Theberton, Middleton cum Fordley, Kelsale, Leiston and Westleton, the proceeds to provide an annuity for his sister Elizabeth, and various substantial sums to his cousins, sisters, nieces and nephews - he had never married. His Clerk, John Barmby, was bequeathed £400. All his wearing apparel went to William Butcher of Yoxford.

Sources

Theberton P.R. / Corder *A Dictionary of Suffolk Arms* / Reynolds & MacLachlan *Guide to Heraldry in Suffolk Churches* / Copinger / Alumni Cantab. / Yoxford P.R. / Wills: PROBII.665.SIG.136 and PROBII.1018 APR 185 / Pevsner *Buildings of Norfolk*

Saltonstall and Base Families 1596 to 1688

Since publishing *The Story of a Suffolk House* in 1994 not only have we found further information regarding the Saltonstalls, but also a splendid painting, entitled 'The Saltonstall Family', now in the Tate Gallery in London and reproduced on the cover of this book.

It is a very large picture, which is odd as the painter, David des Granges, is chiefly known for his portrait miniatures. Des Granges was born about 1611-13, and the dating of this picture would make the artist in his early twenties. There has been some dispute as to the significance of the scene depicted, but after close examination of the original the most likely explanation is as follows: on the bed lies Elizabeth Base, Sir Richard Saltonstall's first wife. He stands beside the bed, holding the hand of his son Richard, who in turn grasps the wrist of his younger sister Anne. Seated beside the bed is Sir Richard's second wife Mary Parken, who is holding her child Philip in his christening cloth. The boy Richard has not yet been breeched, so would be about seven years old, his sister perhaps two years younger. Philip died aged thirty-three in 1668, so was born about 1635. This dates the picture to about 1635, or shortly after, yet looks back five years to 1630 when Elizabeth died. This type of painting was not uncommon at the time - one by John Souch, dated 1635 and now in the Manchester City Art Gallery, shows 'Sir Thomas Aston at the deathbed of his wife'. This too is a large picture, and shows his wife in bed and a second female figure beside it - claimed to be his wife in younger and happier days. It is a much more sombre affair than the des Granges, using dark colours and incorporating religious symbols and looking altogether much more funereal. That the Saltonstall picture shows a similar situation is unlikely: the two ladies are distinct individuals, with different eye colours, and for a conventional deathbed scene the colours are very vivid. The seated woman is too well-dressed to be a nursemaid.

Elizabeth Base was the daughter of Hugh Base and his wife Ann Clarkson, and was baptised on 1st August 1597 at St Gregory by St Paul in the City of London. Ann must have died shortly afterwards as in 1599 Hugh married for a second time to Ann (or Agnes) Venables, a widow who already had a daughter Sarah; two more daughters were born to Hugh and Ann and baptised in the same parish.

By 1604 Hugh Base was living in Halesworth, in Gothic House opposite the church, having purchased it from Thomas Feltham after 1582; in 1607 and 1608 Hugh and his wife appear on the **Rev. John Argall's** Communicants List. By 1609 Hugh had died; his will was proved on 27th March 1609 and the house and other properties passed to his wife for the duration of her life.

After Ann's death Gothic House passed to Elizabeth, Hugh Base's first daughter. She had married Sir Richard Saltonstall, who was descended from a family of yeomen originating in a hamlet called Saltonstall near Halifax, Yorkshire. Their farmhouse is still to be seen there. His grandfather, Sir Richard Saltonstall I, became a very wealthy London merchant, Master of the Skinners Company and a member of both the Muscovy and Levant Companies. He became a Member of Parliament in 1586 and Lord Mayor of the City of London in 1597. In the course of his City business he knew Samuel Clarkson, Elizabeth Base's maternal grandfather. Sir Richard I owned a country estate at South Ockenden, Essex, convenient for the City by water, and in the church there is his monument - a very grand affair showing him with his wife and sixteen children. Nearby is a brass coffin plate inscribed "The Lady Elizabeth Saltonstall her body Ao 1630". This was Elizabeth Base, who died on 21st April 1630.

Her husband - grandson of Sir Richard I and son of Sir Richard II - went to Queen's College, Oxford, becoming BA in 1612, and entered the Middle Temple in 1613. In October 1620 he was granted a pass to travel for one year, with one servant; he agreed not to go to Rome and at the same time took the oath of allegiance. This may have been a 'continental tour' which he undertook before he married and settled down. He was not short of money - in his mother's will of May 1619, proved in June that year, he was instructed to make payments on her behalf to his brothers Bernard and John and his sister Susanna; presumably he had already benefited from his mother after the death of his father, from whom he inherited the South Ockenden estate and other properties. In addition he inherited one of his gilt standing cups, a gilt basin and ewer, his bedding, tapestry and furniture (which could be shown in 'The Saltonstall Family' picture). The gilt basin and ewer had belonged to Sir Richard I and bore his arms and those of Susanna Poyntz, his wife, and were to be passed down to Richard IV. Before Sir Richard III's wife Elizabeth's death in 1630 two children were born - Richard and Anne. In June 1630 he again obtained a pass for travel into "foraigne parts" for the next three ensuing years, and to take with him servants and trunks etc. Could this have been a trading journey, perhaps to New England? There were strong connections with North America: his cousin, Sir Richard Saltonstall of Huntwicke, had been in New England in 1630, helping to found part of Boston, and he returned there the next year. His son (yet another Richard) settled in Ipswich, Massachusetts, in 1635; his descendants still live in the Boston area.

Sir Richard III's brother, Bernard Saltonstall, died in 1632 and is buried at Somerleyton church, Suffolk. In his will of 1630 he was of South Ockenden but moved to Suffolk later; he was unmarried. The mother of Bernard and Richard, Jane Bernard, second wife to Sir Richard II, was related to the Jernegan family who held the manor of Somerleyton. In November 1633 an affidavit stated that having obtained a licence to travel for three years, Sir Richard III had let his lands in Essex "with a great part of his house" until Michaelmas next and was now living two miles out of Essex, in Suffolk. One wonders if his journey was postponed because of his wife's death.

Sir Richard III married again, to Mary Parken, and had more children: Philip, born about 1635 and shown in the family portrait, had a fatal accident in Yorkshire in 1668 when he fell off a horse - this unfortunate occurence is commemorated on a wall plaque in South Ockenden church. Other children there must have been as Sir Richard's will of 1649 refers to "all the rest of my children". In 1643 the Committee for the Advance of Money (to Parliament) assessed him - at Aldersgate Ward, City of London - at £200. In 1649 he was ordered not to pay his brother John the inheritance from their mother, as John was a Royalist.

Sir Richard Saltonstall died in 1649; afterwards his widow Mary stayed on at their South Ockenden estate and as patroness of the church there helped to restore the fabric after a lightning strike in March 1657.

Halesworth Manor Court Roll, at the Court held on 19th October 1641, refers to the inheritance of Elizabeth, Lady Saltonstall, and that after her death the property (Gothic House etc) went to Richard, the first-born son of Sir Richard III and Elizabeth. No one came to the Court or paid the fine to the Lord of the Manor that would register the transfer of the property; the same happened at the Court of 22nd July 1642. At the Court of 19th October 1642 still no one came so it was ordered that the bailiff should take the premises into the hands of the Lord of the Manor. At the last minute, immediately after the session, they were notified by Charles Knight that he was acting for Sir Richard Saltonstall who surrendered the property to **John Bedingfield** Esquire for the fine sum of £25.

At the time these hearings were taking place, Sir Richard III was forty-five years of age and the heir, his son Richard IV, was about eighteen and of age to inherit. He went to Queen's College, Oxford, and entered Gray's Inn in 1641. Later he lived at Chipping Warden, Northants, with his wife Margaret, and according to his will of August 1688 bequeathed no less than £4,000 to his daughter Elizabeth (presumably unmarried), to his son Richard V and daughter-in-law Silence Parkhurst "£100 apiece to buy them mourning". His wife Margaret had all his plate, jewels, gold, his coach chariot and furniture and all his cattle.

Two portraits exist of Richard and Silence, illustrated in *Ancestry and Descendants of Sir Richard Saltonstall*, written by Leverett and Richard M. Saltonstall in 1897 and published in the USA.

Although this appears to end the Saltonstall presence in Suffolk, there was a William Saltonstall, a shopkeeper in Bungay, whose will of 1741 exists but reveals nothing of his background or if there was any connection to this wealthy and illustrious family.

Sources

Communicants List. SROL 124/CIO/1 / Alumni Oxon. / C.S.P. 23.11.1633; 19.5.1657 / A.P.C. 13.10.1620; 9.6.1630 / Wills: Base 1609 PRO 62 Dorset; R. Saltonstall 1618 PROB 11/133; Jane Saltonstall 1619 PROB 11/133; Bernard Saltonstall 1630 PROB 11/161; R. Saltonstall 1649 PROB 11/211 / South Ockenden Parish Registers

Fawether, Samuel *Justice* c1620-56

The long tenure of Halesworth Manor by the **Argentein/Allington** family did not finally end till 1706, but for more than a century before that they had ceased to keep up their manor house and lived at their Horseheath estate in Cambridgeshire. *The Chorographer of Suffolk* (c1605) tells that Sir Giles Allington had let out the site of the manor before 1586, so it had already been alienated more than thirty years when in 1621 it was sold by Thomas Shipdam to Josiah Fawether of Halesworth, together with forty-five acres of land.

Josiah, the father of Samuel, had acquired, by marriage to Elizabeth Kempe of Beccles, the manor of Talmach Hall at Little Bricett, near Stowmarket, but appears to have lived at Halesworth, where he was a Justice of the Peace in 1630. Samuel was admitted to Emmanuel College, Cambridge, in 1641, and by 1653 was back in Halesworth and a Justice himself, helping to administer the Commonwealth's newly-secularised regime. The first volume of the Parish Register begins - "Thomas Debenham of Halesworth... being chosen by the inhabitants of the sayd Towne to serve in the office of Parish Register was appoved and allowed by me and sworne by virtue of an Act of Parliament bearing date the 24 of August in the yeare of our Lord God 1653. Witness my hand the 24 of October 1653. Sam Fawether". In Middleton cum Fordley parish the registers record marriages being performed by "Justice Faierweather of Halesworth", but alas one of Thomas Debenham's first duties was to record the burial of the Justice himself on the 15th December 1656.

By his wife Anne Sedley, Samuel had two daughters and co-heiresses, and their familes held the site of the manor until 1725. Anne lived till 1696, and at that date the property passed to Bridget, wife of Robert Gooch, and Anne, daughter of Elizabeth Reeve deceased - Bridget and Elizabeth being the two daughters of Samuel and Anne. In Brooke church, between Bungay and Norwich, is a ledger slab partly obscured by benches. This reads, with the hidden letters restored as far as possible - "(Here) rest the bodies of Robert G(ooch of Br)ook in the County of Norf(olk aged) 74 and of Bridget his wife (daughter and co-)heiress of Saml. Fairweather of H(alesworth in the) County of Suff. Esq, aged (....) having lived together 50 years (....) buried in the same grave (....) the 19th June 1724". Above are the arms of Gooch and Fawether. In Lakenham church, now a Southern suburb of Norwich, is a slab to Elizabeth wife of Henry Reve of Bracondale, Norwich, who died 15th April 1690 with the arms of Reve and Fawether. In the same church is a slab to her mother, Anne, who died the 17th February 1696.

Sources

McCulloch (ed) *The Chorography of Suffolk* (1976) / Suckling II p331 / Copinger II / Alumni Cantab. / *East Anglian Miscellany* 1922/6502 / Farrer, A. / Blomefield IV p522

Cary, William *Benefactor* 1622-86

Possibly Halesworth's finest secular building is Cary's Almshouse, standing in Steeple End just South of the church. Its founder was William Cary.

William was the eldest child of William Cary of Woodbridge, who died in 1656, by Mary Bolton, also of Woodbridge, who died the next year, but probably had Halesworth connections. Their coat of arms was identical with that of Henry Carey, Lord Hunsdon (1526-96), Lord Lieutenant of Norfolk, but the connection is probably remote. William II moved to Halesworth, but never married. His

An early photograph of the Cary almshouses, Halesworth, built circa 1686

younger brother Thomas married Katherine and had a son Thomas, and four daughters, of whom more later. We know tantalisingly little of William's life at Halesworth, but he was an attorney as was his nephew Thomas II, who also moved to Halesworth and is recorded as Steward of the Rectory Manor from 1688-96. William died in 1686 and a ledger slab at the West end of the church records the bare facts - "Here lieth the body of William Cary, late of this parish gent, who died ye 11th day of July 1686, being aged 64 years".

The most interesting thing about William is his will (P.C.C.127 Lloyd) dated the 1st May and proved the 21st October 1686. All his lands and tenements go to his nephew Thomas, and they are in Halesworth, Woodbridge, Bulcamp, Blyford, other manors, and "two tenements situate on Great Tower Hill, London". Out of the proceeds Thomas was to pay £200 to each of his four sisters - Katherine and Sarah and, when they come of age, Alice and Mary. £20 go to "my most honoured friend **Sr Harry Bedingfield**, now Lord Cheife Justice of the common Pleas" for his advice and for acting as Supervisor. He leaves £5 to the poor of Woodbridge and £10 to the poor of Halesworth. Finally his executors are to purchase a parcel of land "at the South entrance to the Towne here where the Lord's pound now standeth and thereupon to erect a house for the poore, to conteyn twelve roomes besides garretts... all to be bricke from the foundation to the roofe... gabell endes with double chimneys and two chimneys of equal distances betweene each: four fire hearths supplyes twelve roomes" to house twelve aged poor single women or single men, or failing that the churchwardens might admit poor widows without children. All were to wear a badge of silver "as thicke as a halfe crowne and broader than a Crowne" bearing the arms of Cary. William nominates as executors the two Thomases, father and son. Finally he remembers some more lands in All Saints and St Margaret South Elmham, which also go to his nephew, together with all his plate and household goods.

The two Thomases must have followed their instructions faithfully, for the Almshouse as it stands today is remarkably close to that described in the will. However the four sisters were not all paid and as late as 1708 a Chancery suit was brought by Alice and Mary, the two younger sisters, who must by then have long attained twenty-one years, claiming that "Thomas Cary junior, confederating with Thomas Miller and Mary his wife, Thomas Wade and Sarah his wife, William Perkins of Blyford, bone-setter, and others doth refuse to pay the respective legacies".

The Almshouse was replaced as such by a group of bungalows built at the rear, and the old building found excellent new use as the town's library and museum, with the art gallery above. The library has now moved to its new premises and the museum will shortly be moving out, leaving the problem again of finding a worthy use for the ground floor of William Cary's splendid building.

Sources

Muskett *Suffolk Manorial Families*, vol II, 219, 221, 223 (with full text of will) / H.R.M.C.R.

Bedingfield Family 1595 to 1705

The old house to the South of Halesworth church now called Gothic House and Dairy Farm, now two but once one, was described by Suckling as the home of the Bedingfields "who probably built and certainly resided for several generations in this mansion". We now know that it was there for well over a hundred years before the Bedingfields arrived [see **Norton**], and that they occupied it for barely seventy years.

John Bedingfield (1595-1680) was the second son of Thomas of Darsham, and descended from the Bedingfields of Fleming's Hall, Bedingfield, the junior branch to the long line seated at Oxburgh Hall, Norfolk. John's elder brother Thomas became a Justice of the Common Pleas in 1648 and on his monument in Darsham church his widow records that he was appointed "by king Charles I of

blessed memory, upon whose murder he laid down his place and all public employment, retiring himself to this towne where he died March 24th 1660". However the facts deny this. By 1648 the king was a prisoner at Carisbrooke, Thomas was a member of the County Committee through the war, and in 1654 was elected a Knight of the Shire in Cromwell's parliament. Dame Elizabeth, composing his epitaph just after the Restoration, naturally wished to paint a different picture.

John followed his brother into the Law and entered Gray's Inn in 1615, moved to Lincoln's Inn, was called to the Bar in 1630, a Bencher in 1650 and Treasurer in 1659. Meanwhile he had purchased the Halesworth house and its farm in about 1638 and was appointed High Steward of Southwold in 1658 and a Justice of the Peace in 1664. He married Joyce Morgan of Lambeth, daughter of a City merchant, and they produced a large family including six sons who survived to adulthood. An interesting glimpse of John comes in the diary of the notoriously prickly Edmund Bohun of Westhall - "12 May 1677 - again I am left out of the Commission of Peace for this county: many private gentlemen being put in, and the two Bedingfields, father and son forsooth, being nominated: the result of the insatiable revenge of certain persons accustomed to make every thing bend to their own malice and cowardice... It is reported that Sir J.P. has been the means of excluding me". Sir J.P. was John Playters of Sotterley, and the father and son were John and his eldest son Edmund.

John was responsible for much refurbishment of the old house, including the elaborately carved porch, and a fine panelled room upstairs in Dairy Farm. The best interior fittings - the chimney piece and panelling in the parlour - were removed in the 1840's but fortunately recorded by Suckling [Vol II pp335-7] in two drawings by Hamlet Watling. John died aged eighty-five and was buried in Halesworth church, though his monument has since disappeared, leaving all his property to Edmund.

Two of Edmund's brothers achieved remarkable prominence. Henry (1632-87) attended Norwich School and Caius College, then followed his father to Lincoln's Inn where he was called to the Bar in 1657 and a Bencher in 1683. He married his cousin Mary Bedingfield and they had seven children, of whom only two daughters survived infancy. He became MP for Dunwich in 1660 and a Sergeant-at-Law and a Knight in 1684, and followed his father as High Steward of Southwold in 1685. The same year King Charles II died, to be followed by the turbulent three year reign of James II, when Henry rose to new heights - a Judge of the Common Pleas, and, ten weeks later, Chief Justice [see illustration].

Foss was unimpressed - he was "appointed a Judge of the Common Pleas on February 13th 1686 in the place of Sir Cresswell Levinz. It is to be presumed that, either from his own conviction or the arguments of Jeffreys, he acknowledged the king's power to dispense with the penal laws, as two months later, upon the recommendation of the same arrogant patron, he was raised to the head of that Court on April 21st on the discharge of Chief Justice Jones. He did not enjoy this dignity much more than nine months, dying suddenly while receiving the sacrament in Lincoln's Inn Chapel on Sunday February 6th 1687". He was buried in Halesworth church, where his widow erected a handsome marble monument in the chancel. The inscription bears little resemblance to Foss's verdict.

Robert (1637-1711) is referred to by Foss as having been one of Judge Jeffrey's "creatures and boon companions" and having thus furthered his brother's career. He was set up in trade in the City of London by his father and prospered there as a woollen draper, becoming a Common Councillor in 1696, then Alderman, Master of the Merchant Taylors Company and knighted in 1697 "by the King in the bedchamber at Kensington". He was Tory MP for Heddon in 1701, Sheriff in 1703, and Lord Mayor of London in 1707. He married twice but had no children.

Meanwhile Edmund, the eldest son (1631-85) followed his father to Lincoln's Inn and was called to the Bar in 1653. He married Mary Shewbury of Bury St Edmund's, but only two daughters survived childhood. He was, as we have seen, a Justice of the Peace, but died aged only fifty-four and just five years after his father. Once again the diary of Edmund Bohun brings him to life - "May 28th 1678. At Halesworth I found H.Stebbing and Edmund Bedingfield sitting and deciding disputes under the recent statute concerning the poll-tax. We fell into conversation concerning the late treasons, the puritans and their present attempts. I endeavoured to show that their ultimate object was the destruction of the monarchy and the bringing in a republic. I feigned myself to be one of them that I might more easily expose their crimes. E.B. asked me what I would do with the king. I replied that we will destroy him as we before killed his father. He immediately warned me to take care what I said, as if he did not understand my manner of speaking and did not perceive that I was treating satirically what I hated above all things".

Edmund left no male heir, so the properties passed to his next brother Thomas, who had attended Christchurch, Oxford, and qualified as a doctor of medicine. He married well and settled at Isleworth, Middlesex, owning numerous properties there and in London. He was obviously an absentee owner, and when he died in 1691 the Halesworth property passed to his son, also Thomas, who was only fourteen years old. He was admitted to the property, having come of age, on 30th December 1701, but was another absentee owner, and sold the property to William Maggs on 21st April 1705. This ends the Bedingfield presence in Halesworth.

Sources

Suckling II / Black Book of Lincoln's Inn / Bottomley & Chadd *Senescali Sudwoldiensis* / Rix [ed] *Diary & Autobiography of Edmund Bohun* - Beccles, 1853 / Alumni Cantab. / Copinger II / Foss, E. *Biographical Dictionary of the Judges of England* (1870) / Gooch M & S

Betts, William *Lord of Manor* 1650-1709

After the long reign of the **Argentein** and **Allington** families - which lasted more than five hundred years - the first new Lord of Halesworth Manor, in 1706, was William Betts of Yoxford. He was a busy attorney and had been involved in the sale of the Allingtons' Horseheath estate in 1700 to the wealthy Barbados planter John Bromley. It is likely that at the same time Betts took the opportunity of snapping up another part of the crumbling empire - the Manor of Halesworth.

William Betts came from a long-established family at Wortham, near Diss, and married Dorothea, daughter of Thomas Mann of Yoxford and Ipswich, an attorney and Recorder of Ipswich. William then settled in Yoxford, but must have spent some of his time in London, as his fine monument in Yoxford church describes him as principal of Barnard's Inn, one of the Inns of Court. He was also Recorder of Dunwich, which cannot have taken up much time, and owner of five manors, including Halesworth. His daughter Mary married **Edmund Anguish**, brother of Sir Richard Allin Bart. of Somerleyton. After William's death in 1709, Dorothea held Halesworth manor and advowson for a further twenty-three years, and was able to present her grandson Thomas Anguish to the living in 1724.

William's will, proved in April 1710, shows that he had in all five sons and six daughters surviving at that date, and enough properties to endow all the sons. In addition Henry is to get £1,000 "towards buying him a seate in the Six Clerks Office and putting him into the world", while Robert, the youngest, gets the rents from an estate in Godmanchester to support him at University, and if he enters the Church is to be presented to "one of my livings" (Robert was in fact at Peterhouse, Cambridge, but the only livings we know he held were at Bircham Tofts and Bircham Newton in North Norfolk). William gets "my house and grounds in Yoxford" and is to have "the stewardship of my courts for life", while Thomas, presumably already advanced, gets only "his choice of my books". Finally William reminds the family not to release any court books or rolls to clients until their fees have been paid in full!

The eldest son Thomas, born in 1679, was given a superior education at Eton, then Clare College, Cambridge and the Inner Temple. He succeeded his father as Recorder of Dunwich, but obviously had more adventurous ideas and as soon as his father was dead travelled to Jamaica, perhaps dazzled by the vast wealth of John Bromley. Four years later he was back, and in some financial difficulty till appointed High Steward of Southwold, a largely honorific post but yielding a useful stipend. In 1717 the Caribbean called again and he resigned the Southwold post to become Clerk to the Navy Office in Jamaica. By 1721 he was back, having failed for a second time to make his fortune, and resumed his Southwold appointment. After six more years he was dismissed for unsatisfactory service and was "to have nothing more to do or act in this said Court of this Corporation upon any account whatsoever as High Steward". He had to sell most of his manors and moved to Weybread, near his wife's home at Roydon and his own Wortham roots. He died in 1739 and Halesworth Manor passed to **Walter Plumer**.

Sources

Alumni Cantab / Suckling II / Doughty, K.F. *Betts of Wortham* / Bottomley & Chadd *Senescali Sudwoldiensis* (1989) / Will: PROB.11.514.S.77.

Lone, Roger *Petitioner* fl.1675

All we know of Roger Lone is what appears, surprisingly, in the Calendar of State Papers, Charles II:-

"June 16th 1675: Roger Lone of Halesworth to Mr Whale living in Pickedille yard near Pellmell. Request to deliver the enclosed to Lord Berkeley or his own master and desire one of them to deliver it to the King or the Duke.

"Roger Lone to the King requesting him to have re-printed and commended to the world Henry Valentine's Private Devotions. They are grown so proud that they regard not you nor your good Queen but disturb your Parliaments and would do you violence were it not for God our father, to whom with yourself and Bishop Reynolds be all glory, honour and praise. I beseech you to send the enclosed letter to Doctor Wilde that writ 'Iter Boreale':- Roger Lone to Doctor Wilde... I live not far from Norwich but wither you command me I will go. I hope the King and Duke will make good laws that no assize or Quarter sessions be kept without a sermon of one of the Grey Friars: that no town or parish shall be without a minister two Sundays: that no courts baron or leet be kept without the minister of the town: that ministers may receive their tenths: that no merchant shall sell by retail: that no maker of cloth or stuff shall retail any of the same: that no tradesman shall use two trades, that is sell linen and woollen etc."

Dr Wilde was Robert (1609-79), born at St Ives, a prominent Puritan divine. He was ejected from his living in 1662, and wrote and published voluminously. *Iter Boreale* was a collection of his poems, published in 1661.

Sources

C.S.P. Charles II vol 28 item 449 / D.N.B.

Pullyn, Peter *Attorney* 1688-1753

For the leading Halesworth attorney of his day, Peter Pullyn's origins are tantalisingly obscure, and the only reason we know his date of birth is that his age is recorded on his tombstone. Some time before 1720 he married, and married well. His bride was Sarah, daughter and co-heiress of the wealthy John Smith of Holton, whose other daughter Lydia had married Sir Robert Rous of Henham. Peter and Sarah's children were baptised at Halesworth - John Smith in 1720, Lydia 1722, Sarah 1725, Peter in 1726, and finally Catherine. The Rous connection paid off, as by 1730 Peter was steward for all the Rous manors, and when Sir Robert died in 1735 his will left all his manors and lands to his son John and his heirs, failing that to the heirs of the testator, or the children of his sister Turner, or

The Mansion House as it was before the forming of shopfronts in the late 19th century. Drawing based on old photographs

to Peter son of his brother [in law] Peter Pullyn and his children. The will further stipulates that Peter senior is to be steward of all of Sir Robert's properties, which included at least ten manors centred on Henham.

In 1738 Peter is recorded as deputy steward to **Thomas Betts** at Halesworth Rectory Manor, and two years later he was the steward. In 1745 he was appointed Clerk to Southwold Corporation, and in 1747 to the Harbour Commissioners, by which date he was also steward to the Manor of South Elmham. Peter and Sarah lived in the centre of Halesworth in the Mansion House [now 27 Market Place and 46 Thoroughfare - see illustration], which they had purchased from John Prime, and where they were later succeeded by William Norford, John D'Urban, John Woodcock, Robert Gostlin White and Robert Baas - all of whom figure elsewhere in this book.

Here they were involved in an acrimonious dispute with the Rector, Isaac Collman, over the use of a pew in the parish church which Peter considered was his by right of ownership of the Mansion House. This was finally resolved by a Faculty, now in Halesworth Museum, dated 16th June 1742, by the Vicar General of Norwich diocese. Isaac Collman was thrice called in court but failed to appear, so it was pronounced that "a certain seat or pew notoriously situated on the North side of the middle isle of the Parish Church of Halesworth lying between the churching seat on the East and a common seat on the West, containing in length 8' 2" in breadth 6' 4" and of a decent height, to be granted for ever to the said Peter Pullyn, his heirs and assigns, and later proprietors of the said Capital Messuage for them, their children and friends to sit, stand, and kneel in at a time of divine service, to be built, repaired, and decently adorned at their expense as necessary, strictly inhibiting the said Rector and Churchwardens that they do nothing whereby Peter Pullyn is hindered or disturbed in quiet and peacable enjoyment of the said seat or pew under pain of the law".

Peter died on the 24th September 1753 aged 65 and Sarah on the 24th March 1754 aged 52, and both were buried in Halesworth churchyard. Peter's will, proved in December 1753, is mainly concerned to endow their youngest child Catherine, still unmarried, with £1,000. As for Peter junior "whereas he has been guilty of many breaches of his word and very undutifull to his brother" he is to get nothing except "my study of boks" unless his mother sees fit. His mother, dying only six months later, relented and gave Peter one third of her residual estate, shared with his sisters Sarah Wade and Catherine Pullyn. Catherine made good use of her dowry, and married William Elmy of Beccles by whom she had Harriet who married the later Rector of Beccles, Bence Bence, while later she became, through marriage, the aunt of the poet George Crabbe, and was also related to the former Halesworth Rector **Thomas Anguish**.

The unreliable Peter junior was - despite his father's lack of faith - clearly destined to follow the same profession. In 1742 (aged only sixteen) he was appointed one of the Feoffees of the Town Lands, and in 1754 he succeeded his father as Steward of the Rectory Manor. The last reference we have to him is on the 8th December 1772, when **Peter Jermyn** took the Rectory Manor court as deputy to Peter Pullyn. After that Peter Pullyn disappears. It is likely therefore that Peter Jermyn picked up the remains of the Pullyn family practice, and that from then on the succession was Robert Crabtree - John Crabtree - Frederic Cross - Willett Ram, and thence under the name Cross, Ram to the present day.

Sources

Lawrence (1990) / H.P.R. / H.R.M.C.R. / Cross Ram papers SROI (HB26.412/561) / Halesworth Museum (1742 Faculty) / Wills: Peter Pullyn - PROB.11.Dec.1753.805.324. Sarah Pullyn - PROB.11.May 1754.808.144

Kirby, John *Surveyor* c1690-1753

John Kirby, author of the *Suffolk Traveller*, is generally regarded as one of Halesworth's most famous sons. However, after prolonged research, we have concluded that both the date and the place of his birth are "not proven". The Halesworth Parish Registers run unbroken from 1653 and there is no sign in them of his baptism. There was indeed a Kirby (or Curby) family in the town at that time and there was a John, baptised 13 January 1682, son of Stephen, shoemaker, but this John is not our man as he died in 1736 at Halesworth. It is interesting, and faintly comforting, to discover from the pages of *East Anglian*

Portrait of John Kirby by Thomas Gainsborough

Miscellany that Charles Partridge, a keen local historian, pursued John Kirby's origins in 1934, came up against this same brick wall, and also gave a "not proven" verdict. He did however suggest that Stephen could have had a younger brother, born before the Halesworth registers begin, who moved away from the area and produced our John.

Now for the origins of the family. John's grandson, the Rev. William Kirby [see later] in a letter of 1807 says of John "family tradition says that he was descended from an ancient family in the North of England. The ancestor of the Suffolk branch was disinherited during the Great Rebellion and settled at

42

Halesworth". Freeman, in his *Life of William Kirby*, enlarges on this as he understood from William that the family came from Kirkby Stephen, Westmoreland, and that John, a Royalist officer, moved to Halesworth, married a farmer's daughter of Spexhall, and was disinherited. His family, in reduced circumstances, then became shoemakers or rope spinners at Halesworth. Yet another version quoted by J.W.Millard in *East Anglian Miscellany* has John Kirby, gent. of Kirkby Lonsdale, disinherited for siding with the loyalists in the Civil War. Yet another locates the family at Kirby Moorside in Yorkshire.

The quest for Kirby's origins is complicated by the fact that there are thirty-four Kirby or Kirkby place names in England, no fewer than fifteen of these in Yorkshire. To complicate matters still further, we have found a likely candidate in Kirkby Ireleth, near Dalton in Furness in what is now Cumbria but was then Lancashire. This is now known simply as Ireleth, but it figures under its full name in the Calendars for Advance of Money when the victorious Parliamentarians made the "delinquents" pay up. In 1648 John Kirby was held responsible for the debts of Robert Rawlinson of Marsh Grange who had "died a Papist in arms" and was required to pay bonds totalling £150. The Kirkbys were a leading family in the area, having properties at Kirkby Hall, Ireleth, and at Coniston Hall. Could they be our Kirby's ancestors?

The first definite evidence we have of John's existence is his marriage in St Nicholas, Ipswich, on 10 October 1714 - "John Kirby of Erwarton, singleman, and Alice Brown of St Lawrence, singlewoman, were married by Banns". At this time John was occupying "a small overshot mill at the bottom of the Park" at Erwarton, though there are no Kirbys in the registers of that parish. They must have moved immediately after marrying to the Wickham Market area, as their first child, John, was baptised there in August 1715. John was still a miller, probably at Glevering watermill. This is in the parish of Hacheston but is two miles from the village centre and much nearer to Wickham Market. It is therefore not surprising that the first five children were baptised at Wickham, though for the remaining six baptisms they went to Hacheston,the last being baptised there in 1729.

What is rather baffling is how John, presumably a busy miller, managed at the same time to set up as a land surveyor. Suffolk Record Office has twenty of his plans, ranging in date from 1725 to 1745, and all located in the Eastern part of Suffolk, from Rumburgh in the North to Felixstowe in the South. Even the earliest of these are remarkably competent and sophisticated productions, so where and when did he learn surveying? This led to his magnum opus, the *Suffolk Traveller*, and its accompanying map of the County, generally regarded as the first county guide book ever, by "Mr John Kirby of Wickham Market, who took an actual survey of the whole County in the years 1732, 1733 and 1734". This was published in 1735. A second edition appeared in 1764 "With many alterations and large additions by several hands", and third and fourth editions followed.

By 1751 Kirby had moved to Ipswich where he is believed to have owned Roundwood, on the Woodbridge Road. This was sold, long after John's death to "Horatio Nelson K.B. Rear admiral of the Blue" for £2,000. Nelson never slept there, though his neglected wife did. John Kirby died on 13 December 1753 and was buried in St Mary le Tower churchyard, Ipswich. His tomb, now illegible, recorded: "John Kirby died 13 December 1753 aged 63. Alice Kirby widow of the said John Kirby died 28 October 1766 aged 80". This is the only evidence we have of the year of John's birth.

We have mentioned that John and Alice had eleven children. Of these the first four, all boys, are worth exploring further. John the eldest (1715-50) entered the legal profession and was junior partner to Sir Richard Lloyd of Hintlesham Hall, Recorder of Ipswich, Treasurer of the Middle Temple, and later Solicitor General. Lloyd was no doubt responsible for John's appointment as Under-Treasurer of the Middle Temple, but John died early, at the age of thirty-four, and unmarried.

Joshua (1716-74) is the best known of the four. In 1739 he married Sarah Bull of Framlingham and they had two children - Sarah, who later became, under her married name of Trimmer, a celebrated author, and William who died in his twenties. Joshua and his bride moved to Ipswich, where he set up as a house painter (family pride later denied this), but his real ambition was to be an artist and he published numerous topographical drawings over the next few years. In 1747 came a crucial meeting with Thomas Gainsborough, eleven years his junior, who was to become a lifelong friend. This led to the excellent Gainsborough portraits of Joshua's parents painted probably in 1748 (John) and 1757 (Alice), now in the Fitzwilliam Museum, Cambridge [see illustration].

In 1755 Joshua moved to London. His book on perspective attracted great attention and, through the patronage of Lord Bute, he was appointed teacher of perspective to the Prince of Wales, later George III. He lived at Kew Green, convenient for the Palace. In 1768 he became President of the Society of Artists, but there was much infighting at the time within the London art establishment and he was bitterly disappointed when a rival society became the Royal Academy. The King consoled him with the comfortable sinecure of Clerk of Works for Kew and Richmond Palaces, but the next year brought a worse blow with the untimely death of his son. In 1774 Joshua died and was buried in Kew churchyard. In 1788 his old friend Gainsborough was buried beside him.

Stephen (1717-41) probably studied the law with his elder brother John, but died aged only twenty-four. Freeman quotes a touching letter from John senior to John junior on this occasion.

William (1719-91) was another lawyer, practising in Ipswich until he married Lucy Meadows, of the wealthy family seated at Witnesham, just North of Ipswich. They settled at Witnesham Hall in 1750, from where he continued his legal practice and managed to beget ten children. One of these was yet another remarkable Kirby, another William (1759-1850). He entered the Church, became Rector of nearby Barham, and held the living for sixty-eight years. His passion, however, was entomology, on which he became a leading authority. He was an early friend and correspondent of **William Jackson Hooker**, a member of the Linnaean Society, a Fellow of the Royal Society, and one of the founders of the Ipswich Museum. His publications included *Monographia Apium Angliae*, Ipswich 1802, and *Fauna Boreali Americana*, Norwich 1837, based on the findings of Franklin's Arctic expedition, but he will be mainly remembered for the four-volume *Introduction to Entomology*, London 1815-26. As a final footnote, his bookplate was the same crest that had been borne by Lancashire Kirbys two hundred years before.

D.N.B. / H.P.R. / "C.P." in *East Anglian Miscellany*, 9246, 9249, 9254 (1934) / Calendar of Committee for Advance of Money pp436, 890, 891 / V.C.H. Lancashire vol VIII pp303, 306, 313, 396 / Layton's Ipswich church notes - S.R.O.I. / Freeman, J. *Life of the Rev. W. Kirby* (1852) / Millard, J. W. in *East Anglian Miscellany*, no.281 (1901) / *East Anglian Miscellany* 1955/12920 for 'Roundwood' / Owen, F. 'Joshua Kirby' in Gainsborough House Review (1996)

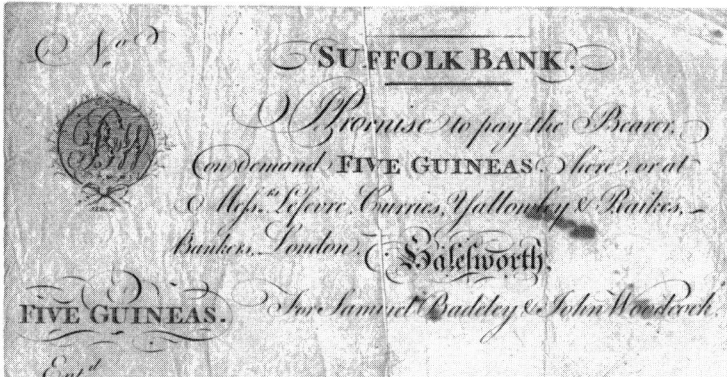

Five Guinea banknote of the Suffolk Bank

BY PERMISSION OF MR HAROLD PRESTON

Badeley Family 1693 to 1899

In 1799 Halesworth, then prospering and expanding with its malting and brewing industry fed by the recently completed Blyth Navigation, was shaken by an impressive bankruptcy. This was the crash of the Suffolk and Halesworth Bank, whose partners were Samuel Badeley and **John Woodcock**.

Samuel Badeley II (1741-1823) came from a Chediston family. His grandfather William had married, in 1693 at Redisham, Sarah Lincolne, and they had four children of whom the third was Samuel I (1709-80). The family appear to have been dissenters, but they hedged their bets as Samuel was baptised on the same day, 6th July, at Chediston church and Walpole chapel. His brother was baptised on consecutive days at Walpole and Chediston,while his sister was baptised at the Chapel exactly one year after her baptism in church. Samuel moved to Walpole, but had business interests in Halesworth where he was one of the first Commissioners of the Blyth Navigation. There is a simple mural tablet to him and to his wife Mary (1719-94) in Walpole church.

Samuel II was baptised at Walpole chapel. He followed his father's business interests in Halesworth, exporting grain via Southwold and building coal sheds on Halesworth quay. He entered into partnership with John Woodcock junior and went into malting and brewing. From this it was a short step to banking, although theirs was not the first Halesworth bank - Gurneys and **Turner** had already opened the Halesworth and Suffolk Bank in 1782. Badeley and Woodcock rather cheekily called theirs the Suffolk and Halesworth Bank. At least one five guinea note issued by them survives [see illustration] and in 1792 Brame Oxford, a developer, took out a mortgage with them for £800 at five per cent on land at Bungay Road. However they could not compete in a world dominated by the apparently bottomless purses of the Norwich Gurneys and the Yarmouth Turners and in 1799 the axe fell. Halesworth Manor Court Book records this - "2 Aug.1803: Isaac Avarne (Rector) cometh with a deed between Henry Jermyn, Thomas Blake and R.G.White (commissioners in bankruptcy of Samuel and Joseph Badeley and John Woodcock junior, Bankers and co-partners).... commissioned by the Government under seal dated Westminster 20 April 1799 regarding the Suffolk and Halesworth Bank". It goes on to detail the sale of most of Woodcock's properties in Halesworth. Poor Woodcock had already died at an early age, so the deeds were surrendered by Elizabeth, eldest daughter of Elizabeth Woodcock, widow. Somehow the Badeleys seem to have survived the shock rather better than the Woodcocks, as in 1812 we find "Samuel Badeley of Norwich, gent" acting together with Gurney and Turner, bankers, regarding the sale of the Dun Cow public house at St Peter's South Elmham.

The family were now firmly of the Church of England, and both Samuel's sons entered the ministry. Samuel III (1770-1854) was schooled by **Dr Forster** at Yoxford and then at Norwich, where Forster had been appointed head. He then attended Trinity Hall, Cambridge, and Lincoln's Inn, was ordained in 1800 and appointed Vicar of Ubbeston, which he held until his death fifty four years later. He preferred however to live in the more urbane surroundings of Yoxford, where he was a neighbour of his old schoolfriend, the diarist D.E.Davy.

The younger son Joseph (1772-1837) was also schooled at Yoxford and Norwich, became Vicar of Blewbury, Berkshire, and in 1831 Rector of Halesworth cum Chediston. He held the living for only four years and died two years after retiring, in 1837. In the 1841 Census his widow Elizabeth, aged 70, was living in Bridge Street with her two unmarried daughters Charlotte and Maria and her companion **Lady Maria Tuthill**, widow of **Sir George Tuthill**. All are described as of independent means, and are ministered to by three female servants.

Joseph's son Joseph Charles (1802-50) attended Corpus Christi College, Cambridge, and in 1833 became Rector of Shipmeadow. The Halesworth living had been held since his father's retirement by the Hon and Rev **Augustus Phipps**, but he moved on in 1839 and the living became vacant. The patron, conveniently, was Elizabeth Badeley, widow, so she was able to present her son. This he held in plurality with Shipmeadow until his death. The 1841 Census records him living at the Rectory with his wife, two children, one male and three female servants. One of those children was to follow him into the Church - John Joseph, Rector of Great Whelnetham from 1873 to 1899.

Sources

Lawrence (1990) / Newby (1936) / Preston, H - *Early East Anglian Banks and Bankers* (1994) / Alumni Cantab.

Part Two

18th Century

Anguish, Thomas *Rector* 1700-63

Thomas Anguish was descended from a long-established family at Moulton St Mary, near Acle in Norfolk, where they were Lords of the Manor and patrons of the living. Another branch of the family flourished as Norwich merchants, where another Thomas became Sheriff in 1596 and Mayor in 1611, and died in 1617 leaving money to establish a boys' hospital. This still survives as a charitable foundation. The Moulton family's fortunes were transformed when Edmund Anguish (1637-1707) married Alice, daughter of Admiral Sir Thomas Allin, the Lowestoft-born hero of the Dutch wars and Comptroller of the Royal Navy. Allin purchased Somerleyton Hall and estate, and when his son Thomas died without issue the property passed to Edmund and Alice's son Richard, who took the name of Allin and became the first Baronet.

His younger brother Edmund, who retained the name Anguish, followed family tradition and entered the Navy - apart from his grandfather the Admiral, his uncle William also served in the Navy from 1666 -78, rising to the rank of Captain. William had commanded the fourth-rate ketch *Deptford*, but incurred royal displeasure in 1674. Pepys records that Captain Anguish, as was all too common at the time, was boosting his naval pay by plying commercially on the side. Unfortunately this came to light when he failed to deliver an important despatch to the Mediterranean station and then ran on to a rock "at which His Majesty was so moved, and I cannot say but with much reason, that the Captain was at once superseded". The King must have relented, as William was re-commissioned three years later, but as a lieutenant, and later commanded the *Swan* frigate. He died in 1689. All we know of Edmund's naval career is that he "perished on the Swan man-o-war in 1706" [family tree], but it is probable he started off under his uncle's command. Naval pay books at the Public Record Office record the loss of the *Swan* on the 17th August 1707 - "the day she was separated from the *Sheerness* in a violent storm and supposed to be lost".

Meanwhile Edmund had married, in 1698 at Thorington, **Mary Betts** of Yoxford, who bore him four children of whom the eldest was our Thomas, aged only seven when his father died. He was educated at Bishop's Stortford and Caius College, Cambridge, where he graduated BA in 1719, MA in 1723, and was ordained at Norwich the same year. He served one year as curate at Barsham, near Beccles, where the Rector - by another naval coincidence - was Horatio Nelson's grandfather, Maurice Suckling. In 1724 however the Rectory of Halesworth fell vacant and the patron was none other than Thomas's grandmother, Dorothea Betts. Thomas was by now married to Mary Elmy of Beccles and they soon had two sons, William and Edmund. Both died in infancy and are commemorated by a ledger slab in Halesworth chancel. There were two daughters, Mary and Ann, and a third son who will be described later.

Meanwhile Thomas had also become rector of Weston, near Beccles. He held the two parishes until 1736 and his tenure appears to have been uneventful. Then however came a rather baffling move, for he left Suffolk and exchanged livings with Isaac Collman of St Nicholas, Deptford - the naval connection again? Collman had only held St Nicholas for two years, having until then been Rector of Shadingfield and Mettingham (so he probably already knew Thomas), and also absentee Rector of Pirton, Hertfordshire.

Slightly more is known of Thomas's Deptford years, as a bundle of letters between him and the patron, Mary Wickham, have survived, and four of his sermons were published - including a stirringly loyal one at the time of the '45 rebellion, when a large army was encamped outside Deptford. In 1750 his wife Mary died, and three years later he married Hannah Taylor, of Henham in Essex, a 40-year old spinster. Anguish was Rector of St Nicholas for twenty seven years until he died in 1763, and was buried in the churchyard there.

His only surviving son, another Thomas, was born in 1724, schooled at Bury St Edmunds, followed his father to Caius College and then went to Lincoln's Inn. He became a Master in Chancery and Accountant General to the Chancery Court, residing in Great Russell Street. He died in 1785 of "indigestion occasioned by eating a quantity of cold oysters whilst he had gout in his stomach". His will mentions estates at Moulton and the advowson of Oulton.

His elder son was another Thomas (1760-1810) who was schooled at Eton, followed his father to Caius and Lincoln's Inn, and was called to the Bar in 1786. He inherited Somerleyton from his bachelor cousin the last Sir Thomas Allin, but was declared a lunatic, his brother George being the "Committee of his estate", He died unmarried and was buried at Moulton.

George (1764-1843) followed his brother to Eton and Caius and was ordained in 1788, later becoming rector of Ashby and Lound on the Somerleyton estate, and of Gislingham. He succeeded Thomas at Somerleyton Hall and in 1835 built and endowed a school for the combined parishes of Somerleyton and Herringfleet, but died unmarried. This was the end of the Anguish male line, but his sister Catherine attained higher social status than them all by marrying Francis Godolphin Osborne, Marquis of Carmarthen and later Duke of Leeds. Her son Richard inherited Somerleyton from his bachelor uncle, but sold it within a year to Samuel Morton Peto. An interesting footnote is that the portrait of Thomas Anguish, Mayor of Norwich, now in the Civic collection there, came from the Duchess of Leeds after her death in 1837.

Sources

Neale, Freda D. *The Rev Thomas Anguish* (Lewisham Local History Soc) /Blomefield IV and XI / Bryant, A. *Samuel Pepys, the Years of Peril* (1935) / *Alumni Cantab.* / Suckling II /Family tree - SROL [ref 317/1/1/13] /Naval pay books - PRO Adm. 33.256 /Charnock - *Naval Biography* (1794)

Jermyn Family 1708 to 1857

The extensive Jermyn family were mainly lawyers, but tended towards antiquarianism in later generations. Walter Rye traced their origins back to Ralph Jermyn of Hempnall, Norfolk, who died in 1637. His son was Robert, his grandson Joseph, and his great-grandson James (1708-78) - the first of the Halesworth Jermyns. One wonders whether there was any connection with the socially superior Jermyns of Rushbrooke, but it was not until three generations later that the Halesworth family started using the arms of Jermyn of Rushbrooke, and Rye thinks any direct connection unlikely. James married Martha Mingay (1708-72), daughter of James of Surlingham, near Norwich. The name of Mingay is fairly common in and to the South of Norwich. One John was Mayor in 1617 and is buried in St Stephen's church, while the name occurs in the same century at Broome, Saxlingham Nethergate and Shotesham.

James, an attorney, founded the Halesworth legal dynasty which continues to the present day [see **Crabtree** and **Cross**]. The first reference we have found to him in Halesworth is in 1737 when his second son Peter was baptised; in 1743 he appears in the books of the Rectory Manor as Deputy Steward to **Peter Pullyn**. He went on to be steward of numerous manors in and around Halesworth, and in the 1750's was closely involved in the early days of the Blyth Navigation. In 1764 he was at the inaugural meeting of the Blything House of Industry and was elected one of the acting Guardians. A ledger slab near the font in Halesworth church records James and Martha, with a remarkable coincidence of dates for the latter - "To the memory of Martha wife of James Jermyn of this parish youngest daughter of James Mingay of Surlingham, Norfolk, gent. She married on Tuesday 27 October 1730 and died Tuesday 27 October 1772 aged 64 years. Also to James Jermyn attorney at law who died 6 January 1778 aged 70 years".

James and Martha had three children - Robert (1733-1812), Peter (1737-1810) and Sarah (1739-93). The two brothers married two sisters, the daughters of Dr Samuel Rye of Halesworth - Robert married Mary and Peter Elizabeth. Sarah cemented a useful legal alliance by marrying **John Tuthill**. The elder son must have been a disappointment to his father as, far from continuing the family legal practice, he went to sea and skippered a vessel in the West Indies trade; his sons were born, in 1771 and 1772, at Stepney, conveniently placed for the London docks. Robert was back in Halesworth soon after and was involved in running a liquor warehouse near the Angel Hotel in partnership with Alderman Skoulding. Around 1790 he moved to Southwold and was appointed Collector of Customs. Liquor was Robert's downfall, however, and in 1802 he was dismissed from the Collectorship for persistent drunkenness, no doubt much to the embarrassment of his younger brother.

Peter Jermyn made up for his brother's erratic career, continued the family practice and prospered mightily. In 1772 he had taken over from his father as Deputy Steward (to Pullyn) of the Rectory Manor, and in 1771 he was appointed Treasurer to the Navigation Commissioners, a post he held until his death. From 1774 he was Town Clerk of Southwold and solicitor to the Harbour Commissioners. He was Clerk to the Ipswich to Southtown (Yarmouth) turnpike trust, and Steward for six Long family manors in and around Saxmundham. In 1776 came the most important appointment of all, as Steward and solicitor to the Rous family at Henham Hall. Sir John, from 1776 Lord Rous (and later Earl of Stradbroke) came to rely on Peter, together with his land agent **John Dresser**, for all matters of business, and even employed him as political agent in the elections of 1780, 1784 and 1790.

Elizabeth died in 1809 and Peter a year later. Their ledger slab adjoins his father's in Halesworth church, and also records the untimely death of Peter junior, of whom more later. There is still no heraldry. Peter's properties were sold at auction by Henry Baxter at the Angel on 11 September 1810. The main item was the capital family house on the Thoroughfare, with coach-house, stables etc and a fine garden with meadow surrounded by a walk and plantations, amounting to four and a half acres, and a second "genteel dwelling house" next door, lately occupied by Mrs Douglas. This whole property was purchased by **Robert Crabtree**, who took over Peter's practice, for £2,107-0-6, and formed the splendid mini-estate that we see on the 1839 tithe map, enlarged by then to seven acres. The house was later rebuilt and is still occupied by Peter Jermyn's successors: Cross, Ram solicitors. The remaining items auctioned were a farm at Holton of 72 acres, 23 acres of pasture in Halesworth, and a 56 acre farm in Chediston. Four weeks later Baxter auctioned the entire contents of the main house: Charlotte Douglas, Peter's daughter, had already moved out and sold her furniture,

Moving to the third generation at Halesworth, Robert Jermyn had two sons - James (1771-1852) and Edward (1772-1848). James was born in London where, according to some authorities, he was called to the Bar, but never practised. However some later critics at Southwold said his "situation in the legal profession had never been higher than an attorney's clerk". He may have spent some time in Peter's office at Halesworth, then followed his father to Southwold. When Robert was dismissed in 1802 James lobbied hard to succeed him but, not surprisingly, failed. He fathered an illegitimate daughter, but was elected Bailiff in 1816, and soon after moved into Reydon Cottage. His cousin Henry Jermyn of Sibton died in 1820 and the following year he married Henry's daughter Emily Harriett, twenty-two years his junior, much against her mother's wishes. Poor Emily bore him two daughters, but died in 1824. Meanwhile James managed to get himself appointed High Steward of Southwold in succession to Henry, a post he was to hold on and off until 1851.

James's real passion was literature, and he built up a vast collection of books and references which were to culminate in his *Opus epithetorum*, but despite his living to the age of eighty-one this was never published. He did, however, publish ten works of a more ephemeral nature. These include a pamphlet in 1827 bitterly attacking D.E.Davy for allegedly defrauding Henry Jermyn, and thereby robbing him (James) of part of his inheritance. James was finally declared bankrupt in 1849, though there may have been an earlier bankruptcy in 1828 when, according to papers in the Cross-Ram collection at Ipswich "James Jermyn of Reydon, insolvent debtor, assigned to the **Rev. J.B. Wilkinson** of Holbrook all books and papers relating to an English Gradus or philological work for £495". After the second bankruptcy James lost Reydon Cottage and moved into lodgings in Southwold, where he died.

Edward Jermyn seems to have led a less troubled life than his brother. He attended Norwich School and then St John's College, Cambridge, where he took BA in 1795 and MA in 1798, was ordained deacon in 1794 and priest in 1796. He was instituted Rector of Carlton Colville in 1806, where the patron was the **Rev. George Anguish**, and remained the rest of his life, in considerable comfort as he inherited in 1812 a property in Mellis worth £40,000 from his Rye grandmother.

James and Edward's uncle Peter and aunt Elizabeth had four children who survived infancy - Margaret, born 1764, Charlotte (1765), Peter (1766) and Henry (1768). Margaret married in 1791, at Halesworth, the Rev. Heneage Robinson. Charlotte must have married a Mr Douglas, as we have seen her living next door to her father in the Thoroughfare in 1810. Peter junior was obviously destined to carry on his father's practice. He married in 1789 Sarah, daughter of George Bitton of Uggeshall, and his father passed on to him the appointment of Town Clerk of Southwold, but the family were dogged by ill-health. In 1794 Sarah died in giving birth to their fourth child, who also died, and in 1797 Peter died, aged only thirty-one.

Peter junior's younger brother was Henry (1767-1820). He was schooled by **Samuel Forster**, son of the Rector of Halesworth, at Yoxford, where fellow-pupils were D.E.Davy and the **Badeley** brothers. When Forster was appoined to Norwich School in 1785 Henry went too. He was admitted to St John's College, Cambridge - Forster's old college - in July 1785, but did not stay. In November the same year he entered Lincoln's Inn, and was called to the Bar in 1790. This must have pleased his father, who now had one son a solicitor and the other a barrister, but the next year Peter senior was bitterly disappointed when Henry, aged twenty-four, married a widow eight years older. This was Harriett née Lucke, widow of Thomas Douglas, and moreover with six children. Rachel Lawrence quotes a letter from Sir John Rous - "Poor Peter is much discomposed by his son Harry having played the fool and married a Widow with six children aged 32 without giving him any notice of his intention. He looks upon it as a fatal Clog to his getting forward in his profession just at a time when he entertained great hopes of his doing well". The consolation was that Harriett must have been a wealthy widow and Henry never really needed to work again.

This enabled him to concentrate on his antiquarian pursuits, which he followed in collaboration with his old schoolfriend David Elisha Davy, though somewhat impeded during the wars by service with the Blything Volunteers, of which Davy was Lieutenant-Colonel and Jermyn a Major. Henry was now living in some state at Sibton Abbey, but his projected history of Suffolk was never published. In 1815 his legal interests revived again and he was appointed High Steward of Southwold, a largely honorific post. He and Harriett had a daughter, Emily, who, as we have seen, married the wayward James of Southwold, her second cousin.

Henry died in 1820 and was buried at Sibton, though no memorial can now be seen there. The next year his library of upwards of two thousand books was auctioned at Sibton Abbey. The collection was more antiquarian than legal, but also included as an afterthought "upwards of 300 yards of fine homespun Suffolk hempen cloth". The manuscript notes, amounting to some fifty volumes, were excluded from the sale and eventually presented to the British Museum. For more than twenty years after his death his cousin/son-in-law, James, pursued his claims against the estate.

The Halesworth Jermyns maintained their interest into a fourth generation. These are the sons of Peter junior (his two daughters died in infancy). The elder was George Bitton Jermyn (1789-1857), baptised at Halesworth on the 4th November 1789, but only eight when his father died. He was schooled at Ipswich and Norwich, and entered Caius College, Cambridge, in 1808. He appears to have interrupted his studies and resumed at Trinity Hall where he took LLB in 1814 and LLD in 1826. He was ordained in 1817 at Ely and was curate successively at Hawkedon, Littleport and Swaffham Prior, where he remained from 1820 until he died. In 1815 he married Catherine Rowland of London, who produced three sons and four daughters but died in 1828. He married secondly Anna Maria Fly, daughter of the Sub-Dean of St Paul's, but she died in 1830. A floor slab in the North aisle of Swaffham Prior St Mary (there are two churches in one churchyard) records these brief marriages - "Catherine Jermyn died 20 January 1828 aged 36. Anna Maria Jermyn died 30 November 1830 aged 39. Anna Maria Jermyn died December 1830 aged five weeks".

George, like his uncle Henry, was a passionate antiquary who also never published. His interest was heraldry and genealogy, and his manuscript notes, mainly prepared in collaboration with his first wife, are preserved in Bury St Edmund's Record Office. He died in 1857 on the island of Madallena, off Sardinia, and was buried there. We have found no explanation of his presence in such a remote spot, though it is tempting (despite nothing in his life to suggest the slightest form of radicalism) to believe he was one of the stream of English sympathisers come to pay homage to Garibaldi, then in temporary retirement on the next door island of Caprera. George's eldest son is commemorated back at Swaffham Prior. This was Hugh Willoughby Jermyn (1820-1903) who became Bishop of Colombo, Bishop of Brechin and Primus of the Church in Scotland.

George's younger brother Henry was baptised in Halesworth on the 11th May 1791. All we know of him, apart from his will, is a tomb in Sibton churchyard telling us that he died on the 21st December 1819 aged twenty-eight, and the arms of Jermyn quartering Bitton. The tomb - once a handsome table-tomb in the neoclassical style of its period - is now in a sorry state of disrepair. His will, brief and hurried-looking, names his uncle Henry as executor and he leaves all his property to "my cousin Harriett Emily Jermyn".

Sources

Rye, W. *Norfolk Families* / Blomefield / H.P.R. / H.R.M.C.R. / H.M.C.R. / Lawrence (1990) / Bottomley & Chadd *Senescali Sudwoldiensis* (1989) / D.N.B. / S.R.O.I. - Cross Ram (HB26/412/51) / Alumni Cantab / Saunders, H. *History of Norwich Grammar School* (1932) / Will of Henry Jermyn junior: Suffolk IC/AA1/240/3

Forster, Thomas *Rector* c1710-85

There is doubt as to Forster's origins: Venn says he was "of Durham" but Saunders says he was "born in Barbados". Wherever his beginnings, he entered Queen's College, Cambridge in 1728, took BA 1731, MA 1735, was ordained deacon at Lincoln in 1734 and priest in 1735. He apparently became Vicar of

Tunstead, in Norfolk, and Rector of Halesworth in the same year - 1746 - but Halesworth was his place of residence. He was inducted on the 14th November, and his wife Elizabeth was soon busy producing children - seven over fourteen years. Rachel Lawrence describes him as "a scholarly man with a reputation as a good preacher" and praises his work as a Commissioner for the Navigation, to which he subscribed £100. He died in 1785, in London, and there is no monument at Halesworth.

Samuel Forster was Thomas's second son, but probably the first to survive infancy, baptised by his father on the 24th August 1752, having been born on the 18th July. He was schooled at Eton, and entered St John's College, Cambridge, in 1772, passing BA in 1776, MA in 1799, DD in 1791 and a Fellow from 1776-84. Ordained in 1776, he followed his father as Vicar of Tunstead from 1776-83, then Perpetual Curate of Walpole from 1784-1810 - the beginning of a notable career in pluralism which was later to include Rector of St Peter Hungate and Perpetual Curate of St Michael Coslany, both in Norwich, from 1797-1810, Vicar of Chesterford, Essex, from 1810, Rector of Shotley, 1817-43, and Rector of Quarrington, Lincolnshire, from 1826. He also found time to be a schoolmaster, living from 1782 at Yoxford Place where he took private pupils who included D.E.Davy, the topographer, **Henry Jermyn**, and the brothers **Badeley**. In 1785 he was appointed High Master of Norwich School, and took ali four pupils with him. There he had to follow a remarkable predecessor - Samuel Parr - and the historians of the school have not been kind to him. One of his pupils, T.S.Norgate, left a detailed pen-picture of a brilliant classical scholar and a vain and lazy fop: "A good natured man, but indolent and exceedingly unfit for the situation, as the event proved. When he left the school after a mastership of about five and twenty years, he had not above seven or eight boys under his care". Forster was the first vice-president of the Norwich Society of Painters; John Crome was his drawing-master, and among his pupils were two more notable painters - John Berney Crome and John Sell Cotman - as well as the architect William Wilkins and the botanist **William Jackson Hooker**.

Forster resigned in 1810 and moved to Windsor, where he tutored a number of Eton boys, including the two sons of the Marquis of Bristol. This stood him in good stead, as he was appointed to their family living of Shotley in 1817, spending there the remaining years of his long life. Davy called on him in October 1823, and records his failing sight, which finally prevented him from carrying out his parochial duties.

He died at Shotley in 1843 and there is a monument in the Georgian chancel of the church. This was placed by his two surviving children - Reinhold Thomas, and Louisa widow of Admiral Sir Edward Berry. It also records that Samuel's wife Elizabeth died in 1807 and was buried in the chancel of St Peter Hungate, Norwich, just a short distance from the Grammar School.

Sources

Alumni Cantab. / Lawrence (1990) / Blatchly, J (ed) *D.E.Davy - Journal of Excursions* (1982) / Saunders, H.W. *History of Norwich Grammar School* (1932) / Harries, R et al *History of Norwich School* (1991)

Norford, William *Surgeon* ?1715-93

William Norford, a surgeon and man-midwife, later becoming a physician, is chiefly memorable for reputedly fathering twenty-six children during the course of three marriages; however only two wives and fifteen legitimate offspring have so far been found. Born sometime between 1715 and 1720, possibly in Norwich, he was apprenticed to John Amyas, surgeon of Norwich. By 1745 he was in Halesworth and married Isabella Knights, daughter of Daniel Knights, surgeon and his wife Isabella. He was obviously practising as a surgeon as an account of 28th November 1748 refers to "Thirteen shillings and sixpence paid Mr Norford the surgeon"; this relates to his attendance on Philip Knights, deceased. In 1754 the Norfords moved into the Mansion House in the Market Place where **Peter Pullyn** had been living. Just prior to this, in 1753, Norford published his first medical work, an essay on the treatment of cancerous tumours; apparently he had great faith in a sulphur electuary and in the use of his own ointment. The book was dedicated to John Freke, senior surgeon at St Bartholomew's Hospital in London. Norford was obviously interested in smallpox and inoculation as he reported only fourteen cases of smallpox in Halesworth in 1754. Later he claimed to have treated some of the best families in the Halesworth area.

In 1759 he married Sarah Miller, a single woman of Halesworth, his first wife having died. The first son of this second marriage, Edward, died an infant in 1761 in Halesworth. In November of the same year William Norford became an Extra Licentiate of the Royal College of Physicians and started calling himself Doctor, which led to later criticisms.

A Manor Court Roll of April 1765 refers to his purchase of Park Close (5 acres) and Pound Pightle, and later the sale of Park Close (also known as Potash Close) in the occupation of **John Durban** [sic], Doctor of Physic, and sold to **James Jermyn**. William is described in the Roll as "of Bury St Edmund's" where he had removed in 1763; he had sold up all his goods and furniture in April. By December he was practising there, and stayed for the rest of his life. His time in Bury was not uneventful: his family increased in numbers and his practice prospered, even to his being summoned to attend the Earl of Bristol.

Opposition was encountered when he first arrived in Bury: a pamphlet published in London in 1764 - *A Letter to Dr Sharpin* - sets out the argument that William claimed he had saved the life of a Mr Rollings, an apothecary, by attending as an uninvited consultant to Dr Sharpin's patient. Moreover, Dr Sharpin and Mr T. Steward, surgeon, had claimed that he was not a fully qualified doctor. This he rebutted by stating that he had practised as such in Halesworth and had not only spread this information around Bury St Edmund's but had also handed around copies of his book of 1753, *Cancerous Tumours*.

He survived these troubles and continued to practise in the town. He also wrote another book, seventy-nine pages in Latin on fevers, published by Green of Bury St Edmund's in 1780. In addition, in 1782, he read a paper before the Royal College of Physicians on the symptoms and treatment of influenza. All this while dining out and entertaining at his own house with his family, and becoming a Governor of the Grammar School - all reported in the *Oakes Diaries*.

Portrait of William Norford by G. Ralph, engraved by J. Singleton.

In 1788 J.Singleton engraved a version of William Norford's portrait [see illustration] painted by one of the leading portraitists of the day, George Keith Ralph, who flourished in London from 1778-1811, but specialised in East Anglian subjects. He crowned his career by becoming Painter to the Duke of Clarence. The portrait of William shows a man of kindly appearance stroking his pet dog.

When William died in 1793, aged ?73 years, his surviving daughters Marianne and Annabella erected a wall tablet, still to be seen in the Cathedral at Bury St Edmund's, which states that he was "universally respected for his professional talents and beloved for his private virtues". Three of his sons are remembered on the same tablet: Thomas MD, "eldest son", born in 1760 at

Halesworth, must have been the eldest child of Sarah, the second wife; James, Lieutenant RN aged 29 and Henry, Captain in the 76th Regiment, as well as the two daughters, must all have been born in Bury St Edmund's. No trace has been found of what happened to the children born to Isabella - it is almost as if they were completely forgotten in their own lifetimes.

Thomas Norford MD went to school in Bury and Ipswich, then entered Caius College, Cambridge, where he became Bachelor of Medicine in 1782, but died at the age of twenty-seven. Charles, the youngest son, followed in the same schools and college, becoming MA in 1803. He was ordained deacon in London and priest in 1801. After a curacy at Leyton, Essex, he went as Rector to Westonbirt, Gloucestershire, where he officiated for sixty years, dying at Clifton, near Bristol, in 1867 aged 90 years.

Sources

H.P.R. / H.M.C.R. / N.R.O. / D.N.B. / Alumni Cantab. / Van Zwanenburg / Dr J. Fiske, S.R.S. (ed) *The Oakes Diaries* / Munk's Roll / S.R.O.B. / *East Anglian Miscellany* / Graves *Dictionary of Artists* / Copsey

Plumer Family *Lords of the Manor* 1739 to 1833

Absentee Lords of Halesworth Manor for nearly a hundred years, the Plumers were based in Hertfordshire, where they held several large estates, and went back at least to the late 16th century. They lived first at Blakesware, near Ware, and later at Gilston Park near Bishop's Stortford. The first Plumer in our area was Walter, who purchased Chediston Hall and its Manors in 1722, and in 1739 purchased Halesworth Manor and advowson from **Thomas Betts**. Walter was an attorney of Gray's Inn, and the properties passed to his brother William who died in 1767. William's son, another William, succeeded and his daughter Jane married the Rev. Joseph Whately. Wiliam's wife was another Jane, and when he died in 1822 she demolished the old mansion at Blakesware and moved to Gilston. Jane was now Lord and Patron and in 1822 presented her nephew **Richard Whately** to the united benefice. She re-married, briefly, Captain Lewin, and in 1828 Robert Ward, who took the name Plumer-Ward. This was his second marriage, the first being to Catherine Maling of Durham, whose elder sister was wife to the first Earl of Mulgrave [see **Phipps, Augustus Frederick**].

Jane died in 1831 and two years later there was a general sale of the Plumer estates, including Chediston, which went to George Parkyns, and Halesworth Manor, which went briefly to John Cutts of Witham before passing to the **Crabtree** family. Robert Plumer-Ward (1765-1846) lived on for a further thirteen years. A barrister, politician and novelist, he was Under-Secretary to Lord Mulgrave at the Foreign Office during the Napoleonic wars, and published several legal works and novels, of which *De Clifford* was the most successful.

The Plumer family houses have not fared well. Blakesware, as we have seen, was demolished by Jane Plumer in 1822 and in 1878 was replaced by a neo-Tudor mansion designed by George Devey. Gilston Park was completely rebuilt in 1852 by Philip Hardwick as a "large asymmetrical mansion of random rubble in the early Tudor style, with Gothic detail in the tower and entrance", and Chediston Hall, described in *White's Directory* of 1844 as "built by William Plumer Esq... a large and elegant mansion in the Tudor style standing on a bold elevation in the Park and ornamented with towers, turrets, pinnacles and an embattled pediment", was completely demolished in the 1950's and its park ploughed up.

Sources

Suckling II / Cross Ram papers: SROI (HB26.412/758) / D.N.B. / V.C.H. Hertfordshire / Pevsner *Hertfordshire*, Buildings of England (1953)

Dresser and Day Families 1746 to 1855

John Dresser qualifies for this book as a property owner, and lived all his life at Blyford Hall, barely three miles away. His father Richard (1691-1780) came from Laxfield and purchased Blyford Hall and its estate of 800 acres in 1744. His wife was Mary Grutson of Kelsale and they had four children, three girls and a son John, born at Laxfield in 1746. Richard became closely involved with his powerful neighbour Sir John Rous of Henham, and was soon acting as agent for his considerable estates, in close cooperation with Rous's attorney **Peter Jermyn**. Richard died in 1780 and his modest stone is in Blyford churchyard, just South of the tower.

John Dresser took over from his father in managing the Rous estates, and soon showed a remarkable gift for making money. In 1782 he purchased the old house in Halesworth now known as Gothic House and Dairy Farm and its farm of over a hundred acres. In 1785 he purchase the manors of Blyford and Thorington Hall and in 1800 that of Wenhaston Grange, and lent Rous £500 to embank the Blyth marshes. He also owned, by the time he died, land at Bulcamp, Laxfield, Stradbroke, Horham, Hoxne, Wilby and Caister-by-Yarmouth. He became High Sheriff in 1809, the *Ipswich Journal* for 11th March telling us "At the County Court John Dresser Esq. was proclaimed Sheriff for this County. At the same time **Robert Crabtree** gent. was declared Under Sheriff".

He never married, but his sister Sarah provided a large brood of nephews and nieces on whom to lavish his wealth. She married Richard Day of St John's Hall, Ilketshall and had four sons and four daughters. John died in 1822 and his will has cash bequests totalling £83,000 - quite apart from his lands, which mainly survived intact, and went to his nephew Jeremy. In the chancel of Blyford church is a handsome tablet telling us "John Dresser esq. was born at Laxfield May 30th 1746 and died at Blyford Hall in this parish Feb 18th 1822. He served the office of High Sheriff for this county for 1809. In testimony of gratitude for his great kindness and liberality to all the descendants of his late sister Sarah Day of St John's

Ilketshall, his nephew the Rev.Jeremy Day MA, whom he thought proper particularly to distinguish by his bounty, has erected this monument to his memory".

The recipient of all this bounty had been born in 1774 at St John's. He attended Norwich School under Dr Parr, and in 1790 entered Gonville and Caius College, Cambridge, taking BA in 1795 and MA in 1799. He was ordained Deacon in 1796 and Norfolk Record Office has a letter of recommendation from Thomas Holmes, Rector of Woodton, Thomas Reeve, Curate of Ilketshall St Lawrence, and P.Forster, Rector of Hedenham. These are supported by a testimonial from the Master and Fellows of Caius,and a letter appointing him Curate at Holton St Peter in 1795 for the yearly allowance of twenty-five pounds. He was ordained priest on 23rd December 1798 at Hingham, but soon returned to Cambridge. He became a Fellow of his old college and stayed for twenty-three years, becoming successively Dean, Steward and President. A college living fell vacant at Hethersett, near Norwich, and he was Rector there until his death in 1855.

Like his uncle he never married, but his brothers and sisters provided plenty of nephews and nieces. His fortune was considerable, as he inherited the bulk of Dresser's estates. He added to these, buying in 1823 Carman's Farm (the site of the Manor) in Halesworth, with its house and forty-five acres. Apart from Hethersett Rectory he owned a house in St Stephen's, Norwich, and another in Southwold. James Maggs records that he "sold to Capt.Rayley R.N. house and premises of Jeremy Day at Long Island Cliff 6 April 1853".This was no doubt useful when visiting his properties in East Suffolk, though by 1853 he was ailing and probably reluctant to travel. He was Lord and Patron of Blyford, but at Halesworth was beginning to reduce his holdings. In 1844 he gave four acres on the Bramfield Road to **Samuel Blois Turner** who was married to his niece Marion Day, on which to build his new house - South Lodge. In 1848 he sold Gothic House to **Thompson George**, and sold a strip of land adjoining Pound Street (London Road) for building development.

His will runs to thirty-one pages, which must break the record for Halesworth, and presents a vivid picture of an early Victorian bachelor-cleric. His lands are listed as being in Halesworth, Blyford, Ilketshall St Andrew and St Lawrence, Pulham St Mary, Broome, Ditchingham, Wrentham, Wilby, Norwich, the Mells estate, marshes at Wheatacre Burgh, a farm at Caister, Linstead Parva and Stradbroke. These are shared between his surviving brothers and nephews, and his nephew-in-law Turner. £2,500 each goes to his five nephews and nieces. The will is dated February 1852 and witnessed by John Crabtree and Frederic Cross. Three years later he added a lengthy codicil covering his personal effects: his books are to be shared by his nephews: his manuscript sermons to be burned: niece Catherine to have four silver boats and ladles: Gordon's sherries to his two brothers: niece Ann gets a silver tea service, the sofa in his study, and twenty dozen wines from his cellar: Edward Walker has the gold watch, chain and seal: the residue of wines and spirits go to the executors "for their own use".

Jeremy died on the 1st November 1855 and the will was proved in London a month later by his brother John and nephew Richard Day French. In Hethersett church a new pulpit was installed in his memory.

One nephew followed Jeremy into the Church - Richard Day was Vicar of Wenhaston from 1831 to 1852.

Lawrence (1990) / H.M.C.R. / Will (Dresser) P.C.C.PROB.11/1654 / Will (Day) P.C.C.PROB.11/2223 / Gooch M&S / Alumni Cantab.

Suggate, George *Watchmaker etc* 1751-1844

There were two George Suggates, father and son, and between them they dominated the clock, watch, and jewellery trade in Halesworth for the best part of a century. George Suggate senior (1720-1807) was apparently not a native of Halesworth and had married Ann Holgate on 21st February 1742 at Hoo, a tiny village near Framlingham. They were, however, in Halesworth by 1745 when their first child Elizabeth was baptised, to be followed by Mary in 1748 and George in 1751. In some entries the name is written "Southgate", of which Suggate and Sugget may be corruptions. The business must have been flourishing by 1764, when George advertised in the *Ipswich Journal* "wanted: a good hand", and he appears in the 1793 *Universal British Directory* as Suggatt G: watchmaker. He probably retired around 1790-1800, and died on 10th May 1807. His will describes him as brickmaker and farmer, a diversifying trend which his son was to continue. There is a watch by him in the Ipswich Museum.

George junior had married Ann Felgate of Bawdsey, but they never had any children. He appears in the directories of 1823, 1830 and 1844, variously described as watch and clockmaker, silversmith and jeweller. Haggar and Miller conclude that the watch mechanisms were bought in, but several of his watches survive, including one in Ipswich Museum, and a number of clocks, including a fine one in the Crown Hotel at Southwold and another in the Angel at Halesworth [see illustration].

He diversified further, especially into property development. In 1807, immediately after his father's death, he was assessed for Poor Rates on his own house, a brick kiln, a dwelling and a pightle - **Langslow's** Land - and Hatcher's chandling office, at a total value of £37. By the tithe map of 1839 he owned and occupied a house and garden in the Thoroughfare, where Lloyd's Bank now stands, and Street Field - six acres on Quay Street. He owned the former Pound Pightle (Langslow's Land) on Soaphouse Hill, with a large house and three acres occupied by **Samuel Blois Turner** - properties totalling over twelve acres. His brickfield was just beyond the parish boundary in Holton, now Halesworth cemetery, and his farm must also have been outside the parish.

His biggest clock was most probably the one he installed in the church tower in 1826, when a cupola was erected on the roof of the tower to house a clock-bell. The clock, exterior dial, and striking mechanism were all installed by George, and after that he sent regular bills to the churchwardens for winding and maintenance. He was no longer involved in chandling. Hatcher and Suggate had advertised "Tallow chandler wanted" in the *Ipswich Journal* in 1802 and 1809, but in 1812 there was a notice announcing the dissolution of the partnership, which

Clock in the Angel Hotel, Halesworth, signed
Geo. Suggate, Halesworth

John Hatcher was carrying on.

George's biggest property development began in 1831 when he was admitted to six acres of land fronting on to the Holton Road (now Quay Street), formerly of Elizabeth **Woodcock**. He mortgaged the land to Henry Huson in 1838 for £4,000 and the deed refers in part to a house with coachhouse, stable, surgery etc. occupied by Edwin Haward, surgeon. This is what is now 47 Quay Street, the first house in what was later known as Suggate Terrace. On George's death the six acres passed to Sarah Felgate "with the houses thereon built" and she paid off the mortgage. In 1862 the *Halesworth Times* carried an advertisement: "To let a genteel residence on Suggate's Terrace".

George died early in 1844 and was buried at Halesworth church on 5th February, though surprisingly no monument can now be traced. The main beneficiaries of his will, proved on the 14th June 1844, were his executrixes Emma and Sarah Felgate of Bawdsey who were presumably his nieces.

Haggar and Miller believe the business was taken over by George's foreman, Samuel Chilver junior. His father, also Samuel, is buried in Halesworth churchyard - "Samuel Chilver, watchmaker, died 1835 aged 73, for 50 years in the employ of George Suggate of this town". However there is no mention of a Chilver in *White's Directory* of 1855, and it seems that by then **Peter Canova** had taken over as Halesworth's leading watchmaker.

Sources

Haggar and Miller *Suffolk Clocks and Clockmakers* (1974) / SROL: Poor Rates (124/G9/6) / SROL: (clock) - (124/E2/1-6) / Deeds of 47 Quay Street (Mrs R. Nichols) / H.M.C.R. /H.R.M.C.R. /H.P.R.

Woodcock, John *Banker* 1751-1801

John Woodcock and **Samuel Badeley** were joint owners of the "Suffolk and Halesworth Bank" which failed dramatically in 1799, leaving the town's attorneys and financiers picking up the pieces over the next ten years or more. The

Badeley family are well documented, but John Woodcock's origins are difficult to verify.

There was a large Woodcock presence at Middleton cum Fordley, where the Manor was held by three John Woodcocks in succession from 1616 to 1681. However the last of these Johns died in 1681, leaving his widow Catherine and three daughters. These were another Catherine, who married John Martin of Brundish, Frances who married the Rev. Thomas Meadows of Benacre, and Honour who remained unmarried. There are however two ledger slabs in Middleton church to John Woodcocks who died in 1689 and 1715, so this indicates a continuing family presence in the village which may connect with the Halesworth Woodcocks. Another possibility is raised by the sale of the British Fishery assets at Southwold in 1772 when a Mr Woodcock of Blackwall (East London), reputed to own several busses (fishing boats) at Southwold, purchased "a large building on the Common upon brick arches, 120 by 43 feet" for £310.

"Our" John Woodcock was married to Elizabeth Garneys, and her family is better documented. Her father was John Garneys (1728-98), a surgeon of Yoxford who also held the Manor of Westleton Cliffs from 1770, passing at his death to his widow, and then in 1809 to Elizabeth Woodcock. John Garneys was the third son of Wentworth Garneys of Kenton, near Debenham, and the family had lived there or at nearby Mickfield since the 16th century. John Garneys the surgeon, in his will dated 1797, confirmed settlements made at the marriage of his daughters - Elizabeth to John Woodcock, merchant of Halesworth, and Charlotte to the Rev. William Kett of Melton - and appointed as executors the two sons-in-law.

John and Elizabeth were living in Halesworth by 1778. At a Manor Court on the 13th December 1777 John had been admitted to the Mansion House, until then owned and occupied by **John D'Urban** MD. They soon started a family, all baptised at Halesworth and eventually numbering twelve. They were Elizabeth in 1780, John 1783, Ann 1784, Joseph 1786, Thomas 1788, Charlotte 1789, George 1790, Charles 1791, William 1794, Mary 1795, Susanna 1796 and Henry 1798. It appears that John's father, another John (1719-1811) joined them there, as at a later Manor Court on the 2nd August 1803 the house is described as the "dwelling house late of John Woodcock the younger deceased... wherein he did formerly dwell, and John Woodcock the elder, his father, did lately dwell". One wonders whether or not it came as a surprise when the elder John's will was proved in March 1811, and found to be concerned entirely with his nonagenarian involvement with one Amy Mayhew and her son "John Mayhew otherwise Woodcock, son of me and of the said Amy, born at Pulham 5th January 1809".

By 1792 John junior had entered into partnership with Samuel Badeley as the "Suffolk Bank", or the "Suffolk and Halesworth Bank", their cheques being signed "Halesworth, for Samuel Badeley and John Woodcock" [see **Badeley, Samuel** for illustration]. The earliest mortgage we have found was in the same year to Brame Oxford, who was busy developing land around Quay Street and Bungay Road (Station Road) for £800 at five per cent. The 1793 directory lists Badeley and Woodcock, bankers, and John Woodcock, brewer and maltster. By that date John had acquired the Bridge Street brewery, later to be owned by Paget, **Turner** and **Hooker**, and the King's Head in Quay Street. Several other public houses followed, including the Hawk and the Blue Boar (later White

The Red House [left], formerly the residence of John Woodcock II.

Lion), with many other properties, including a meadow and coal sheds by the Quay. By 1798 he was a churchwarden, and one of the feoffees of town lands... but trouble awaited.

The banking enterprise was in direct competition with Gurney's and Turner's "Halesworth and Suffolk Bank", which had the resources of two major East Anglian families behind it. On 20th April 1799, at Westminster, a Commission of Bankruptcy was issued against "Samuel Badeley and Joseph Badeley and John Woodcock the younger, Bankers and co-partners lately carrying on their trade at Halesworth". The lawyers immediately got busy sorting out a tangle of property ownerships, but the strain was too much for John Woodcock - by December 1801 he was dead, aged only fifty.

Some time before the bankruptcy John and Elizabeth and their twelve children had moved out of the Mansion House, leaving John senior in sole possession. They moved to a house [see illustration] of which no trace remains. It was a three-storeyed house in red brick, with sash windows, three bays wide, with on its left a two-storeyed wing of similar style. It stood immediately to the West of where the United Reformed chapel now stands in Quay Street and was demolished in the 1980's to make way for a traffic roundabout. The house is fully described in the auction particulars of 1811 as having on the ground floor a dining room 23' x 19', and drawing room 20' x 17', with all the usual offices, on the first floor seven bedrooms and three dressing rooms, and on the second floor three bedrooms, nursery and servants' rooms - as the auctioneer says "fit for the reception of a large genteel family". Outside was a large garden, and beyond this

SUFFOLK AND NORFOLK.

PARTICULAR

WITH

Conditions of Sale,

OF A

SPACIOUS DWELLING-HOUSE,

IN HALESWORTH,

WITH

COACH-HOUSE, STABLING, ATTACHED AND DETACHED OFFICES,

AN EXCELLENT GARDEN,

And 77 A. 3 R. 15 P. of most rich Pasture, Arable, and Meadow Land,

ADJOINING THERETO;

A MOST

DESIRABLE FARM,

COMPRISING

102 A. 3 R. 4 P. of highly cultivated Land,

LYING IN

Pulham St. Margaret and Stratton St. Mary, in Norfolk;

A FREEHOLD DWELLING-HOUSE AT SOUTHWOLD,

IN SUFFOLK;

ALSO

The Growing Crops of Grass, &c. on certain Lands

IN HALESWORTH;

AND OTHER VALUABLE PROPERTY;

WHICH ARE INTENDED

TO BE SOLD BY AUCTION,

BY HENRY BAXTER,

On MONDAY, the 10th Day of JUNE, 1811,

At Three o'Clock in the Afternoon,

AT THE

KING's ARMS, IN HALESWORTH,

IN THE FOLLOWING LOTS.

Cover of auction catalogue for the Red House, 1811, printed by Thomas Tippell

two paddocks, and then "Great Pond Piece". In this was the Great Pond which was the source of water for the brewery: no problem when brewery and house were both in the Woodcock ownership, but now subject to an easement for the pipeline from the pond to "the brewery belonging to Messrs Turner and Co", and running right through the garden of the Woodcocks' house. The house figures later in the archives of the Independent chapel, which was built in 1836. In order to get their plot of land the Trustees had to purchase the house "as far as the three stories are continued, late the property of John Woodcock Esq. deceased". Having built the chapel they sold the house, which from 1852 housed the Blything Hundred Savings Bank and the Halesworth Institute, with its reading rooms, and later still became a Temperance Hotel.

John's will was dated 25th November 1801 and proved on the 18th June 1802. It lists his numerous properties and claims that the debts arising from the bankruptcy have now been paid off without affecting these properties. It appears that the properties had already been passed to the two eldest sons, John and Joseph (aged only eighteen and fifteen at the time) as the next item says that the Manor of Westleton Cliffs is to go to Elizabeth for life and then to be shared between the other nine children. His widow is to get a life annuity of £150 per annum and his father £100. Then comes the difficult part - legacies of £3,000 each to the four remaining sons and five daughters. The trustees are named as Isaac Avarne, Rector of Halesworth, **Francis Robinson** of Westleton, and William Kett, John's brother-in-law, and they are asked to permit John's father to live rent-free in the Mansion House, and Elizabeth to live in their present house. They are also to pay premiums of up to £315 each to place the boys in a trade or profession.

It was not until 1811 that the brewery and its chain of public houses were sold to Paget, Turner and Hooker for £28,000 - on the face of it just enough to pay nine legacies of £3,000 each - but it is likely the money got used elsewhere, as the shares of Thomas, then of Carlow in Ireland, and of Ann, then of Ipswich, were not paid until 1835. Elizabeth senior seems to have led a peripatetic life as a widow: in 1812 she was at Bungay, in 1822 at North Walsham, and in 1836 at Ipswich. She sold various properties piecemeal, in 1816 was still advertising the main house in the *Ipswich Journal* for sale or to let, and in 1833 failed to repay a mortgage of £3,000 to Francis Robinson "at his house in Dunwich", as a result of which Robinson was admitted to seven acres of land.

As for the children, our information is sketchy. Elizabeth was apparently dead by 1813. John appears in 1809 as treasurer of the Halesworth Association for Prosecuting Felons, but by 1821 "had lately died intestate". Ann was a spinster living with her mother in Ipswich in 1836. Joseph is referred to in 1812 as of Laughton, Lincolnshire. Thomas became a successful solicitor, added an "e" to his name, and was in practice with **Robert Gostlin White** in Halesworth, appearing as White and Woodcocke in the Law Lists of 1811 and 1819. Charlotte married a Dr Dunne of Dublin. We know nothing of the others.

Elizabeth senior outlived her husband more than forty years. The family at least had the wherewithal to put up a tablet of black and white marble in Westleton church - "Sacred to the memory of John Woodcock, late of Halesworth, who departed this life December 7th 1801 aged 50 years, and of Elizabeth his wife who died April 11th 1842 aged 84 years".

Sources

Lawrence (1990) / Suckling II / Copinger II.198 / Muskett I.192 / H.M.C.R. /H.R.M.C.R. / H.P.R. / Preston, H. *Early East Anglian Banks and Bankers* (1994) / Auction: SROL (996/2) / Will: John senior - NCC.1811.60 Mullenger / Chapel minute book: SROL (230/1/15) / Will: John junior - SROL (996/6)

Langslow, Richard *Physician* 1752-1812

In the summer of 1799, a difficult medical case was placed in the hands of Dr Richard Langslow. A fifteen-year old boy, John Day, a pupil at **Mr Tanqueray's** school at Halesworth (in what is now Gothic House, London Road) became ill with symptoms which turned to typhoid fever. He had sucked some ice after taking exercise on 5th April. His fever became worse, even though he was bled and took copious quantities of medicine, and eventually developed 'gangrene'. Dr Langslow operated on the boy's affected back and used nitrous gas; he was assisted by Mrs Tanqueray and two nurses. The boy happily recovered and went home to Peasenhall.

When Dr Langslow sent in his bill, Mr Bobbit, a wealthy tanner of Yoxford and the boy's stepfather, refused to pay - the sum being £76.6s.6d - although the doctor had warned him it might well reach £80, and he had already had £30 on account. The resulting law suit came before the Bury Assizes on 20th March, 1800 and Langslow published his own detailed account of the treatment in a pamphlet the same year [see illustration].

Published with it was an *Address to the Inhabitants of Halesworth*, 18th July 1796, which set out his problems with rival doctors on his arrival in the town and his reasons for dispensing his own medicines.

In 1801 and 1802 further pamphlets appeared, one refuting a rival publication of 1800 and listing his successful cases, including attendance on Lady Rous at Darsham Hall, the other referring to a row over apoplexy between Langslow and Dr Girdlestone and Mr Crowfoot of Beccles. There was also an argument with John Walker, a phlebotomist (blood-letter) at Walpole, near Halesworth.

So it seems that D.E.Davy was right in *Athenae Suffolciensis* in saying that Langslow "obtained a fair practice, but uneven temper and irritability caused many disputes, so he left Halesworth and went to London".

Richard Langslow was born at Church Stretton, Shropshire, on April 3rd 1752. His father, also Richard, was a surgeon and apothecary, and Richard the younger was presumably apprenticed to him. He moved into Ludlow about 1783, perhaps aiming for a better class of medical practice as he had married a Ludlow lady of good family in 1781. She was Sarah Phillips, whose grandmother was daughter of Sir Edward Acton, baronet, of Aldenham Park, Shropshire; her grandfather Robert Phillips was headmaster of Shrewsbury School in 1727.

While living in Ludlow, the Langslows baptised five sons, two of whom died young and were buried at Church Stretton. Presumably Richard's family stayed in Ludlow (the youngest boy was baptised there in 1791) while he went up to Edinburgh University as a mature student to attend medical classes for a year. In 1791 he obtained his medical degree at Glasgow University, having "practised medicine in England for 18 years" - that is since 1773, when he was aged twenty-one.

From Ludlow he moved to London and became Physician to the Lying-in Charity, but this can only have been a brief appointment as by about 1792 he had health problems and as a result "was invited to reside at Halesworth, and was employed by some of the most considerable families in that neighbourhood" according to evidence given in the 1800 law suit.

In 1793 at the August Manor Court hearing, Richard Langslow took over Pound Pightle in Pound Street, consisting of three acres of land, formerly in the occupation of **Dr John D'Urban**; this is the land on which the present Rifle Hall and the house now known as The Elms were built, but then was presumably a convenient meadow for horses.

Richard had obviously settled in the town in style - a later Court Roll of 30th October 1797 admits him to premises "lately built" in Quay Street (now known as Quay House), previously tenanted by John Rye, surgeon,"now decesed". In 1799 he even attended a patient in far-off Bath.

He had a partner, Miles Rudland, who described himself as "surgeon, apothecary and man-midwife"; in the *Ipswich Journal* of 27th April 1805 there is a formal notice of dissolving the partnership. Two years later Rudland announced the opening of a consulting room at the Griffin Inn, Yoxford. Another partner, Mr Courtenay, also dissolved the partnership in 1805.

Richard had advertised for an apprentice in 1799. This was probably when

Bishop Burnett, who paid a £126 premium, came to work for him, and quite soon left his employment (though Langslow claimed he ran away); Burnett eventually became a surgeon. Richard's son, also Richard, helped him too - he is mentioned in the Day case, although he was only thirteen at the time. Bishop Burnett was making up medicines at the age of sixteen years.

By June 1805 Dr Langslow must have moved back down to London. An auction notice by Henry Baxter advertised the sale of Quay House, to be followed by a sale of furniture and effects on June 5th and June 12th respectively.

THE

CASE

OF

Mafter Day of Yoxford,

WITH

Comments

ON THE

LATE TRIAL

BETWEEN

R. LANGSLOW, M. D. & Mr. BOBBIT,

To which is prefixed a second edition of

AN ADDRESS

TO THE INHABITANTS OF

HALESWORTH & the NEIGHBOURHOOD,

upon a subject which

nearly concerns their healths & welfare,

FROM

R. LANGSLOW, M. D. A. M.

Member of the Royal Medical Society of

EDINBURGH,

AND

Late Phyfician to the Lying-in Charity,

LONDON.

Facts are stubborn things.

BUNGAY;

PRINTED FOR THE AUTHOR BY C. BRIGHTLY.

1800.

Even allowing for the auctioneer's enthusiasm, the Langslows had lived in a very comfortable way: "A desirable dwelling house... Lately been nearly rebuilt & fitted up at great expense - suitable accomodation for a genteel family. Also 3 acres of excellent pasture land on Soap House Hill, in the occupation of **George Suggate**, junior". The effects comprised "A handsome gig or curricle, a very capital mare, a handsome pony... mahogany dining furniture... mahogany bedsteads... goose feather beds, wool mattresses... Turkey carpets... ten beautiful painted elbow chairs... pier glasses, mahogany chests of drawers... a chamber horse... a large mangle... 200 volumes of books... brewing utensils... etc, etc"

The house was sold; a Court Roll entry of 15th February 1806 shows Richard Langslow as "of the City of London, Doctor of Physic, and Sarah his wife" surrendering Quay House to William Hamilton, Doctor of Physic. Links with Halesworth continued, as debts unpaid to Richard's practice had still not been

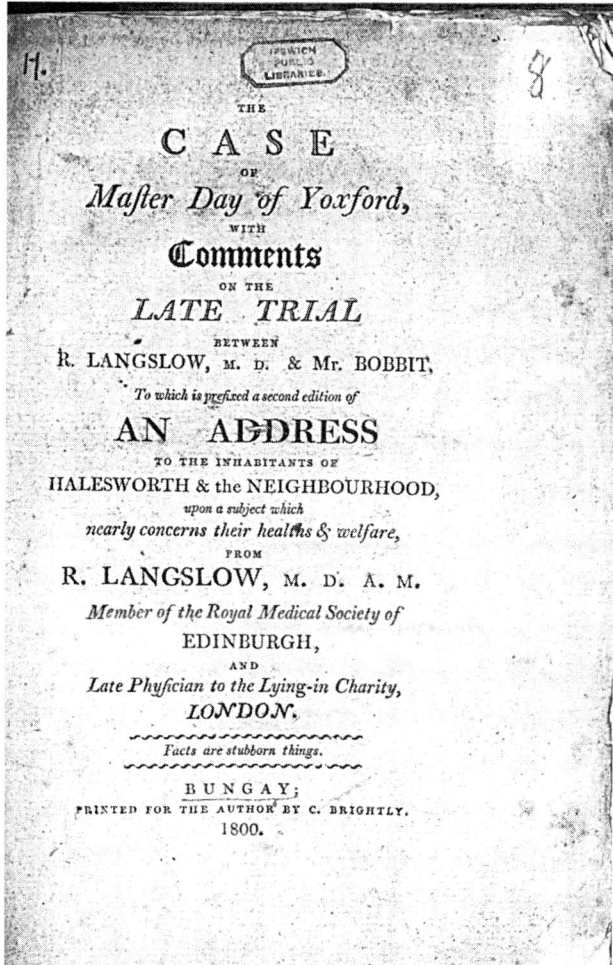

67

settled by early 1807; a threat of legal action was published in the *Ipswich Journal* of 24th January 1807.

The move to London was not permanent - perhaps health problems arose again, for in the Court Roll of August 11th 1808, recording the transfer of Pound Pightle to George Suggate, Richard is described as "late of Halesworth and now of Tiverton". His fourth son, Edward William, died there aged 19 years on 14th December 1807.

A further and final move was to Clifton, near Bristol, as he is recorded as dying there in 1812. He was interred at Clifton in the New Burial Ground, and his wife, who died in 1816, is buried with him in the same vault. In Bristol Cathedral is a memorial tablet to "Richard Langslow of Ludlow, Shropshire, and of Halesworth, Suffolk and of Clifton, Glos. M.D. and sometime Physician to the Lying in Charity, London. Born 3rd April 1752 died at Bristol Hot Wells, 24th December 1812".

The Langslow children, of whom only two lived to maturity, led interesting lives. Richard junior married Lydia Coles of Highgate, London, in 1813 and made a career in the Bengal Army, part of the East India Company. He became a captain, but we do not know if he was an army surgeon. The family travelled extensively, their eight children were born in St Helena; Nepal; USA; Highgate, London; Bedfont, Middlesex; Strand-on-the-Green, London; Dieppe; Euston, London.

Robert, the youngest son, born 1791, became a barrister. He entered Jesus College, Cambridge, in October 1809, then went to the Middle Temple. He was called to the Bar in 1823, having previously married Sarah Jane Henrietta, the twelfth and youngest child of the author William Makepeace Thackeray. By 1832 he had been appointed Attorney General of Malta, but was pensioned off with a grant of £300 when this office was abolished. By 1840 he was a judge at Colombo, but was suspended in 1843 and removed from office in 1844 for "dilatoriness in discharge of his duty". He died in London in 1853.

Dr Richard Langslow's claim to interest in medical matters results from a link to Henry Hill Hickman, a pioneer of anaesthesia. Hickman came from the same area as Langslow and is thought to have been encouraged to take up medicine by Richard's father. There is also a link at Clifton, where the Langslows finally settled, perhaps renewing old connections with the Pneumatic Institution, founded by Dr Thomas Beddoes, and where Sir Humphrey Davy worked. Davy discovered nitrous oxide; Richard Langslow had used nitrous gas in the treatment of Master Day in 1799.

He also practised inoculation against smallpox, then a dreadful scourge; Dr Jenner's discovery of vaccination in 1796 was only just becoming generally known. It was a long time before it became effective - in January 1877 the *Halesworth Times* reported an outbreak of smallpox in the town; the long-disused pest house on Loam Pit Lane had to be re-opened.

Sources

H.P.R. / The Langslow family / Smith, Dr W.D.A. Leeds University (1972) / S.R.O.I. 5347.9 / Alumni Cantab. / Ipswich Journal

Robinson, Francis *Man of Property* 1756-1843

Francis Robinson never lived in Halesworth but he owned at different times much property there. There were indeed many Robinsons in Halesworth in the 18th century, but we have found no connection with the Dunwich family of which Francis was a member. These latter Robinsons have been admirably described by Ormonde Pickard in his book *The Little Freemen of Dunwich*, so we will concentrate here on Francis Robinson's Halesworth interests.

He was baptised at All Saints church, Dunwich, on 15th April 1756 - not 1753, as stated on his monument - the son of Francis Robinson and Rebecca Ladbrook, who had been married there in December 1754. Francis senior, who died in 1790, had elevated himself well above the general level of the "little freemen" and fishermen of Dunwich who were his ancestors. The elder Francis was a tenant farmer of 187 acres in Dunwich, and from 1766 also at Scot's Hall on the Blois estate, now part of the Minsmere bird reserve. He was also, which is more relevant to Halesworth, a merchant trading from Walberswick quay, exporting grain, cheese and butter to London and Rotterdam and importing wine and spirits from the continent and coals from Newcastle. When the Blyth Navigation commenced operation in the 1760's he purchased land adjoining the canal basin at Halesworth and set up a "coal bin" there to which coal was carried by wherry from Walberswick.

The younger Francis worked closely with his father and was elected Bailiff of the decayed Borough of Dunwich for the first time in 1779 and was re-elected frequently after that, often in double-harness with his younger brother John. He took over Scot's Hall, became a Justice of the Peace, acquired the title "Esquire" and was a Southwold Harbour Commissioner from 1810 until his death. He further developed his father's trading activities, and seems to have ploughed much of the profits from these into property speculation and development in Halesworth.

Halesworth in the early 19th century was something of a boom town, its expansion fed by the Blyth Navigation and the growth of the brewing and malting industries. Its population rose sharply from less than 1,700 in 1801 to more than 2,600 in 1851, then commencing a slow decline to a trough of just over 2,000 in 1931.

Francis Robinson invested in Halesworth at just the right time to benefit from this growth, and from the bankruptcy of **John Woodcock** in 1799 and subsequent death in 1801.

The trustees of Woodcock's will included Francis Robinson of Westleton. In 1809 Francis "of Scot's Hall, gent." purchased, for £1,055 (as part of a deal totalling £6,000), various lands in Holton parish, part of which then penetrated well into Halesworth, abutting Cakerow Street (Holton Road), from Charles Long of Saxmundham. In 1822 Francis advanced £3,000 on mortgage to Elizabeth Woodcock, widow of John, against the messuage and close "Seven Acres". This was a key site for the expansion of the town North of the river which occurred at this time, and when Elizabeth failed to redeem this in 1833 "at his house situate in Dunwich" the property passed to Francis.

Only three years later Francis sold the former Woodcock house and adjoining garden ground to the Trustees of the Independent Chapel [see **Dennant, John**], and in the next few years the rest of the seven acres was sold to the brothers Benjamin Prime, farmer, and Edward Prime, bricklayer, who proceeded to build on the site. Their development, mostly in the "white" brick then so fashionable, consisted of Chapel Terrace on Quay Street, a new road still called the New Cut, and houses fronting the Bungay Road (Station Road), including the impressive Magnolia House of 1841 [see **Rugby, Lord**]. On the tithe map of 1839, Francis also owned Low Meadow and Street Meadow, some five acres altogether, adjoining the canal basin where his father had set up his "coal bin" in the 1760's. There was more land too, as in 1859 Frederick Robinson "late of Cliff House, but now of the Bedford Hotel, Covent Garden" sold twelve acres he had inherited from Francis to the East Suffolk Railway Company.

Back at Dunwich, Francis had purchased, in 1807, ninety acres which the Corporation had enclosed from the Common and proceeded to transform it into a mini-estate with an impressive seaside villa surrounded by extensive planting. D.E.Davy in 1823 "called on Mr Robinson at his new house on the Heath which he has lately built in a most singular situation. It stands in Dunwich on the bare heath... on so bad a soil and so bleak a spot that none of the trees, of which - he has planted many, have hitherto grown". Pigot in 1830 was more polite - "the two principal residences are those of Lt. Col. Barne and the seat of Francis Robinson Esq... Mr R. has adorned the summit of the cliff with plantations that have a pleasing effect". Cliff House is now the centre of a large caravan site, and the trees are splendid in their maturity. In the 1841 Census family members living at Cliff House are Francis, 88, independent, John, 45, farmer, and Maria, 20, independent.

Francis was buried in the churchyard of the new St James's church [see **Appleton, Robert**] under a massive cast-iron pedestal inscribed "Sacred to the memory of Francis Robinson Esq. of Cliff House, Dunwich. He departed this life April 7th 1843 in his 91st year" - still convinced that he was three years older! His obituary a week later in the *Ipswich Journal* was rather backhanded - "The integrity of his character seldom failed to produce a ready and cheerful acquiescence in the recommendations or judgments he so forcibly expressed". Davy commented - "I am not sure whether he ever married: but he left only natural children".

His nephew John inherited Cliff House, and was living there in 1851 as "landed proprietor and Bailiff of Dunwich, unmarried, aged 53, born Westleton" with a cook, a groom and a yard man. Presumably Frederick of the Bedford Hotel was another nephew - or were they both "nephews"? John was buried next to Francis in St James's churchyard - "John Robinson Esq, many years a member of the Corporation and resident at Cliff House in this ancient borough. 29th July 1860 aged 63".

Sources

Lawrence (1990) / Pickard, O. *The Little Freemen of Dunwich* (1997) / H.M.C.R. / H.R.M.C.R. / Dunwich parish registers / Davy (ed Blatchly) *Journal of Excursions through the County of Suffolk* (1982) / Ipswich Journal 15.4.1843

Tanqueray, Thomas *Schoolmaster and Clergyman* 1763-1841

At the time of researching the history of Gothic House, Halesworth [see *The Story of a Suffolk House*], and its period of use as a school, we admitted failure to find biographical details of one of the school's owners, Thomas Tanqueray. Further searches have revealed the interesting story of Thomas and his family.

As was surmised he was of Huguenot extraction - but three generations back. David Tanqueray, his grandfather, was born in St Lô, Normandy, was naturalised in England in 1708, and worked as a goldsmith in London in the parish of St Martin in the Fields. He married Anne, daughter of David Willaume, a very successful goldsmith and silversmith, who was born in Metz and had premises in St James Street, London, in 1697 and later in Pall Mall. David Tanqueray was able eventually to become a landed gentleman and Lord of the Manor of Tingrith in Bedfordshire. When David died his wife Anne carried on his business and had her own silver mark, which can be seen on a silver salt now on display at the Victoria & Albert Museum. The Willaume/Tanqueray workshops made silverware of the highest quality for royalty and the best families of their day.

After settling in Bedfordshire, the family dropped the trade connection and settled into rural life. David and Anne had two sons, both of whom took Holy Orders. The younger son, the Rev. Thomas, married his cousin Mary Willaume and became Rector of Tingrith. They had three sons and two daughters; all three boys eventually entered the Church - the eldest, Edward, following his father as Rector of Tingrith. Charles, the youngest, moved to Norfolk, becoming curate at Lingwood and later Rector of Belaugh, where he died in 1856.

Thomas, the middle son of Rev. Thomas and Mary, was born at Tingrith on 16th May and baptised 25th May 1763; a copy of his birth certificate is in the Norwich Diocesan Registry Ordination papers. He had different ideas of a career, and opened his school at Gothic House, Halesworth, before March 1798, well before the Case of Master John Day became headline news in the *Ipswich Journal* [see **Richard Langslow**]. Mrs Elizabeth Tanqueray figures in the reports of the case, so they must have married before this time. In 1798 there were sufficient scholars to contribute £4 to the local fund against the threat of a French invasion.

An advertisement in the Ipswich Journal of 6th July 1799 states:-

"At Mr Tanqueray's school in Halesworth young gentlemen are instructed in the Greek Latin and English languages and the useful branches of the mathematics. The vacation will terminate on15th July. N.B. The number of pupils is limited to 24 boarders."

Harrison Packard of Middleton, Suffolk, was at the school before entering Caius College, Cambridge, on 22nd October 1800, and paid a return visit after matriculating, when he scratched his name and the date - 10th October 1801 - on a window pane in the house.

On 19th June 1801 Tanqueray received his Scholastic Licence from the Bishop of Norwich. Over the years he advertised in the *Ipswich Journal*, reporting dates of vacations and terms for boarders. The Christmas holiday in 1804 ended on 15th January; the summer holiday in 1805 started on 20th June and ended on 22nd July. In 1807 a notice stated that as Mr Tanqueray had been very unwell the new term was deferred until 26th January, giving him two weeks to recover.

By 1809 the strain was beginning to tell, and by the end of the year he decided to follow the example of his brothers and enter the Church. A notice was given in Halesworth church on 19th November 1809 that "Thomas Tanqueray of the same parish schoolmaster did intend to offer himself as candidate for Holy Orders at the ensuing Ordination and that no objection was alledged". The notice was witnessed by Isaac Avarne, Rector; John Wilkinson; James Reeve; S. Revans, surgeon; William Nichols and John Hatcher, churchwardens. The Letter Testimonial confirming his learning and good behaviour to the Bishop was signed by Avarne, Daniel Packard - Rector of Fordley cum Middleton (and father of Harrison Packard) - and the Rector of Bedfield.

Having become a deacon, Thomas was appointed to the curacy of Holton on 21st December 1809, succeeding **John Brewster Wilkinson** and **Jeremy Day**. He held this curacy until 1813, when he was licensed as a curate in three Norwich parishes on 27th December - St James, St Michael Coslany and St Paul's. At the same time he was engaged as an usher at Norwich School from 1813 to 1819.

Before this move Mrs Parker of Norwich had announced that she had taken over the premises "lately occupied by the Rev. Tanqueray". This appeared on 29th June 1811, so it seems possible that he may have stayed at Gothic House as a tenant while serving the Holton parish. Mrs Parker only stayed a year; she and her husband moved to Bocking, Suffolk, to start another school, and auctioned all their household and school effects on 27th June 1812. Four years later **Joseph Harvey** was in residence at Gothic House and had set up his Academy.

The Rev. Thomas moved again when on 12th January 1815 he was appointed curate at Ludham, Norfolk, and presumably had to buy his own house, as in his will of 1840 he leaves his copyhold dwelling house "now occupied by the Rev. Walter Apsley Bathurst [Vicar of Ludham]" and a cottage adjoining, to his wife Elizabeth. Bathurst - a relative of Rt. Rev. Henry Bathurst, Bishop of Norwich from 1805 to 1837 - was inducted in 1833, and about this time the Tanquerays moved to Gorleston. Rev. Thomas appears as of Gorleston in the Clergy List of 1841, but with no appointment to a living, so presumably they were enjoying a seaside retirement.

He died on 1st December 1841, aged 77 years; his wife died on 22nd December 1843, aged 73 years. They never had any children. In his will, in addition to the Ludham properties mentioned above, Elizabeth also inherited their Gorleston house "lately purchased of Catherine Bristow" and various other properties, with all his money, securities, shares in the public funds and furniture - altogether quite an impressive list for a retired schoolmaster.

Sources

N.R.O. Diocesan Records / Tingrith Parish Records / Tanqueray family pedigree / Saunders, H.W. *History of Norwich Grammar School* (1932) / Alumni Oxon. / Records of The Huguenot Society

Cufaude, John *Attorney* 1765-1837

To the South of the tower of Halesworth church stands a simple but handsome tomb inscribed - "John Cufaude for many years an inhabitant of Halesworth. Died 19th January 1837 aged 72 years. Martha, beloved wife of John Cufaude of Halesworth. Died 20th March 1833 aged 49 years".

John Cufaude was an attorney in Halesworth from at least 1797 when he is described in the Manor Court Rolls as deputy to John Barmby the Steward of the Manor. He was born and baptised on 29th September 1765 at St Michael at Plea, Norwich. His father, John Cufaude the elder, attorney-at-law, and all his father's family were baptised in various Norwich parishes: his mother, Sarah Ellis, married John the elder in 1761 at St Giles church, Norwich.

The Cufaudes owe their unusual name to their place of origin - they were an old family seated in Hampshire and holding the manor of 'Cufauds' from the Crown as a Manor of Basingstoke; their name was spelt variously as Cuffold, Cowfold and Cuffeld, all sounding rather rustic, though Simon de Cufaud, who died in 1619, claimed descent from the Plantagenets. This Simon married Frances Godfrey, a daughter of Richard Godfrey of Hindringham, Norfolk, an eminent lawyer, whose wife Joan was a daughter of **Robert Norton**, the builder of Gothic House in Halesworth.

John Cufaude the younger must have moved to Great Yarmouth, where the family had connections (his uncle Matthew was buried in St Nicholas church, Great Yarmouth, in 1796). John was apprenticed to a Yarmouth attorney, John Bell, and became a Freeman by right of this apprenticeship in 1788. Not long after this he moved to Halesworth and set up as an attorney on his own account; his working life was a busy and successful one, although he appears never to have taken a business partner.

In the *Ipswich Journal* for 7th April 1798 he advertised for an articled clerk; later advertisements show him acting as Halesworth agent for the Norwich Insurance Office, as agent for the sale of various properties in the town and acting for at least three bankruptcies. In 1807 a sale notice refers to him as being of Halesworth and Bungay, so presumably he had a branch office there.

The Manor Court Rolls from 1797-1822 show him acting for the transfer of lands and properties, sometimes in conjunction with other Halesworth attorneys, such as **Robert Gostlin White** and **Robert Crabtree**. In 1816 he paid £285 to the Court for premises which he tenanted. The Law Lists show him practising up to 1835; after this he moved to Great Yarmouth, his wife Martha having predeceased him. His sister Ann had married John Davie of Yarmouth, their son Cufaude Davie was a well-known druggist and chemist in the town.

John Cufaude and his wife Martha had two sons - John Lomas, baptised 28th January 1811 and William Henry, baptised 19th April 1813 - and two daughters: Ellen Martha (1812) and Frances (1815). All were born and baptised in Halesworth. Both the boys attended Harvey's Academy in what is now Gothic House. In 1822 John inherited property in St Saviour's parish, Norwich, under the terms of the will of his father, John the elder.

John Lomas Cufaude followed his father's profession and is listed in *Whites*

Directory of 1844 as an attorney at 5, Regent Street, Great Yarmouth. He became Clerk of the peace and Clerk to the Board of Guardians at Yarmouth and according to *Palmer's Perlustration*, built No.19, Britannia Terrace, near Britannia Pier. Late in life he married Marianne Clarke of Norwich, and died in 1872 aged 61 years. William Henry Cufaude became a surgeon and reputedly died in the USA.

John Cufaude's will, proved 7th August 1840, indicates that he owned several properties: his own freehold house and stables in the Thoroughfare; several properties in Pound Street (now London Road) in Halesworth; an estate in Benhall, Suffolk; the Norwich property left him by his father; a "capital messuage and shop next the Quay in Great Yarmouth" occupied by his nephew the chemist, with the houses in the yard. It is curious to note that his will, although dated and witnessed in 1836 refers to his wife who had died in 1833 as if she were still alive and his children as if they were still minors. Could it be that this busy lawyer never had time to revise a much earlier will?

An interesting possible connection is with Francis Cufaude of King's Lynn, a painter who was apprenticed in London in 1722 to Thomas Proctor, but returned to East Anglia and is credited with portraits and decorative work. He may have returned to London as a son - also Francis - was born at St Marylebone in 1756. At the sale of the contents of Cockfield Hall, Yoxford, in 1996 a portrait by him, dated 1746, of Sir Charles Blois, 2nd Baronet, was catalogued. In Ipswich Museum is his double portrait of the Gosnold twins, dated 1749.

Sources

I.G.I / H.P.R. / H.M.C.R. / Soc. Gen. / White / Farrer / Palmer / Gentlemans Magazine / Great Yarmouth Parish Registers / Visitation of Hampshire

Dennant, John *Minister* 1766 - 1851

Halesworth had no dissenting chapel until the last years of the 18th century, though this is offset by the fact that Walpole, only two miles away, has one of the oldest Independent chapels in the country. In 1793 this lack was rectified, and the *Evangelical Magazine* said "It is a little singular, notwithstanding Halesworth is a considerable market town, that there never was a dissenting Meeting House of any description in the place before, and as there is but one sermon in the week in the parish church the necessity appeared the greater".The new chapel was a modest structure tucked away in a yard off Pound Street (London Road). It made a rather hesitant start, until a new pastor arrived in 1796.

This was John Dennant, a poor Debenham boy who had virtually no schooling, but at the age of twenty heard a call. In 1791 he entered the Training Academy at Hoxton, in North London, and was accepted for the Independent ministry. In 1794 he married Sarah Green of Laxfield, and after a brief spell at Bicester was appointed pastor at Halesworth in 1796. The chapel soon flourished and within a year had to be enlarged to seat, it is said, six hundred, and in 1803

Portrait of John Dennant, 1826

it was again enlarged and galleries installed.

This modest but thriving meeting house was barely fifty yards from the Halesworth Theatre (now the Rifle Hall) where the David Fisher company held a season of plays and concerts every autumn. In 1808 the dynamic pastor and the ebullient actor-manager clashed. Dennant preached a sermon denouncing the theatre as "the resort of the most worthless characters in existence" and full of "love intrigues, blasphemous passions, profane discourses, lewd discriptions, and filthy jests". This sparked off a flurry of controversy which has become known as the Halesworth Pamphlet War.

The town's two printers were kept busy over the next few weeks, with Harper working for Dennant and his friends and **Tippell** for the defenders of the theatre. In all fifteen broadsheets were produced, with the devil having the best tune in the shape of the *Halesworth Dunciad* by the poetical tanner **John Hugman**, whose first lines are worth quoting:-

Dennant, great censor-general of the stage
I've read thy learned pamphlet page by page:
Good Heaven! what brilliant satire fires each line,
Flash after flash, how awful! how divine!......

The anonymous *Halesworth Review* - possibly by **James Jermyn** of Southwold - ran to two issues and struck a rather personal note by suggesting that if "the daughters of Venus" were driven from the theatre they might go to Dennant's door "and perhaps triumph over even his chastity". On the same side came *Stanzas Objurgatory* by Mrs Douglas, Peter Jermyn's daughter, and on Dennant's side *Gentle Strictures on the Halesworth Review* by Mr Thornby, and *A poem or satire on vanity*, anonymous, but probably by Dennant. Finally, David Fisher summed up good-humouredly with a song on stage beginning:-

If you please Sirs might I be so bold as to say,
For I fancy I've somehow been missing my way,
Is this pray the playhouse 'bout which there's a pother
Or have I mistaken *this* house for *that* other.
Tol, lol, de rol, etc.

The Pamphlet War and its protagonists were memorably brought back to life in 1990, in the very building which had been Fisher's theatre, in a dramatised version written and produced by the late Donald Newby. Neither side really won or lost the war, and the theatre flourished in Halesworth until the general collapse of the Fisher circuit in the 1840's.

By 1834 the time had come to move the chapel to a new building in a better position and a committee was formed to further this. In May 1836 the Court Rolls record the sale by **Francis Robinson** of "garden ground as staked out 62 by 154 feet... abutting on the King's highway to Holton" to the trustees of the chapel - William Lincolne, John George, J.Corbyn tailor, Daniel Gobbett draper, Nath.Steptoe, Robt.Aldred of Wissett, Robt.Haward of Bramfield, **Joseph Harvey** schoolmaster, John London hatter, John Jillings, Wm.Gayfer, John Dennant ironmonger, William George farmer" - a broad cross-section of the town's middle-class at the time (the Dennant is John junior, recorded in the 1841 Census as aged thirty and living in the Thoroughfare with his wife and son). The architect for the new chapel was James Fenton of Chelmsford, a chapel specialist. Tenders were received and the chapel completed in a remarkably quick five months for a total cost of £1,938.7.8, having saved by re-using the pews and galleries from the old chapel. The exterior remains as built then, but internally it was completely remodelled in 1893 by Edward Boardman and Sons, architects, of Norwich, who had recently completed the impressive Prince's Street Chapel in that city.

Dennant retired after forty-four years' ministry in Halesworth in 1840. He is commemorated by a tablet in the chapel - "In affectionate remembrance of the Rev.John Dennant, first pastor of this church. He honorably and successfully sustained that office from 1796 - 1840 and entered into his last rest the 20th January 1851 in the 85th year of his age". He must have owned the old chapel personally, as the Court Rolls record in March, 1852 his (posthumous) surrender to Garrould Oldrid of "two newly-erected tenements on the North side of Pound Street in front of the dissenting meeting-house with blacksmith's shop and other buildings erected thereon which John Dennnant purchased on 2 April 1805 from Daniel Cook... with edifices or buildings standing thereon late used as a dissenting chapel and now as a Methodist chapel". A suitable use had been found for the old chapel, and the Methodists were to remain there until they built their own new chapel further up London Road in 1877. The old chapel is now a pair of houses.

Sources

Newby (1936) / Gooch, M: *The Halesworth Theatre*, in Suffolk Review (1995) /H.R.M.C.R. / H.M.C.R. / Brown, Haward & Kindred

White, Robert Gostlin *Attorney* 1767-1828

In Halesworth churchyard, beneath the East window, is a classical stone memorial - somewhat damaged now - inscribed with details of the White family. On the North side is Robert Gostlin White, who departed this life 18th October 1828 aged 61, also Elizabeth White his widow, who departed this life 25th September 1831 aged 68 years. On the East side is Mary, the late wife of Robert Gostlin White of Halesworth, Attorney-at-Law. She departed this life the 15th December 1795 aged 29 years. Near her remains, which are deposited in the vault beneath, lies the body of Robert James White, their infant son. On the South side is Emma White, third daughter of Robert Gostlin White and Mary his late wife, who died 26th June 1812 aged 20 years, and Mary Ann, their eldest daughter, who died 26th March 1836 aged 45 years. In total Robert Gostlin's name appears five times.

The Gostlin Whites were members of a family of professional men with ramifications into the **Jermyns** and **Tuthills**, leading local families. Robert Gostlin was baptised on 4th July 1767 at Great Yarmouth, the son of Robert White and his wife Sarah, who had previously baptised an earlier Robert (1763) who presumably died an infant; they later baptised Henry Gostlin (1769) and Sarah (1771) - all at Yarmouth. The lists of Freemen of Yarmouth include various Whites in several trades: in 1762 Robert, son of Mr Robert White, was admitted by birth, and

Monument to Robert Gostlin White in Halesworth churchyard

in 1790 Robert Gostlin White, gent. son of Robert White, surgeon, was admitted - also by birth. In 1796, Henry Gostlin White, clerk, was admitted; he later became Chaplain to the Duke of Kent and a distinguished preacher. Apparently Robert White the surgeon moved to Bury St Edmund's, as he is located there in Venn's *Alumni Cantabrigiensis*.

On 1st October 1789, Robert Gostlin White married Mary Yarington at St Peter Mancroft, Norwich, and their first daughter Mary Ann was born at Yarmouth. Two subsequent daughters - Emma (1791) and Sophia (1792) and a son Robert James (1794) who died an infant, were born in Halesworth, so by 1791 Robert Gostlin was established in the town in the office of **Peter Jermyn** the elder, attorney.

He built up the practice with a number of official appointments. In 1792 he and Peter Jermyn the younger were appointed Clerks to the Blyth Navigation Commissioners; in 1793 he was temporary Deputy Steward to Rectory Manor; in 1799 he was Clerk to the Turnpike Trust from Yoxford to Aldeburgh. In 1801 he was Clerk to the Guardians of the Poor for Blything Hundred; 1805 saw him named as Clerk to the Commissioners of Southwold Haven. In 1806 he acted with **Robert Crabtree** as Solicitor for the Maltsters Committee; in 1810 he was Clerk to Minsmere Level Drainage, and in 1814 he was Clerk to the Ipswich and Southtown [Yarmouth] Turnpike. All these appointments ran for many years and were a useful steady source of fees.

He found time for a second marriage, to Elizabeth Meadows, spinster, in 1797. She came from a well-connected Suffolk family. Their children included Robert Meadows (1798), John Meadows (1799), Anna Clementina (1805) and Harry (1806) - all baptised in Halesworth.

In 1802 the Law List shows Robert Gostlin on his own, but from 1803 onwards he had a partner - Thomas Woodcocke. In the same year he moved into the handsome house in the Market Place, now called Mansion House, which came onto the property market after the bankruptcy of **John Woodcock**. The *Ipswich Journal* carried advertisements for the auction sale by Henry Baxter on 19th October 1802 at the Three Tuns Inn (now the Social Club): "Lot 1. A capital messuage... suitable for the residence of a large genteel family... every requisite convenience... and a good garden. Lot 2. A messuage... with a capital shop... adjoining Lot 1, now in the occupation of Mr Thomas Bayfield, woollen draper, as tenant [this is now Patrick's Newsagents]". Robert Gostlin paid £820 for the premises and was admitted to them at the Halesworth Manor Court on 2nd August 1803 - things apparently did not move too fast. An excellent plan of the two buildings and the garden is in the Halesworth Museum collection, but unfortunately is not dated.

Robert Gostlin figures frequently in the Court Rolls in property transactions, but never became Steward - this distinction was reserved for John Barmby, from **John Ingham's** office in Yoxford. The *Ipswich Journal* posted numerous advertisements bearing the name of his firm, either as receivers in bankruptcies or as solicitors for property sales, in addition to the regular notices of meetings (held in various hostelries) of the official bodies mentioned above.

In 1804 he acted for Mr Swan, selling his two post windmills on Soaphouse Hill; in 1814 he sold them again for Mr Panchen. These mills stood at the top of London Road, behind what is now Kerridge's Garage.

Although he must have made a good living from his practice, Robert Gostlin's will - written as early as 1813 - was very pessimistic: his wife Elizabeth was sole beneficiary, there were numerous debts, and he could only bequeath his blessing to his children. When he died in 1828 his finances had improved and he left a large fortune, although the children still did not benefit. The *Gentleman's Magazine* published an obituary stating he had been "upwards of forty years a solicitor in Halesworth".

The sons from his second marriage did well in life. After attending Norwich School under Edward Valpy (Headmaster 1811 to 1829), the two older boys' paths diverged. Robert Meadows went to Magdalen College, Oxford, where he began a most successful career as Vice President in 1837 and Doctor of Divinity in 1843. He held the Rawlinson Professorship of Anglo-Saxon from 1834 to 1839. In 1842 he decided to move out into the wider world, going first to Yorkshire, then Lincolnshire, and finally settling as Rector of Little and Great Glemham, Suffolk. *White's Directory* of 1844 notes that he is the incumbent "for whom a new Rectory House has been built". He did not stay long to enjoy the new abode, as by 1846 he was Rector of Slimbridge, Gloucestershire, a wealthy college living, and stayed there until his death in 1865.

John Meadows went into his father's office after leaving school, but had bigger ideas and went up to London, where he formed a partnership with Thomas Borrett, a son of Giles Borrett, lawyer, of Great Yarmouth; Thomas Borrett was married to Laura, daughter of **Sir George Leman Tuthill**. The chambers were in Great St Helen's, Bishopgate. John Meadows married Anne, daughter of **Robert Crabtree**, whose wife Elizabeth was sister to Sir George Leman Tuthill, so they were all connected by marriage. The practice grew to become a leading

Parliamentary specialist firm, and they were solicitors to the Ecclesiastical Commissioners. John Meadows lived in Blackheath and later in Stanhope Place, Hyde Park; he died in 1863 at Weymouth. Of his long list of published works - entirely on legal subjects - one was published at Halesworth in 1829.

Harry, the youngest son, also went to his father's office and after his death continued with Robert Gostlin's official appointments. He married Elizabeth and had at least two children. Maggs's *Southwold Diary* has a sad notice of Harry's death: "Mr Harry White, solicitor, died at Loddon Asylum, 22nd June 1846. He was Clerk to the Port of Southwold". In Blyford churchyard are the following memorials: "Harry White Esq. Late of Halesworth, solicitor, died July 22nd 1846 aged 40. Elizabeth his wife died 1853 aged 42".

John Meadows White and his wife Anne had a daughter and two sons. Lewis Borrett (born 1827) went to Oxford, became a Doctor of Divinity and Rector of St Mary Aldermary in the City of London, and Prebendary of St Paul's Cathedral. He conducted the service of dedication of the Mrs Crabtree Memorial Homes in Halesworth (these still stand between the church and Gothic House) on 5th July 1859. He had a son, the Rev. Lewis Meadows White, who became a celebrated musician and organist.

Their second son, Frederick Meadows White (born 1829), had a distinguished legal career. After Oxford he became a barrister in the Inner Temple and Queen's Counsel in 1877, becoming Recorder of Canterbury in 1883. He married yet another Crabtree - Ann - and they had four sons and nine daughters. In the Suffolk Record Office at Lowestoft is a photograph of three of his daughters, one of whom was then one hundred years old.

Sources

Alumni Cantab. / Alumni Oxon. / H.P.R. / Lawrence (1990) / Rye, W. *Norfolk Families* / H.M.C.R. / Copsey / Halesworth Times

Hugman, John *Poet and Tanner* 1770-1846

The Hugmans were a remarkably prolific Halesworth family, mostly connected with the tanning trade, with mentions from at least 1706 (baptism of John, son of John, glover) to 1884 (burial of Anna, widow of Joseph, schoolmaster). The repetition of the same Christian names - John, Joseph, Benjamin, Robert - makes them difficult to disentangle, but we can be fairly definite about John Hugman the poet. He was baptised on the 4th April 1770, the son of John, a tanner, and Susan. He married, on 3rd May 1795, Mary Anne Reeve, and he was buried in Halesworth churchyard, where a headstone survives, on 5th December 1846.

The family tannery seems to have been located at the corner of Mill Hill Street (now Rectory Lane) and Parson's Lane, running down to the river, where its noxious effluents no doubt found their way eventually to the Blyth. There are references to it, in Hugman ownership, in the Rectory Manor rolls from 1765 to 1874.

In *Pigot's Directory* of 1830 Joseph Hugman is a currier and leather-cutter, and in White, 1844, Benjamin is the currier in Mill Hill Street, while Mr John and Mr Joseph are living, presumably in retirement, in the same street. In the 1841 Census John, aged 70, independent, is living alone in Mill Hill Street while Joseph, 60, currier, is round the corner in Mill Hill.

So much for tanning: now the poetry. John's first publication was the *Halesworth Dunciad*, his contribution to the Pamphlet War of 1808, which has already been quoted in connection with **John Dennant**. This was printed by **Thomas Tippell**, the prolific Halesworth printer and publisher, and was followed in 1825 by *Original poems in the Moral, Heroic, Pathetic and other styles, by A Traveller*, running to forty-two pages. This was a great success and ran to eighteen editions, of which all from the sixth to the last were printed by Tippell. The fifteen poems include a *Monody on the Death of Nelson, Neja the Maid of the Blyth, On the greatness and fall of Buonaparte*, and a *Volunteer Song*, written in 1804 while on garrison duty at Lowestoft. Lord Cranbrook describes these as "pretty poor doggerel", but we will quote the chorus of the last and think of John Hugman on Lowestoft beach playing his part in the tyrant's downfall:-

...Then sleep, dear girls, at Love's command
Nor dream of Gallia's roar,
While we, the guardians of our land,
Are watching on your shore.

Doggerel maybe, but superior doggerel when compared to Samuel Hart's somewhat later *The Queen*:-

I was then on my travels, the day being fine,
These words I composed then came to my mind.
I arrived at Halesworth, there was great preparation,
They were celebrating Victoria's coronation!

This local laureate described himself as "curer of corns, bunions, rheumatism, scrofula etc... poems and pieces composed and arranged on any occasion", so he may (like John the tanner) have been preoccupied with his unpoetical activities.

It was a poetical age, and another Hugman caught the versifying bug. This was John's son Robert, baptised 7th June 1813, who changed his name to the more euphonious Hughman. He was a schoolmaster at Yoxford and published *Suffolk* at Halesworth in 1846. David Elisha Davy, in his *Diary*, says "Mr H. being ashamed of his name, though it has been known and respected in Halesworth for several generations, has changed it to Hughman, and is the master of a very respectable school at Yoxford". Lord Cranbrook, that stern critic, says his poetry is "no worse, though certainly no better, than some of his father's doggerel".

Sources

H.P.R. / H.R.M.C.R. / Cranbrook *Parnassian Molehill: an anthology of Suffolk Verse* (1953) / Copsey

Tuthill, Sir George Leman *Physician* 1772-1835

George Leman Tuthill became an eminent physician. Born in Halesworth on 16th February 1772 and baptised on 3rd March, his parents were John Tuthill, attorney-at-law, and Sarah, only daughter of **James Jermyn**, also an attorney, of Halesworth; John and Sarah had married on 4th February 1771 in Halesworth. It is thought that John was a son of James and Elizabeth Tuthill of Wenhaston, baptised on 19th February 1737, although Tuthills were numerous in East Anglia - as were the Lemans, whose pedigree appears in Suckling's *Antiquities of Suffolk* Volume II, opposite page 185. In spite of this Wallace Morfey claims that John Tuthill came from Norwich to work in Halesworth as a junior partner to Peter Jermyn. On their marriage lands at Sotherton, Suffolk, were settled on Sarah by her father.

Further children were born to the Tuthills: Sarah (1773), Elizabeth (1774), Hannah (1776), Martha (1778) - and Margaret Jermyn (1782) who will be mentioned later. There was also Harriet, who died an infant.

George Leman went from Bungay Grammar School (under the Rev. English and Rev. Reeve) to Caius College, Cambridge, becoming BA in 1794. On 24th April 1798, George, described as of St Marylebone, London, married Maria Smith at Halesworth. Her father Richard Smith, surgeon of Halesworth, had been apprenticed to Samuel Rye, surgeon of Halesworth, but moved out to Sotherton in 1780; he died on 28th January 1788. Maria's sister Elizabeth married **Joseph Badeley**, Rector of Halesworth.

George and Maria presumably lived in London after their marriage, George improving his medical knowledge there. Nothing is heard of them until a report of their imprisonment in France. This story features in *Englishmen in the French Revolution* by John G. Alger (1889). After the Peace of Amiens in 1802 there was a rush of English to Paris, only for war to be declared on France again on 18th May 1803; in June an order was made to detain all the English, including the eight hundred or so that resided in Paris, and they were sent to Fontainebleau. Alger lists the members of the gentry that were released by various means, and mentions that "Mrs Tuthill, a great beauty, managed to present a petition to Napoleon while out hunting, and gallantly obliged him to concede her husband's release".

A Halesworth Court Roll entry of 1806 certified that George Tuthill and Maria his wife had come before the Steward of the Court on 14th October 1805, and that at that date they were of "St Germain in the Empire of France". By 1808 they were certainly back in this country, as on 3rd October that year they came to Halesworth for the baptism of their only child, Laura Maria Love Tuthill.

In 1809 George gained his MA at Cambridge, and in 1811 they were living in Soho Square, where the Land Tax Assessment lists them as tenants to Charles Sayer and paying £10.10.0 on a value of £120, implying a middling size dwelling of a type no longer to be seen there. George gained his licence to practise on 25th November 1812, became MD in 1816 and Fellow of the College of Physicians on 30th September 1817. About this time he became Physician to Westminster, Bridewell and Bethlehem Hospitals, and published an address to the governors of those institutions regarding reforms.

On 28th April 1820, as evidence of a remarkably rapid rise to prominence in the profession after his delayed start, he received the honour of a knighthood at Carlton House from the hands of the newly-succeeded King George IV. His skill in the classics was brought to public notice when his translation from the original Latin of the *Pharmacopoeia* of the Royal College of Physicians was published in February 1824. It is claimed that he compiled the book in Latin himself, but the edition in the Wellcome Library, dated 1824, carries a copy of a preface to an edition of 1809 [see illustration].

J.B.Scott, the Bungay diarist, records meeting Sir George at the University Club in London on 21st October 1827, so in spite of his exalted position he had maintained his local links, perhaps from his schooldays. He was a popular lecturer and the *Gentleman's Magazine* claimed later that he had "the largest class in Physic" in London - perhaps he won the sympathy of students by his help in reforming the College of Physicians. He retained all his hospital appointments up till his death on 7th April 1835, aged 63 years, of inflammations of the larynx. He died at his home in Cavendish Square where he had lived since 1826 at least, as listed in *Pigot's London Directory*. The Tuthills had moved from No.9 in 1826 to Nos. 24, 25 and 26 where they were in the 1830 Land Tax list, paying £1.2.0. The site of these houses is now a large modern office block. Sir George had collected a fine library, sold after his death by Sotheby's.

For some reason not so far established, Sir George was buried six days after his death in London at St Michael's church, St Albans, Hertfordshire. A handsome altar tomb in the churchyard bears the inscription "Beneath this tomb are deposited the remains of Sir George Leman Tuthill, Knt. MD... A man no less distinguished for his medical knowledge, his literary and scientific attainments, than esteemed for his amiable and benevolent disposition". The officiating vicar was the Rev. F. Beauclerk DD - in fact Lord Frederick de Vere Beauclerk, fourth son of the Duke of St Albans. He was ordained deacon at Norwich in 1795, and was a famous cricketer of his day. Could Sir George have known him when in

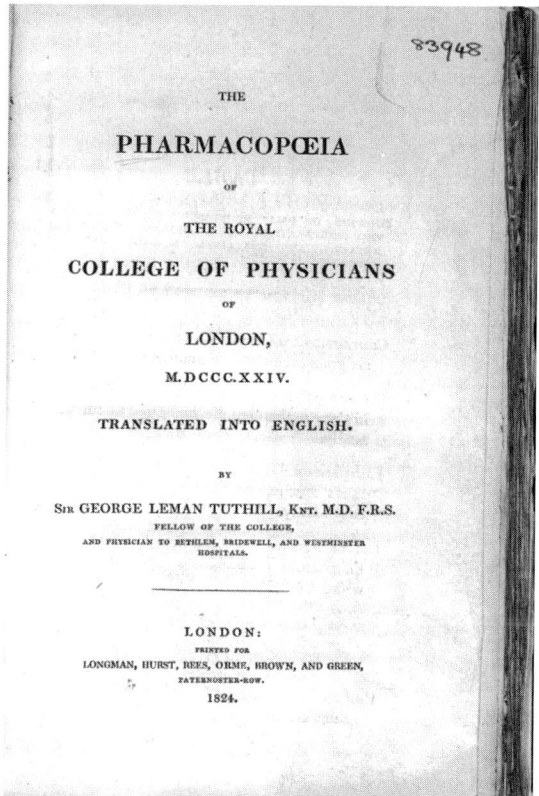

THE

PHARMACOPŒIA

OF

THE ROYAL

COLLEGE OF PHYSICIANS

OF

LONDON,

M.DCCC.XXIV.

TRANSLATED INTO ENGLISH.

BY

Sir GEORGE LEMAN TUTHILL, Knt. M.D. F.R.S.
FELLOW OF THE COLLEGE,
AND PHYSICIAN TO BETHLEM, BRIDEWELL, AND WESTMINSTER
HOSPITALS.

LONDON:
PRINTED FOR
LONGMAN, HURST, REES, ORME, BROWN, AND GREEN,
PATERNOSTER-ROW.
1824.

Norwich, or through his London connections? At any event his wife, Lady Maria, chose not to be buried with him but at Cransford, Suffolk.

The Tuthills' daughter Laura had married Thomas Borrett, the lawyer partner of **John Meadows White**, in Halesworth on 3rd February 1836, after her father's death. The Borretts were an old-established Suffolk family in the Stradbroke area, although Thomas's father Giles Borrett was of Great Yarmouth. Sir George Tuthill had purchased Cransford Hall and manor in 1832, presumably as a country retreat; after his death his will instructed his executors to sell it so that the interest from the capital could go to his widow. In the *Ipswich Journal* in 1831 the estate was reported sold for £2,525. *White's Directory* of 1844 states that "Lady Tuthill is lady of the manor and owns the Hall and a great part of the soil", so somehow she had either circumvented the terms of her husband's will, or had repurchased the property. Another puzzle is her listing in the 1841 Census as being at Bridge Street, Halesworth, though she may have been visiting her Tuthill sisters-in-law, and her death on 23rd January 1845, at Halesworth.

In Cransford church is a wall tablet recording her death and also commemorating her husband. She was buried there on 29th January by her express wish in her will. At this time Thomas and Laura Borrett were living at Cransford and at Gloucester Place, London, and later at Bryanston Square. They had a family of three sons; Laura died on 20th February 1863 and Thomas on 3rd February 1875. There are wall tablets in Cransford church to their memory, also to their son and heir George Tuthill Borrett, born January 1838, died February 1892. He had married Ellen Holmes of Brooke Hall, near Norwich, whose grandmother was Margaret Jermyn Tuthill, daughter of John Tuthill and sister of Sir George Leman. Two of Sir George's spinster sisters - Hannah and Martha - lived on in Halesworth: Hannah died in 1847, aged 71, and Martha died at Holton in 1856, aged 70, but was buried at Halesworth.

We believe Sir George Leman Tuthill was the first pupil of Bungay Grammar School to receive a knighthood.

Sources

D.N.B. / Copinger / Munk's Roll / Gentleman's Magazine / H.P.R. / H.M.C.R. / Alumni Cantab. / Rye, W. *Norfolk Families* / van Zwanenburg / Hertfordshire Record Office / Scott, J.B. *Diary* / London Metropolitan Archives / Wellcome Library / Wills: PROB 11 1848 392; PROB 11 2022

Crabtree, Robert 1772-1840 and John 1806-70 *Attorneys*

The Crabtrees, uncle and nephew, were the leading lawyers in Halesworth throughout much of the 19th century. Robert was the younger son of John Crabtree I, a Halesworth grocer who had, however, been born in London in 1740

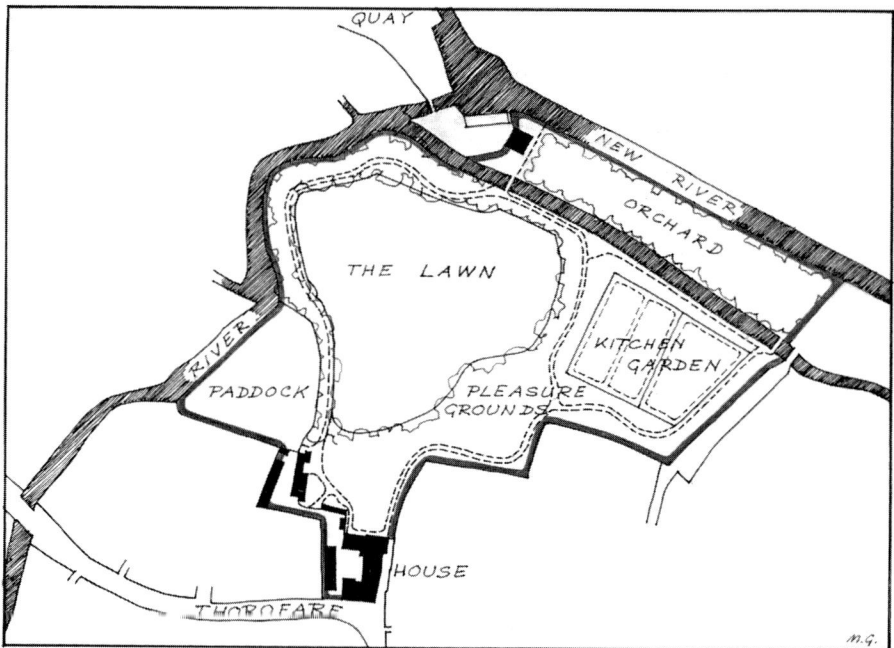

Plan of John Crabtree's house and grounds, based on the 1839 Tithe Map

and had married a London girl - Philippa - who was baptised at St Vedast, Foster Lane, in 1742. They had six children, who were baptised variously in London and East Anglia - Philippa (1764) at St Vedast, John (1769) at Halesworth, Samuel (1770) at Halesworth, Robert (1772) at St Michael Coslany, Norwich, Mary Ann (1781) and Lucy (1783) both at St Botolph without Aldersgate, London.

The eldest son, John II, seems to have stayed in London, as he is described in 1804 as a cotton merchant of Newgate Street. He married in 1802 Sarah, one of the five daughters of **John Tuthill,** whose sister Elizabeth was already married to Robert Crabtree. They had three children: John III (1806) born at Christchurch, London, Mary (1810) at Newington, Surrey, and Fanny (1814) at Lambeth. Sarah died in 1821 and John in 1835 and both were buried at Halesworth.

Meanwhile Robert had moved to Halesworth and married in 1798 Elizabeth Tuthill, younger sister of Sarah and a niece of **Peter Jermyn.** They had six children of whom Mary was to marry her first cousin John III and Maria was to marry John's later partner **Frederick Cross.** Robert is shown in the Law Lists as a sole practitioner in Halesworth from 1802 to 1825, but no doubt worked closely with Peter Jermyn, to whom he was Deputy Steward of the Rectory Manor in 1802, and whose practice he took over in 1811. This is recorded in the court book of Halesworth Manor on the 29th October 1811 - after reporting the death of Peter Jermyn, Robert Crabtree is admitted to Jermyn's property in the Thoroughfare with the adjacent messuage occupied by his daughter Charlotte Douglas, having paid £2,107.0.6 to the trustees of Jermyn's will - John Dresser, the Rev Thomas

Courtroom sketch of Judge Worlledge by Thomas Churchyard, dated 1862

Halesworth County Court 20th Feby 1862.

Sheriffe, and banker James Turner. This takeover was viewed askance by Jermyn's son Henry (his elder brother Peter II had died prematurely in 1797) who had been called to the Bar, but had offended his father by marrying "the widow Douglas" and was probably happier anyway pursuing his antiquarian interests than running a busy solicitor's office. Robert consolidated the well-established practice, took over the stewardship of all the Rous manors, and was soon solicitor to most of the landed gentry in his quarter of Suffolk. He was soon appointed Town Clerk of Southwold, and an Under Sheriff for the County, a Trustee of the Blyth Navigation and from 1808 Captain in command of the 1st troop of Yeomanry Cavalry. In 1815 he purchased an acre of land at the rear of the Thoroughfare house, running down to the Quay and the navigable river - no doubt another stage in building up the splendid seven acre mini-estate as it shows on the 1839 Tithe Map [see illustration]. Robert and Elizabeth died within six months of each other in 1840, and are buried just to the South of the parish church.

One of Robert's articled pupils had been a person of more than usual interest, now better known as an artist than an attorney. This was Thomas Churchyard of Woodbridge (1798-1865), articled to Robert from 1816 to 1820 for a premium of £100, probably lodging in the Thoroughfare house. He then set up his plate in Woodbridge, and practised there for the rest of his life, marrying and rearing an over-large family. In 1832-3 however he decided that painting was his true calling and tried unsuccessfully to set up as a professional in London. He gave up after a year and returned to Woodbridge, but from then on, although a busy solicitor, his passion was painting. The two disparate callings left his financial affairs in ruins and he died virtually bankrupt, leaving little to his widow and three unmarried daughters but a vast stock of paintings and sketches which he was sure would make their fortunes. Alas, it took more than a hundred years for his true worth to be appreciated, and the poor girls would be amazed to see the prices his work fetches today.

No pictures have been discovered from Thomas Churchyard's Halesworth period - perhaps Robert Crabtree kept him too busy in the office - but there is one of his courtroom sketches still surviving. This shows Judge Worlledge and is inscribed "Halesworth County Court, 20th July 1862". [see illustration].

John III, born in London in 1806, had meanwhile moved to Halesworth, where he is recorded as Deputy Steward to his uncle Robert for the Rectory Manor in 1831. The next year he married Robert's daughter Mary, his first cousin, at Halesworth church. In February 1833 a son was christened Robert at Bungay St Mary. This was a bare eight months after the wedding, so is that why they travelled to Bungay? The boy must have died in infancy, as he is not recorded living with them in the 1841 Census, and they appear to have had no more children.

Meanwhile John had become Robert's partner, as they are recorded in the Law Lists of 1833, 1835 and 1840 as "Robert and John Crabtree". In 1832 he became one of the Town Land Trustees, and in 1838 he was a trustee for the new Halesworth Gas Light Company regarding their land on Wissett Road "whereon the works of the said Company are now building". In 1844 he purchased the Lordship of the Manor of Halesworth and later several other manors including Rendham Barnes and Earl Soham. Also in 1844 he took over from Robert as Under Sheriff for the County, and in 1845 as Clerk of the Mary Warner charity at Boyton, where he was soon involved in their highly profitable quarrying for coprolite [see **Packard**]. He was steward for all the Rous manors, and in 1846 while giving evidence to the Parliamentary Select Committee on Railway Bills he was asked "You are professionally concerned, I believe, for a great number of noblemen and gentlemen about your part of the country, are you not?" at which, we presume, he blushed modestly.

It looks likely that John remodelled the Thoroughfare house to its present form, as the Rate Books record - "1839, Crabtree Robert, House and garden - £65.3.9. 1842 Crabtree John, House and garden - £105.0.0". The latter valuation probably marks the rebuilding between those dates. Meanwhile the garden behind had by now taken its full extent as recorded on the Tithe Map with a layout almost like a miniature landscaped park stretching down to the "navigable river", comprising in all seven acres with a central lawn surrounded by tree belts, stables, kitchen garden, and a footbridge over the "old river" to an orchard between the two rivers. At the 1841 Census John and Mary were living there with Mary's unmarried sister Elizabeth and four female servants, and it was the same in 1851. In 1856 however Mary died, Elizabeth moved out, and John's sisters Mary and Fanny moved in, as the 1861 Census records John aged 55 born Christchurch London, Mary his sister aged 51 born Newington Surrey and Fanny aged 46 born Lambeth, again with four servants.

John was now the great benefactor. In 1859 he built and endowed the Memorial Home adjoining the churchyard in memory of Mary - "a handsome, commodious and comfortable building for the use of destitute widows" which was dedicated by Mary's nephew the Rev **Meadows White**. In 1867 the annual treat for the workhouse children took place "in the beautiful grounds of Mr John Crabtree's house" ending with three cheers for Mr and the Misses Crabtree, and in 1868 John gave a dinner of roast beef and plum pudding to upwards of forty members of the Adult School, with which Mary and Fanny were closely involved.

John died on the 30th June 1870, and not for the first time, or the last, an eminent lawyer was intestate. However the inheritance was simple enough, as the two sisters were his only next of kin, and an administration was granted at

Ipswich on the 18th August, with effects estimated at under £50,000. His funeral took place on the 5th July, when all shops and offices closed from 10am to 1pm ; on the 28th November Mary and Fanny were admitted to all his properties in Halesworth Manor. He is commemorated by the stained glass window at the East end of the South aisle in Halesworth church.

Mary Crabtree, born 1810, and Fanny Crabtree, born 1814, now took over all John's properties and the "effects under £50,000". They also became the ladies bountiful of Halesworth. They had long been involved with the Adult School, which was intended to give a second chance to illiterate adults, and the *Halesworth Times* in 1862 reported that the school "after three or four winters will continue under the superintendance of the Misses Crabtree". After the death of John they were on their own and their gifts multiplied - in 1871 they gave thirteen tons of coal for the poor of the town, and in 1878 they paid for repairs to the Market Place, "the property of the Ladies of the Manor". About 1880 they sold the site of the Patrick Stead Hospital to the trustees for a modest £200, and in 1887 they built the Town Rooms, the cost being shared with Frederick Cross and his daughter Mary Elizabeth, their second cousin. They still managed to live in reasonable comfort in John's old house, though their 1871 census entry hints at increasing eccentricity - "Mary Crabtree, head, 61, no profession, born Newington Butts; Fanny Crabtree, wife, 57, no profession, born Old Kent Road". A coachman, housekeeper, cook, parlourmaid, housemaid and kitchen maid complete the list.

Mary died in 1887 and Fanny in 1890, and both were buried in the Holton Road cemetery. The West tower window in the parish church is of stained glass in their memory, and they were the last of the Halesworth Crabtrees.

Sources

Lawrence (1990) / Morfey, W. *Painting the Day* [Churchyard] (1986) / Blake, R. *The Search for Thomas Churchyard* (1998) / Halesworth Times / Halesworth parish collection: SROL ref 124 / Newby (1964)

D'Urban, Sir Benjamin *Soldier* 1777-1849

Arguably the most eminent person born in Halesworth, Benjamin was the son of Dr John D'Urban (1721-82) whose antecedents were - despite the French-looking name - most probably of English stock. It was likely that John was the first to insert the apostrophe. There are indeed two villages in the Eastern Pyrenees, one called Durban-Segalas near Foix, and another - Durban-Corbieres - near Carcassone; after the Battle of Toulouse in 1814 Sir Benjamin claimed to have exchanged genealogical notes with the Marquis D'Urban (de Durban?) who lived in that area. However there were Durbans, or Durbins, in and around Bristol by the 16th century. John's grandparents moved to Norfolk: they were Walter, son of Richard, of Cheddar (1648-1724) and Bridget, whose headstone survives in Long

Portrait of Sir Benjamin D'Urban by Thomas Mogford

Stratton (St Mary's) churchyard just East of the chancel - "Bridget the wife of Walter Durban of this parish who died ye X of April 1714 Anno. aetat. suae 80". Their son Richard (1681-1763) married Mary Myles, and their son was John.

Our knowledge of John's earlier years comes from the *Chirurgical Works* of his future father-in-law Benjamin Gooch, of whom more later. He says that John had

PRIVATE COLLECTION

studied under a regular surgeon till the age of twenty, when he enlisted in the Navy and qualified as a surgeon for a small man-o-war, but instead became first mate to the surgeon, Mr Green, on the first-rater *Royal Sovereign*, then preparing for war. Green fell sick and John found himself in sole charge of the 850 crew, with four mates to assist him. He remained in the Navy until 1748 when the War of the Austrian Succession finally ended. Gooch then tells us that he went back to his medical studies in London, Paris and Edinburgh, taking his MD there in 1753 at the age of thirty-two. Gooch also tells us that John and he corresponded regularly throughout his naval career, so they must have known each other before 1741 - Long Stratton and Shotesham, where Gooch lived, are only four or five miles apart.

In the same year that he qualified John married Gooch's only child Elizabeth (1736-1810) at St Margaret's, Westminster. They remained in London for some ten years, during which John was physician-accoucheur at the Middlesex Hospital, and he may have had a Royal appointment, as his family still have a mourning ring for King George II. Their first child, Shute, was born in London in 1761, and the next, Elizabeth, in Halesworth in 1764, so the move occurred between those dates. In 1763 **Dr William Norford** moved from Halesworth to Bury St Edmund's and D'Urban took over his house, so it is likely he took over his practice as well.

The house they moved into still survives in the Thoroughfare, named the Mansion House, where it is now a cafe and an art shop, the shopwindows having been cut early this century. It is one of the largest houses in town, oak-framed under its 18th century plastered facade, and having two fine panelled rooms on the ground floor. Before the D'Urbans it had been owned by John Prime, **Peter Pullyn**, and **Dr Norford**, and after them by **John Woodcock**, **Robert Gostlin White** and **Robert Baas**. It is described in an auction advertisement in the *Ipswich Journal* of 13th July 1799 - "vestibule, good stairs, breakfast Dining and drawing rooms 20 x 18 feet each, kitchen, offices, cellar, shop. 6 chambers and closets, 3 garrets, chaise house, stable, garden etc. situated in the centre of Halesworth, a suitable dwelling for a merchant or banker with a large family, for many years in the occupation of John D'Urban". John also rented Pound Pightle, three acres of land on Pound Street, which had also been owned by William Norford. Both doctors presumably used it to pasture their horses.

Five more children were born at Halesworth - Elizabeth (1764) who married William Blythe, Sophia (1767) who married Dr Richard Fulcher, Charles (1769) who died less than one month old, Dorothea (1772) who died aged thirteen, and finally one healthy boy, Benjamin (1777). Shute, the eldest, had died aged fifteen. Meanwhile Benjamin Gooch had retired because of ill health, and come with his wife to live with their only child at Halesworth, where he died in 1776. This house therefore saw the birth and the death of two famous Benjamins.

John soon moved with the remainder of his family to Shotesham, but was obviously in ailing health, as he wrote his will in 1778, though it was not proved until November 1782. The only property listed is a farm in Stratton St Mary and adjoining parishes. This is to go to his son Benjamin at the age of twenty-one, or failing that to his three sisters. Forty shillings goes to the poor of "Shottisham" and the same to Long Stratton. The residue goes to Elizabeth, who is appointed sole executrix. At the end of the will John says "and lastly I hope and trust that the same almighty providence who has preserved me so often through the multifarious... dangers of the ocean on board the Royal Sovereign and other ships of war during seven years and upwards against the united fleets of France and Spain will... have mercy upon me and bless also my wife and children for ever. Amen".

The father of Benjamin Gooch (1708-76), also Benjamin, was Rector of Ashwellthorpe. Benjamin senior had been born in 1670, the son of Henry, husbandman, of Wreningham. He attended Norwich School and Caius College, Cambridge and was Rector of Ashwellthorpe, the next village to Wreningham, from 1693 until his death in 1728. He was buried however at Carlton Forehoe to be beside his first wife Ann Phyllis, who died in 1701 at the age of thirty-two. He remarried, and Benjamin was born in 1708. He was apprenticed to David Amyas, a leading Norwich surgeon, studied at St Thomas's Hospital in London, and then became assistant to Dr Robert Bransby at Hapton, only a mile or two from Ashwellthorpe, and later at Shotesham. Bransby had no son to inherit the practice, so it is no surprise that his daughter Elizabeth married Benjamin.

Benjamin and Elizabeth had only one child, also Elizabeth, who as we have seen married Dr John D'Urban in 1753. Benjamin soon became one of the foremost surgeons in Norfolk, travelling widely as a consultant. The squire of Shotesham, William Fellowes, was his close friend and ally, and in 1754 he built the Shotesham Infirmary, probably the first cottage hospital in the country, where Gooch presided. Benjamin's work now frequently called him to Norwich and he had a house there from at least 1759 to 1766. He was early involved in proposals to set up a county hospital, and this finally materialised in 1771, largely as a result of Fellowes's exertions. It thrives to this day as the Norfolk and Norwich Hospital, and the lecture hall there was named in 1973 the Benjamin Gooch Hall.

Gooch's health was never very good and in 1757 he suffered a serious breakdown, going to Bath to recuperate. He did not waste his time there and in 1758 published *Cases and practical remarks on surgery*. His numerous other writings were published as *The Chirurgical Works of Benjamin Gooch* in 1792, long after his death. His health however continued to deteriorate and his and Elizabeth's last years were spent at Halesworth with their daughter, Mrs D'Urban.

Benjamin died there in February 1776, just a year before the birth of his youngest grandchild, who was named after him. His will names lands in Framlingham and elsewhere, which are to go the D'Urbans and then to the grandchildren. It is odd that these Framlingham lands do not recur later, but there is a D'Urban's Farm about a mile West of the town. His wife is to be sole executrix, and the will is dated 6th November 1775. The witnesses are three Halesworth attorneys, James and **Peter Jermyn** and **John Tuthill**, and the will was proved in London on 20 March 1776.

Elizabeth, his widow, moved back to Shotesham with the rest of the family, where she lived for a further eight years. Her will, as of Shotesham, mentions no real property, but leaves £3,500 in capital stock to her trustees Robert Fellowes and her nephew Robert Francis of Norwich to be invested to give an income to her daughter and her three granddaughters Elizabeth, Sophia and Dorothea. The executors are Elizabeth D'Urban and Robert Francis, and all other personal estate goes to Elizabeth. The will is dated May 1784 and was proved in London in February 1785. Benjamin and Elizabeth are buried at Shotesham All Saints, just East of the chancel. Beside them are John and Elizabeth D'Urban, Shute, aged fifteen, and Dorothea aged thirteen.

Benjamin D'Urban was born on 16th February 1777 and baptised at Halesworth church two days later - "Benjamin son of John D'Urban MD and Elizabeth his wife - Knighted, afterwards governor of Cape of Good Hope". By 1793, aged only sixteen, he was serving with the Dragoon Guards. It was the year war broke out with revolutionary France and Benjamin's rise was rapid - Lieutenant 1793, Captain 1794, Major 1799 - pausing only in 1797 to marry Anna, daugher of William Wilcocks of Norwich, when he was twenty and she only eighteen. The wedding was at St James, Piccadilly, though Benjamin is believed to have been stationed at Norwich at the time. The Peninsular War broke out in 1808, and Benjamin was sent as a Colonel, to stiffen up the Portuguese army, rising to Brigadier-General in 1811, commanding a Brigade of Portuguese cavalry under the future Duke of Wellington. He was at the battles of Busaco, Albuera, Badajoz, Salamanca, Vittoria, Nivelle and Toulouse, latterly as Quartermaster General of the Portuguese army. At the end of the war he brought them home in such good order that the Regent of Portugal conferred a life pension and made him a Knight of the Order of the Tower and Sword, to be followed, on returning to England, by the K.C.B.

While he was in the Peninsula Anna was living at Yarmouth, and we have a glimpse of her in Palmer's *Perlustration* - "when a boy the editor was delighted to visit Lady D'Urban because her appartments were adorned with prints and drawings of battles and sieges and was much frequented by the military officers quartered in the town, whose gay uniforms and clanking swords excited his youthful imagination". He also records in his diary "I attended Mr Nicholl's seminary, Among my schoolfellows were William and Walter D'Urban, sons of General Sir Benjamin, both fine handsome fellows".

Soon after the end of the war Benjamin found a new metier as Colonial governor, of Antigua in 1820, Demerara in 1824, and Guiana in 1831, but his major appointment came in 1833 as the first Governor of the Cape of Good Hope. Here he was responsible for the abolition of slavery, setting up the first Legislative Council, and the annexation of Natal, which led to the re-naming of Port Natal as Durban in his honour. Lady D'Urban died at Cape Town in 1843. His last colonial posting was a less happy one. Canada and the United States were locked in bitter disputes over the Oregon/Columbia border, and the government needed a strong commander-in-chief. In 1847, at the age of seventy, Sir Benjamin exchanged the sunny Cape for wintry Montreal. The Governor General, Lord Elgin, was unhappy with D'Urban's appointment. Benjamin's health was failing, there were riots in Montreal, and on 25th May 1849 he died. Elgin refused to attend the funeral but enough people did to make the cortege a mile long. He was buried in the Montreal military cemetery under an impressive obelisk, but even here he was not allowed to rest in peace. The cemetery became redundant after British troops left the country in 1870, then vandalised and derelict. Finally a new Field of Honor was set up at Pointe Claire on Montreal Island with D'Urban and his obelisk at the centre and the graves of the re-interred soldiers around it. This was re-dedicated in 1945.

Sources

John D'Urban: Gooch, Benjamin *Chirurgical Works* (1792) / H.P.R. / H.M.C.R. / Will - NRO.U.99.f.516.
Benjamin Gooch: Batty Shaw, A. *Benjamin Gooch* in Medical History XVI/I, Jan 1992 / Batty Shaw, A. *Benjamin Gooch., letters to Messenger Monsey* in Norfolk & Norwich Inst. for Medical Education journal, Autumn 1993 / D.N.B. / Will of BG: PCC.PROB.11/1017 / Will of EG: PCC.PROB.11/1126
Benjamin D'Urban: H.P.R. / D.N.B./ *Gentleman's Magazine* - obituary, 1849 p647 / Palmer / Palmer, F.D. *Leaves from the diary of C.J.P.* / Shaw, W. *Knights of England*

Easterson, Thomas *Ironfounder* 1777-1858

Halesworth had a busy iron foundry through the 19th century. It was set up in the early years of the century by Thomas Easterson and his aptly-named partner Tubal Cain Seaman. Thomas gave his place of birth as Ipswich, and he may have been the son of another Thomas, born in 1750, son of Thomas and Susan at Woodbridge, where the name Easterson occurs frequently. In 1820 at his marriage he is described as bachelor of Halesworth. His bride was Mary Hopson, born at Halesworth, but the wedding was at St Matthew, Ipswich. Both were of relatively mature years: Thomas, 43, and Mary ten years younger, and they soon produced a family - Thomas, born in 1822, Elizabeth (1823), Mary Ann Amelia (1824), Emma (1827) and Ellen (1830) who died in infancy.

The foundry was certainly well-established by 1813 when the firm advertised in the *Ipswich Journal* - "Panel'd iron chests, suitable for parish registers or coun-

Billhead of Thomas Easterson, dated 1837

try houses, manufactured and sold by Messrs Easterson and Seaman, iron founders of Halesworth". Three years later a notice appears in the same paper of the dissolution of the partnership, with Thomas continuing the business. The premises figure in the Manor court books where in 1807 John Girling surrendered for £98.11.0 to Thomas Easterson and Tubal Cain Seaman, ironfounders and whitesmiths, a messuage now occupied by Dorothy Boone, Easterson and Seaman being admitted to one moiety each. In 1817 Easterson is recorded as buying out for £50 the moiety owned by Seaman and his wife Elizabeth of the premises "now used as a selling shop", late of Dorothy Boone. It seems therefore that there was a shop fronting the Thoroughfare (probably now Pearce & Kemp) with the foundry behind it built, or rebuilt, later as the Vestry minutes of 1839 record a rating assessment - "New iron foundry of Mr Easterson - £14 at present, it not being completed". This shows clearly on the 1839 tithe map as a courtyard-like group of buildings where the central car park now is.

By 1830, in *Pigot's Directory*, Seaman was running his own foundry at Woodbridge, and Easterson's bill head of 1842 reads "Halesworth Iron Foundry, Dr. to T.Easterson, manufacturer of iron ploughs, ploughshares case-hardened, chaff engines, improved kitchen ranges, stoves etc". An advertisement in the *Halesworth Times* of 1855 has "Easterson and Son, iron and brass founders and implement makers, patent turnip-cutters, improved ploughs, chaff engines, horse works for driving machinery; stove, kitchen range and fender warehouses. N.B. all work done on the premises from well-seasoned stuff". Another line was cast iron copings for brick bridges, and one of these survives at Wissett with the inscription "Easterson, Halesworth" and the date 1847. The 1851 Census records the family living in the Thoroughfare, with Thomas, 73 (employs eleven men and boys), Mary 64, and Thomas 29, Amelia 26, and Emma 24 - all single and living with their parents.

Thomas died on the 30th March 1858, having moved to a house in the Market Place, and within three months Thomas junior had sold the business to Messrs Bond and Silver, later Bond and Robinson. It was again sold in 1865, to Edwin Headley, who continued until his death in 1902. Thomas junior soon transformed himself into a farmer at Bawdsey, and his mother must have joined him, as she died there in 1868. Thomas and his sister Mary inherited land in Chediston Street and the Thoroughfare shop, and still held these in 1880, though by then he was "Thomas Easterson of Deerbolt Hall, Earl Stonham, gent" and Marianne Amelia was still a spinster and living with him.

One of the Easterson foundry buildings still survives, adjoining the public car park, and is now used as workshops. The tall brick chimney was demolished during the Second World War, as it was believed to be a useful landmark for enemy aircraft.

Sources

H.P.R. / H.M.C.R. / Ipswich Journal / Halesworth Times

Baas, Robert *Gentleman* 1778-1875

Robert Baas was a native of Great Yarmouth. Palmer records him joining the newly raised Corps of Infantry Volunteers shortly after its formation in 1798 as "Ensign Baas". In 1800 he became a freeman of the Borough, not by birth but by apprenticeship to Samuel Barker Esq. However he moved to Chediston Hall in 1811, where members of the Beales and Baas families were already established. In Chediston church is a plaque "Sacred to the memory of members of the Beales and Baas families who resided at Chediston Hall". The earliest Beales died in 1787 and the earliest Baas in 1806. They must have been tenants of the Hall, which had been owned, with the Manors of Chediston, since 1722 by the absentee **Plumer** family of Hertfordshire. In 1833 it was sold, so evidently the Beales-Baas's had to vacate.

Robert moved to Halesworth, living with his unmarried son in the spacious house in the Thoroughfare previously owned by **Robert Gostlin White**, who had died in 1828. In the 1851 Census he is described as a widower, living with his son and daughter, two sisters older than himself, and three female servants. He was a Trustee of the Blyth Navigation and Treasurer of the Halesworth Gas Light Company. The *Halesworth Times* reports his death on 2nd April 1875 aged ninety-eight - "the beau ideal of a fine old English gentleman". He was buried in Chediston churchyard, but a handsome stained glass window was dedicated in 1877 in the North aisle of Halesworth church, inscribed "Robert Baas for 40 years and upwards resident in Halesworth, for 23 years previously in Chediston, died 2 April 1875 in his 98th year, also Frances Baas his eldest and only surviving daughter, died 28 July 1876, likewise buried at Chediston. Window erected by his son and brother".

The son, Robert Beales Baas was born in 1808 at Yarmouth, and qualified as a solicitor in Hilary Term 1830. By 1833 he was practising in Halesworth in partnership with Harry White, son of Robert Gostlin White. From 1845 to 1883 he was practising alone but with London agents White and Borrett. These were Harry's brother John Meadows White and his partner Thomas Borrett, practising as solicitors in London. In 1852 he was appointed Solicitor to the Blything Hundred Savings Bank and in 1875 took his late father's place as a Trustee of the Blyth Navigation. He was an officer of the 7th Suffolk Volunteers, as the *Halesworth Times* of 24th February 1874 records his retirement as Captain commandant after fourteen years in the Corps, and a dinner at the King's Arms at which he was presented with a timepiece, supplied by Sergeant **Canova**.

Finally, the name Baas was probably a variant of Base, a family represented in both Halesworth and Beccles inthe 16th and 17th centuries [see **Saltonstall**]. We have however found no definite connection.

Sources

Palmer / The Law List

Tippell, Thomas *Printer* 1780-1855

Thomas Tippell was born at Stuston, near Diss, and baptised there on 10th December 1780, the son of Jonathan and Mary. His wife was Prudence, a Halesworth girl, born c.1786, but we know no more about her or her origins as we have not traced their marriage.

Thomas was in Halesworth by 1806, when the Poor Rates book records - "Tipple, late Allcock - value £9 - rates s7/6". This indicates that he had taken over the business of John Turrill Allcock in the Thoroughfare, who had in turn taken over from William Gilbert. Allcock had been a printer and bookseller and run a circulating library in the building known as the Old Guildhall. In 1806 Thomas advertised for an apprentice in the *Ipswich Journal*,and later the same year advertised the range of goods on offer at his shop. He received a licence for his printing press in 1814, but had clearly been printing long before that, as in 1808 he was much involved in the Pamphlet War [see **Dennant, John**], printing most of the contributions on the pro-theatre side. He advertised again for apprentices in 1813, 1818 and 1826, presumably keeping one apprentice at a time. He appears in *Pigot's Directory* of 1826 as a bookseller and in 1830 as bookseller and stationer, while in *White's Directory*, 1844, he has three entries: as "Bookseller, printer and stamp office", as "Savings Bank at Mr Tippell's" and as "Norwich Union Insurance Society at Mr Tippell's". In the 1841 Census he is living in Thoroughfare with his wife Prudence, sons Thomas and James - the latter an apprentice - and one female servant.

Thomas and Prudence had ten children, all baptised at Halesworth: Sarah in 1812, Thomas 1815, William 1816, Mary 1817, Prudence 1818, Lucy 1819, Emma

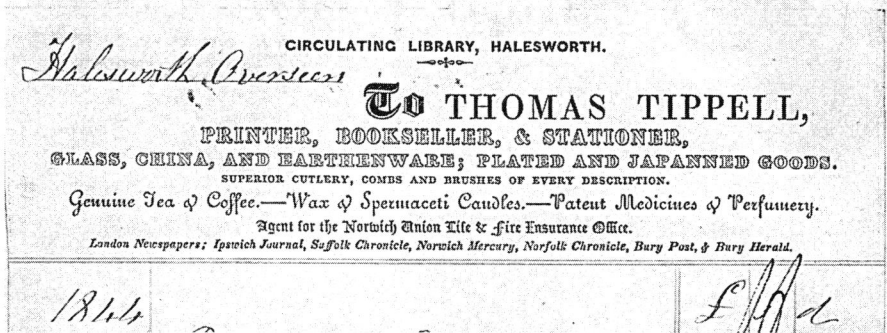

CIRCULATING LIBRARY, HALESWORTH.

Halesworth Overseers

To THOMAS TIPPELL,

PRINTER, BOOKSELLER, & STATIONER,

GLASS, CHINA, AND EARTHENWARE; PLATED AND JAPANNED GOODS.

SUPERIOR CUTLERY, COMBS AND BRUSHES OF EVERY DESCRIPTION.

Genuine Tea & Coffee.—Wax & Spermaceti Candles.—Patent Medicines & Perfumery.

Agent for the Norwich Union Life & Fire Insurance Office.

London Newspapers; Ipswich Journal, Suffolk Chronicle, Norwich Mercury, Norfolk Chronicle, Bury Post, & Bury Herald.

1844

Billhead of Thomas Tippell, dated 1844

1821, James 1823, John 1824, and Louisa 1827 - but the only ones of whom we have later records are Thomas, Emma and James. By the 1851 Census he had further expanded his business as he "employs three, and three as a coal dealer", while a billhead of 1842 describes the business fully - "Printer, bookseller and stationer, circulating library, glass, china, earthenware, plated and Japanned goods. Genuine tea and coffeee, wax spermaceti candles, patent medicines and perfumery. Agent for Norwich Union Life and Fire Offices. London newspapers, Ipswich Journal, Suffolk Chronicle, Norwich Mercury, Norfolk Chronicle, Bury Post, Bury Herald".

By 1855 the business is described as Thomas Tippell and Son, but on 20th November, in one of the first issues of the *Halesworth Times*, "Died in his 74th year Mr Thomas Tippell, for fifty years printer and bookseller of Halesworth". Six days later he was buried in the new cemetery on the Holton Road.

Thomas junior took over, but less than four years later he died, still a bachelor, aged forty-three, and was buried at Holton Road on 1st April 1859. James took over and in the 1861 Census was living over the shop in the Thoroughfare as bookseller and printer, aged thirty-eight, with his wife Harriet, four children and two servants. In March of the same year the *Halesworth Times* announced that its own offices were removing to J.Tippell in the Thoroughfare, having until then been owned by George Rackham, but two years later "James Tippell has relinquished the bookbinding and stationery department to William Pickin Gale". This was the first step to a complete takeover, as in July 1867 "Old Guildhall printing offices - James Tippell after thirteen years has transferred the business to W.P. Gale". Nothing more is known of James until a further notice in the *Halesworth Times* on 15th December 1874 - "Death - Tippell, James, in Kensington, many years resident in Halesworth and for some time publisher of this paper, aged fifty-one". Typically of Halesworth continuity, the premises are today still a stationer's and newsagent's.

Tippell's, in its prime, had been a busy publisher and a printer of considerable quality. We have already mentioned their part in the Pamphlet War, in which they printed **John Hugman's** *Halesworth Dunciad*, Charlotte Douglas's *Stanzas Objurgatory*, and both issues of the anonymous*Halesworth Review* (possibly by

97

James Jermyn). This did not, however, prevent him from printing John Dennant's collected sermons of 1812 to 1830. Also for John Hugman he printed eighteen editions of his collected poems from 1825 to 1836, and for another local poet, James Bird, *The Vale of Slaughden* in 1819. Among numerous official publications were the bye-laws of the Blything Union in 1818, the rules and regulations of the Blything Hundred Savings Bank, and the Poll Book for the East Suffolk division in the general election of 1835, the latter being a particularly good example of the quality of Tippell's printing. More unusual works included a catalogue of the sale of **Henry Jermyn's** library in 1821, James Magg's *Handbook to the port and shipping of Southwold*, and *An authentic copy of the poll book of the late election of a churchwarden for the parish of Halesworth, at which election the Methodists were so decisively defeated*, in 1812.

Sources

Copsey / Halesworth Times / H.P.R. / Stuston parish registers

Packard, Harrison *Cleric* 1783-1860

There are two lasting memorials to Harrison Packard - one is a handsome wall tablet in Middleton church, near Westleton. The other is his name scratched on a pane of glass in a back window at Gothic House, London Road, and dated October 10th 1801, when the Halesworth house was **Mr Tanqueray's** school.

Harrison Packard was born in Middleton, the elder son of the Rector, the Rev. Daniel Packard and Ann his wife, who are both commemorated on the same wall tablet as their son. Harrison was baptised there on November 15th 1783. His father, Daniel, was born in Woodbridge, the son of another Daniel, a merchant in that town, who had married Sarah Harrison, also of Woodbridge, in 1748/9. She was the sister of the Rev. Joseph (or John) Harrison, Rector of Middleton and Vicar of Westleton, whose wall tablet is also in Middleton church. He held the patronage of the church and on his death transferred it to the Rev. Daniel, who in turn left it in trust for his son Harrison, the trustees being David Elisha Davy and **Henry Jermyn**.

Young Harrison Packard seems to have had a career in the church mapped out for him. He attended Mr Tanqueray's school in Halesworth and from there went to Caius College, Cambridge, and matriculated at Michaelmas 1801, the date of his visit back to his old school. Becoming BA in 1805 and MA in 1808, he was ordained deacon at Norwich in 1806 and priest in June 1808.

In 1809 Mr Charles Blois of Yoxford granted him the living of Blythburgh and Walberswick, in succession to his father, who had held it from 1779 under the patronage of Sir John Blois. About this time Harrison married Esther, daughter of the Rev. Francis Leggett of Sibton, and in 1811 their first son Francis was born. For unknown reasons they moved to Blaxhall, where Harrison opened a school in the parsonage house. An advertisement placed in the *Ipswich Journal* for 5th

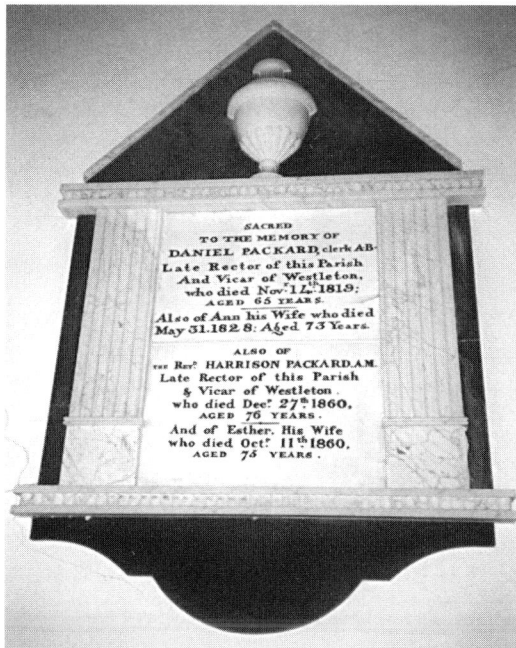

Tablet to Harrison Packard and his father in Middleton church

August 1815 announces:-

"The Rev. H. Packard intends to instruct in English, Latin, Greek, mathematics, geography, composition etc. Terms - under 10 years £35 above 10 years £40. Entrance 2gns. No extras except washing. Accomodation for day boarders £20 p.a. The Seminary will open on 7th August"

Two more sons were born at Blaxhall - Joseph and William in 1813 and 1814, but by 1816 when another son Daniel was born the family had moved to Stutton, the seat of the Jermy family. The Rev. Harrison accumulated other livings: Bruisyard in 1814, and perpetual curate of Butley from 1814-25. Eventually he settled down at Fordley and Middleton, where he stayed until his death in 1860.

Francis Packard, the eldest son, became a surgeon in Halesworth, and according to Van Zwanenburg, was in financial difficulties in 1838 and had moved to Walton, near Felixstowe by 1841.

Joseph too became a doctor, in Leiston, and had a son Harrison Joseph in 1859. The fourth son, Daniel, became a priest, following his father to Caius College and being ordained deacon at Lincoln in 1835 and priest at Norwich in 1841. He became curate at Harpenden, Hertfordshire, in 1845 and Chesterford, Essex, in 1850. He married Sarah Devereux of Beccles in 1835, and took her off to Australia where he became incumbent of Walkerville, South Australia, in 1859.

In *White's Directory* of 1844, their father is listed as incumbent of Fordley cum Middleton, Peasenhall and Westleton; however he chose to live in Yoxford near to the Blois family, his patrons. Daniel Packard, his younger brother, is listed as a farmer and gentleman, of Mill Farm, Middleton, and held the Lordship of Austin's Manor, Middleton.

When Rev. Harrison wrote his will on 31st October 1860, shortly before he died on 27th December, he was living at Darsham. He left all his effects and money to his unmarried only daughter Jane, but they only totalled under £300.

In *Pigot's Directories* of Saxmundham, 1830 and 1839, a James Packard, brazier and tinsmith, is listed. His grandfather John, also a brazier, was of Woodbridge; his father was John Harrison Packard, born in Woodbridge in 1780, died at Hasketon in 1829, and first cousin to the Rev. Harrison Packard.

Portrait of Sir William Jackson Hooker, drawn and engraved by Mrs Dawson Turner, 1813

James's younger brother Edward was born at Hasketon in 1819, but by 1843 he also was established in Saxmundham. In *White's Directory*,1844, he is "wine & spirit merchant" and in *Kelly's Directory* of 1846 he is "chemist and druggist". In 1843 he had started producing fertilisers at Snape, and in 1850 signed an agreement with the trustees of the Boyton Charity, whose agent was **John Crabtree**, to allow the digging of coprolites for use as fertilisers.

By 1851 he had bought land at Bramford, near Ipswich, and by 1854 had erected a sulphuric acid works there. Shortly afterwards Joseph Fison set up a phosphate works on an adjacent site. A merger, resulting in Fison, Packard & Prentice, was formed in 1929, becoming eventually the well-known firm of Fison's. James's son Edward, born in 1843 at Saxmundham, became a JP, Mayor of Ipswich in 1887 and was knighted in 1922.

Sources

Alumni Cantab. / White's Directory / Parish registers / Diocesan registry / Will: Probate Registry 98/12/1209 / Suckling / Packard, W.G. "To the memory of my father Sir Edward Packard KB JP", *History of Fison's Ltd* / *Cox's County Who's Who* (1912)

Hooker, Sir William Jackson 1785-1865 and Sir Joseph Dalton 1817-1911 *Botanists*

The first of that remarkable father and son double act, the Hookers of Kew, lived at Halesworth eleven years, and the second was born in the town. William's father was Joseph, born at Exeter, who claimed relationship with Richard Hooker the 16th century theologian; his mother was Lydia Vincent of Norwich, related to George Vincent the Norwich School artist. Joseph was a merchant's clerk, living in Magdalen Street, when William was born there on the 6th July 1785. He was named after his godfather, William Jackson of Kent, a childless uncle of whom the Hookers had great expectations. William attended Norwich School under **Dr Forster**, and at the age of eleven inherited in trust the Jackson estate in Kent. He was early encouraged in his botanical interests by the Norwich doctor, James Smith, founder of the Linnaean Society, but after school was sent to learn estate management at Starston Hall, near Harleston, presumably on the assumption that he would take over the Kentish estate.

A meeting with **Dawson Turner** of Yarmouth changed this. The Turners, with their partner Samuel Paget, had just bought the Halesworth brewery and maltings from **John Woodcock's** executors, with several public houses, for £34,000 and needed another investor. In 1809 William took a quarter share for £8,000 and agreed to move into the brewery house and superintend operations. We believe this was not the house now known as Hooker House, but its predecessor on the same site [see **Patrick Stead**], but it had a large garden and a stove (heated greenhouse) in which William could rear exotic orchids. His investment was amply covered by the Kentish estate, which eventually sold for £14,000, and his parents soon moved in, father having presumably retired.

Dawson Turner was to prove a hard taskmaster. A passionate amateur botanist, he kept Hooker hard at work illustrating his book on seaweeds, for minimal payment and no public recognition, just as he was to keep John Sell Cotman employed on illustrating his antiquarian works. However William got his reward - in 1812 he was betrothed to Turner's eldest child Maria, aged sixteen, and in 1815 they were married. Four children were born and baptised in Halesworth - William Dawson (1816), Joseph Dalton (1817), Maria (1819) and Elizabeth (1820). By the time of Elizabeth's birth William had moved to Glasgow, but travelled by ship, Leith to Yarmouth and return, for the birth and christening. In the register he is described as "L.L.D. Professor of Botany in the University of Glasgow", rather than the plain "Brewer" of the earlier births.

William appears to have been a reluctant brewer, and he wrote to a friend "If you hear of anyone who can employ a poor botanical author and give him something for his work, bear me in mind". He published several botanical works while at the brewery, and in 1820 came the Glasgow appointment. Though no longer resident, he remained a partner in Turner's enterprise. The main brewery had been sold to Patrick Stead in 1821, but the Rectory Manor books record in 1821 the purchase by Paget, Turner and Hooker of the "Ax", late Fighting Cocks, in Chediston Street for £400, and as late as 1830 their sale of the King's Head in Quay Street for £740 to Dowson and Rathbone, brewers of Gillingham.

Meanwhile William's career progressed at Glasgow University, and he was dubbed a Knight of Hanover in 1836, travelling by ship again, Leith to London, to collect the honour. Finally in 1841 came his appointment as the first Director of Kew Gardens, which post he held until his death, enlarging and transforming them into one of the world's leading botanical gardens and building the superb Temperate and Palm Houses. The history of Kew, and of William's botanical acheivements, is amply recorded elsewhere, but an unusual sidelight comes in a letter from William Gifford Palgrave, a Turner relation serving with the East India Company, dated 28th November 1848 at Rajcote - "Dear Uncle Hooker... you have, I hope, had no more threatenings of Chartist attacks on the Palm House. Your affectionate nephew, W.G.Palgrave".

Sir William died, loaded with honours and with his son already installed as Deputy Director, on the 12th August 1865. He was buried in Kew churchyard and there is a tablet to his memory in the church. It was not until 1930 that a tablet to both the Hookers was unveiled in Halesworth church.

Joseph Dalton Hooker was presumably given his second name in honour of the great Mancunian scientist John Dalton. The second son of William Jackson Hooker, he was born at Halesworth on the 30th June 1817, but at the age of four moved with his parents to Glasgow. He attended high school and university there, and qualified as Doctor of Medicine in 1839. The same year came a remarkable opportunity when, no doubt through his father's influence, he enrolled on the *Erebus* under Captian James Ross, nominally as surgeon but really as botanist, to explore Antarctica, also visiting Australia, New Zealand and the Falklands.

Portrait photograph of Sir Joseph Dalton Hooker, by Maull and Co., 1855

While in Antarctica the Ross ice barrier and Mount Erebus were named, and on the expedition's return in 1843 Hooker published his botanical findings.

In 1847 he became engaged to Frances Henslow, daughter of the Rev. John Stevens Henslow (1796-1861), Professor of Botany at Cambridge and Rector of

Hitcham in mid-Suffolk, who managed to combine the two jobs by spending each Summer Term at the university and the rest of the year at Hitcham. Frances had to be patient, however, as Joseph was about to set off on another major expedition to India, where he spent the next two years trekking in the Himalayas and Sikkim, climbing to over 19,000 feet and sending home the first Rhododendrons. He returned home in 1851 with more crates full of specimens, and promptly married Frances.

He was by now a close friend of Charles Darwin, with whom he corresponded regularly, and Hooker later said "I believe I was the first to whom he communicated his then new ideas on the subject [of evolution]". In 1855 he was appointed assistant director to his father at Kew Gardens, and Darwin wrote to congratulate him "though the income is but a poor one". After the death of Sir William in 1865 Joseph succeeded to the Directorship. In 1873 he was elected President of the Royal Society, but the same year Frances died, aged only forty-nine, leaving four sons and two daughters.

Joseph re-married three years later. His bride was a young widow, Hyacinth Jardine, née Symonds, who gave birth to two more sons. The following year Joseph was knighted. In 1885 he retired from Kew and spent the next twelve years publishing his magnum opus, *The Flora of India*, in seven volumes. He was now living at Sunningdale, was awarded the Order of Merit in 1907, and died there on the 10th December 1911, aged ninety-four. He was buried near his father in Kew churchyard, and in the church is a tablet very similar to his father's.

Sources

D.N.B. / Allan, M. *The Hookers of Kew* (1967) / Allan, M. *Beer and Botany* T.S.N.S. vol 14 / Lawrence (1990) / H.P.R. / H.R.M.C.R. / Letter - SROL (363/B2/7-11) / Russell-Gebett *Henslow of Hitcham* (1977) / Darwin, F. *The Life and Letters of Charles Darwin*

Wilkinson, John Brewster *Cleric* 1785-1862

The name Wilkinson was very widespread in the 17th and 18th centuries over North Suffolk and South Norfolk, with families at Walsham le Willows, Thetford, Stradbroke, Bury St Edmund's and elsewhere. The Wilkinsons of the Halesworth area trace their origins to Hustings Wilkinson of Chediston, who died in 1663. After two generations came John of Halesworth (1709-57) who married, in 1737, Ann Brewster of Wrentham (1713-80). The Brewsters were a family long-established at Wrentham, where they held the principal manor from 1576. After five generations came Humphrey, who died unmarried in 1797, when the manor passed to his aunt Frances Meadows and his first cousin John Wilkinson, son of Ann Brewster. Frances and John sold the estate in 1810 to Sir Thomas Gooch of Benacre, who promptly demolished the hall (illustrated in Copinger vol II), sold the materials by public auction, and added the estate to his already extensive holdings. This John (1743-1818) was baptised at Halesworth but lived at Holton. He married Jane Brettingham (1756-90) at St Clement's church, Norwich. Their stone in Holton churchyard records - "John Wilkinson, gent. of Halesworth, died 23 July 1818 aged 74 and Jane his wife died 10 May 1790 aged 34".

The Wilkinsons had been property owners in Halesworth for some time. In 1740 John Wilkinson, gent. was admitted to Seven Acre Close and Hempland, and in 1800 the existing Town feoffees - John Wilkinson and **Peter Jermyn** - nominated four of the next generation to join them. These were John Wilkinson junior (aged fifteen), **John Woodcock** junior, John Hatcher junior and **John Hugman** junior. In 1814 the Rev. Lombe Atthill was admitted, on payment of £525 to John Wilkinson, to a messuage with yards and gardens where the postal sorting office now stands.

John Brewster Wilkinson, named for his grandmother, was baptised at Halesworth on 25th June 1785. His siblings were also baptised there - Harriet in 1787, George in 1788 and Jane in 1789. John attended Bungay Grammar School where a fellow-pupil was John Barber Scott the Bungay diarist, who was to be a lifelong friend. Our John entered St John's College, Cambridge, in 1803, taking BA in 1807, MA in 1810 and BD in 1817. He was a Fellow of the College from 1809 to 1832, then in Scott's words - "29 May 1832: J.B.W. married to Jane, daughter of John FitzGerald MP for Seaford, at Trinity church, Marylebone, London". John FitzGerald had been John Purcell, of Kilkenny, but took his mother's maiden name on marrying another FitzGerald cousin. They lived at Wherstead Lodge, near Ipswich, from 1825 to 1835, then moved to Boulge Hall, near Woodbridge. Wilkinson thus became brother-in-law to Edward FitzGerald the poet, best known for his *Rubaiyat of Omar Khayam*.

John Brewster became Rector of Freston the same year, and having acquired the advowson of Holbrook presented himself as Rector there the same year. Both villages are within a few miles of Wherstead, and the Wilkinsons were to stay at Holbrook for twenty-six years. J.B. Scott was a frequent visitor, and provides an interesting glimpse of John Brewster's character on 20th August 1858, when he spends a pleasant hour with the Wilkinsons - "He amiable, clever, and as eccentric as ever". Though long resident at Holbrook he still retained his properties in and around Halesworth, and *White's Directory* in 1844 tells us that in Holton the land is mostly owned by John Brewster - "The Hall, a neat mansion, the property of J.B. Wilkinson, is occupied by the Rev. Richard Day. The living is in the incumbency of Rev. W.T. Worship who erected a neat Rectory House in 1838". By 1855 (in White) J.B. Wilkinson had sold the Hall to **Andrew Johnston**, though it was still unoccupied.

John Brewster in extreme old age was, despite living at Holbrook, still a feoffee of the Halesworth town lands, and this caused some problems when it was proposed that his copyhold properties should be enfranchised (made freehold). The Vestry minutes record:-

"31 March 1853: Enfranchisement of the copyhold parts of the unappropriated estate, of which the Rev. J.B.Wilkinson is the only surviving tenant.

26 May 1853: The Lord of the Manor is unwilling to enfranchise in the lifetime of the Rev J.B.Wilkinson.

6 April 1861: Considering the great age of the Rev. J.B.Wilkinson it was decided to go ahead with the enfranchisement."

John Brewster appears to have given up his Holbrook living in 1858 and retired to London. He died on 20th June 1862 at 18 Sussex Gardens, Middlesex, a then highly fashionable address in Bayswater.

His will, written as of Holbrook on 23rd October 1855, is commendably brief and leaves everything to Jane Teresa - there is no mention of any children - and makes her executrix. It is witnessed by **John Meadows White**, solicitor, of Whitehall Place. There is an undated codicil leaving some farm buildings adjoining the Rectory garden at Holbrook to Charlotte Pytches, obviously a tidying-up of boundaries. The will was proved by Jane Teresa, widow, relict and sole executrix, on 29th July 1862.

Sources

Society of Genealogists - "W" box / Copinger II / H.P.R. / Alumni Cantab. / H.R.M.C.R. / Vestry minutes: SROL (214/A1/1-7) / Probate registry ref. 98/12/1210

Turner, James *Banker* 1786-1820

The Turner family were based in Great Yarmouth, where they held a dominant position through the 18th and much of the 19th centuries. Halesworth people today look to Norwich or Ipswich for "big town" services, or to Lowestoft at a more local level, but at the period we are writing about the most important link was to Yarmouth. Water transport was dominant, and the short road trip to Bungay or Beccles gave access to regular river services to Yarmouth. When the railway first arrived at Halesworth in 1854 the link was to the North, via Beccles, and it was only in 1859 that the much longer connection to Ipswich was completed. It is not surprising therefore that when Halesworth's first bank opened in 1782 it was a branch of Gurneys and Turner of Great Yarmouth.

The Turners of Yarmouth traced their origins to Mulbarton, a few miles South of Norwich, where there were Turners at least from the early 16th century. After six generations of yeomen came Francis (1681-1720), who moved to Yarmouth, practised there as an attorney, and became Town Clerk. His son, another Francis (1716-90) attended Caius College, Cambridge, where he graduated MA in 1740, and then became a notable pluralist, being minister of St George's, Yarmouth - the handsome Wren-like brick church of 1714, now a theatre - from 1742 till he died, and at the same time Master of Yarmouth Grammar School from 1742 to 1758, and Rector of three of the South Elmhams - All Saints, St James and St Michael - from 1743 to 1790. This last is an interesting coincidence with another of our characters, **Samuel Blois Turner**, who was Rector there from 1862 to 1882, but we have been unable to find any definite connection between the two fami-

Banknote of the Halesworth and Suffolk Bank, dated 1818

lies. Francis married Sarah Dawson and had four sons. The third of these, Joseph (1745-1828), graduated from Pembroke College, Cambridge, in 1767, stayed on to become a Fellow, and was Master of the College from 1784 to 1828 and Dean of Norwich from 1790. By another coincidence Samuel Blois Turner was a student at Pembroke under his mastership.

The second son, James (1743-94) was the founder of the family Bank. He married Elizabeth Cotman, a member of a long-established Yarmouth family but apparently not related to the artist John Sell Cotman, who will figure later in our narrative. The years 1750 to 1800 saw the great expansion of provincial banking and in 1781 James, in conjunction with the Quaker Gurneys of Norwich, set up Gurney and Turner's "Yarmouth and Suffolk Bank" with headquarters in his house on South Quay. The next year, wishing to expand further into Suffolk, James founded the "Halesworth and Suffolk Bank" in what is now Barclay's premises on the Thoroughfare. While still under overall control from Yarmouth, this soon developed independently and had its own sub-branches at Bungay, Eye, Framlingham, Harleston, Saxmundham, Woodbridge and Yoxford. Soon after opening the Halesworth bank had to face local competition from **Badeley** and **Woodcock's** "Suffolk and Halesworth Bank", but this ended in their dramatic failure in 1799.

James had two sons - Dawson (1775-1858) and James (1786-1820). Dawson is undoubtedly the best-known of the family. After attending Paston School at North Walsham he entered his uncle's college, Pembroke, in 1792 but never graduated. This must be because his father's death in 1794 caused him to hurry back to Yarmouth and take control of the Bank. Two years later he married Mary Palgrave from Coltishall, near Wroxham, who was to bear him eleven children of whom three died in infancy. Dawson inherited - and made - a vast amount of money, but his lifelong passion was his academic interests, possibly heightened by having been obliged to leave Cambridge prematurely. Botany was his first enthusiasm and he made himself the leading authority on seaweeds (*fuci*), publishing the definitive work on the subject with the (unacknowledged) help of his future son-in-law **William Jackson Hooker**. He later turned more to art and antiquities, and built up a remarkable collection of Italian and Dutch old masters, and of Norwich School contemporaries. John Crome became drawing master to the Turner daughters, but handed over in 1812 to John Sell Cotman, whom Dawson persuaded to move to Yarmouth. Cotman stayed there for twelve years, very much at the beck and call of his enthusiastic but dominant patron. The result was the production of countless architectural drawings and etchings and the publication of the *Architectural Antiquities of Norfolk* in 1818, the *Sepulchral Brasses in Norfolk* the following year, and the *Architectural Antiquities of Normandy* in 1822, with drawings by Cotman and text by Turner.

Of Dawson Turner's large family the two eldest are the most interesting. Maria (1797-1872) married, in 1815, Dawson's botanical collaborator William Jackson Hooker, and Elizabeth (1799-1852) married Francis Cohen, who converted to Christianity from Judaism and took the name Palgrave from his wife's mother's family. He became Deputy Keeper of His Majesty's Records and was knighted in 1832. Their son, Francis Turner Palgrave, born in the Turner house at Yarmouth, became Professor of Poetry at Oxford and produced that favourite anthology *The Golden Treasury*. Mary Turner died in 1850, and the following year Dawson remarried, his bride being Rosamund Duff, thirty-six years his junior. They went to Gretna Green for the wedding, which alienated many of Dawson's family; J.B.Scott, the Bungay diarist, says on the 5th November 1851 - "Hear of Dawson Turner's deplorable marriage and his leaving the house on the Quay at Yarmouth".

Dawson's younger brother James was the only member of the family to live in Halesworth. He followed Dawson to Pembroke College in 1803 but like him apparently never graduated. He took over control of the Halesworth bank in 1808 and in the same year married Mary Ann, daughter of James Sayers. Gurney and Turner's now had a clear field, after the collapse of Badeley and Woodcock, and soon exploited this in another area. Dawson was already involved in brewing at Yarmouth, in partnership with Samuel Paget. - a member of an old Yarmouth family, Mayor in 1817, who fathered two remarkable medical men. These were George Edward Paget, Professor of Physick at Cambridge, and Sir James Paget, first Baronet, surgeon to Queen Victoria and the Prince of Wales, who gave his name to the present Yarmouth hospital. Badeley and Woodcock had owned the brewery in Bridge Street, Halesworth, and after their bankruptcy this was acquired by "Samuel Paget, Dawson Turner and James Turner of Yarmouth" and reported to a Manor Court in October 1812. They had paid £28,000 for the whole package, including several public houses and another maltings (incidentally a marginal note says "**Patrick Stead** admitted 2 August 1837"). Dawson's botanical friend W.J. Hooker was persuaded to take a quarter share and was installed in the brewery house.

James and Mary Ann had one child, James Sayers Turner, but two years later, in 1812, Mary Ann died. Four years later James married Charlotte Herbert, but in

1820 he died, aged only thirty-four. There is a slab in the North aisle of Halesworth church commemorating Mary Ann who died on the 21st April 1812, and James who died on the 2nd January 1820. His will, dated 7th June 1819 at Halesworth, is firstly concerned with the future of his only son James, and £4,000 is to be placed in government stocks for him to have at twenty-one. However James was not the only child, as £300 is to go, at majority, to "Elizabeth Keogh, my daughter by Susan Keogh", and Charlotte is to be guardian of both children. Charlotte will be well recompensed, however, for "life or widowhood" with £3,000 in the Equitable assurance office and quarter shares of both the Halesworth and the Yarmouth breweries. The executors are to be Charlotte, her father William Herbert, and James's brother Dawson. The will was proved in the Prerogative Court of Canterbury on the 11th April 1820.

Sources

Turner, H. *The Turner family of Mulbarton and Great Yarmouth* (1907) / Alumni Cantab / Palmer / Bidwell, W.H. *Annals of an East Anglian Bank* (1900) / Preston, H. *Early East Anglian Banks and Bankers* (1994) / D.N.B. / Allan, M. *The Hookers of Kew* (1967) / H.M.C.R. / Will: SROL (749/1/883)

Stead, Patrick *Maltster* 1787-1869

Halesworth, in the middle of the 19th century, was dominated by two redoubtable Scotsmen - **Andrew Johnston** and Patrick Stead.

Patrick Stead was born on 1st December 1787 at Stead's Place, Leith Walk, Edinburgh, and baptised at Leith, South, church on the 13th December. His parents were David Stead, card manufacturer, and his wife Janet, née Anderson, and the witnesses at the baptism were George Stead, shipmaster, and John Hewit, shoemaker. Stead's Place took its name from David Stead's factory. Patrick was probably a younger son, as another David was made a Burgess of Edinburgh by apprenticeship in 1802. Patrick is believed to have been educated at Perth Academy, but unfortunately they have no records early enough to confirm this. He married Susan, eldest daughter of Fulton Alexander of Hermitage, who in later censuses gives her place of birth as Paisley, Renfrewshire. Nothing else is known of Patrick Stead's life before moving to England.

Newby thinks he probably worked for Truman's in London for a time before settling in Great Yarmouth by at the latest 1822. By this date he was also malting at Beccles and Halesworth, but his centre was Yarmouth and his business was mainly corn exporting and coal importing. Palmer records him as living in South Town Road, on the Suffolk side of the river, sometimes known as "Little Yarmouth", and having his business there. This led to a contretemps at the general election of 1826 when Patrick voted, but was rejected by the returning officer as not being a freeman of the Borough. This so rankled that eight years later, when the Municipal Commissioners were inquiring into the affairs of the

The Patrick Stead Hospital, Halesworth, photographed soon after completion

Lansdowne Park, Helensburgh, photographed in 1923

Borough, Patrick insisted on appearing and "addressed the Commissioners at very considerable length". Again he claimed entitlement to freedom of the Borough for the inhabitants of Southtown, and thus exemption from the duty on import of coal. He quoted the services he had rendered in setting up postal communication to the South and West of England at great expense to himself - presumably on his grain ships. Town Clerk - "If admitted, the whole coal trade would go to Little Yarmouth". Stead - "They are driving the shipping of non-freemen from Yarmouth to the New Port". The picture of a prickly and argumentative Scot is lightened however by personal reminiscences in the diary of C.J.Palmer, where he records convivial evenings with Patrick, and in 1824 their joint membership of the new Rowing Boat Club with its uniform of "blue jackets, Guernsey frocks, green belts,white trousers and straw hats with green ribbons".

In Halesworth Patrick had purchased from Paget, **Turner** and **Hooker** the brewery and malting in Bridge Street which had been managed until 1820 by the great botanist, and reluctant brewer, William Jackson Hooker. Patrick had a partner and fellow-Scot John Robinson - it seems he was initially in charge as Pigot in 1830 has "Maltsters - Robinson, John Joseph". About 1837 Patrick decided to move to Halesworth and to concentrate his business there. More land was purchased to the East of Hooker's house and later a separate malting complex built to the East of the public quay. Newby records the characteristic cast iron tie-plates bearing dates 1838, 1840 and 1842. We are fairly sure that the Steads never lived in Hooker's house, but largely rebuilt it before moving to Halesworth. In January 1840 the Vestry minutes state "The assessment for the new dwelling house of Mr P. Stead fixed for the present (it not being completed) at the sum of £20". By census day 1841 they were installed there - Patrick, Susan (they never had any children), two female servants and one male. When looking at the present house - now named Hooker House, but really Stead's House - one must remember that it was about twice its present size, and had a spacious garden stretching down to the river.

The story of Patrick Stead's expanding business has been admirably recorded by Rachel Lawrence in 1986 and 1990, so this must be only a brief summary. Water transport was the key, with Patrick at his own expense canalising a further stretch of river to serve his first new maltings - malthouses numbers 2 - 5, and building a cut from the canal basin to serve the second block - malthouses numbers 1, 6 and 7, and (his own design) the new steam-heated tower-kiln. However the Blyth Navigation only got his malt as far as Southwold, where it was transshipped to sea-going vessels, and here he was in constant dispute with the Harbour Commissioners, dominated by the big landed proprietors. These were busy reclaiming their marshes from the salt waters of the Blyth estuary, thus reducing drastically the tidal flow at the harbour mouth, and causing silting up at the bar. Patrick's ships were frequently held up by this, with disturbing effects on his business. However when the harbour was passable the business prospered, and Stead's was now the largest maltings in the country, averaging £3,800 per annum in malt despatched to Truman's in London.

Patrick Stead must by the 1850's have been tiring of his constant battles, and it was Truman's who resolved things for him, by buying all his Halesworth properties for £18,000. They were leased back to him to continue to operate for a few more years, but in 1851 **Robert Burleigh** moved in as manager and in 1854 took over. It is somewhat ironical to think that this was the year the railway arrived in Halesworth, though it was not till 1859 that the link to Ipswich was completed, thus sounding the death-knell of the Navigation and of Burleigh's dependence on it. The orientation of the business then turned towards the railway sidings under Burleigh and his successor Parry, and a large new malting was built there.

Patrick and Susan returned to Scotland, and Susan's Paisley origins may have led them to the West rather than the East side. They settled at Helensburgh, which was then a highly fashionable address for wealthy Glaswegians. It had been laid out in the 1770's as a new town on the shores of the Clyde estuary, but really took off in the 1850's when first the paddle steamers and then the railway from Glasgow arrived. Large stone houses fronted onto broad tree-lined roads, and the Steads' new house was one of the largest, named Lansdowne Park and standing in elaborately laid out grounds. The Steads were living there by the 1861 Census, with one male and two female servants. The house survives, little altered, as a girls' boarding house for Lomond School, but the grounds have been much reduced by housing developments [see illustration].

Patrick died on the 28th June 1869 at Birnam, Perthshire, where they were presumably on holiday (the Perth link again?). Susan stayed on at Lansdowne Park, still keeping three servants at the 1871 Census, but died there on the 1st June 1875. Meanwhile back in Halesworth there were great expectations, as it was widely known the Steads intended to endow a hospital. The Vestry meeting on 18th April 1870 instructed the clerk to obtain a copy of Patrick's will. This showed that after a life interest to Susan and legacies to various next of kin, the residue would come to Halesworth. After long negotiations the town's share was agreed at £26,000, though the next of kin did not do too badly out of a total of over £55,000. A Trust was set up, land purchased on the Bungay Road, plans prepared by London hospital specialist Henry Hall FRIBA and the building [see illustration] erected for less than £5,000, leaving a substantial endowment. The building still flourishes as the Patrick Stead Hospital. It is not, however, the Steads' only monument, as in 1872 a splendid stained glass window was dedicated in the South aisle of the parish church, with the inscription "In Memoriam of Patrick Stead, born at Stead's Place, Leith Walk, for many years a resident in Norfolk and Suffolk. Died at Birnam, Perthshire, 1869. Placed by his widow".

Stead's buildings in Halesworth have fared less well. Half his house was demolished to make way for the new link road; its garden has been built over; his maltings have been demolished, except the Easternmost, "Malthouse No.7", which has been converted to flats but still displays the 'P. Stead' tie-irons, dated 1842. It represents, however, not more than a twentieth of the entire complex.

Sources

Newby (1964) / Lawrence (1986) / Lawrence (1990) / General Register Office for Scotland / Palmer / Palmer, F.D.(ed) *Leaves from the Diary of C.J.Palmer* (1892) / *Great Yarmouth* - Report of Municipal Commissioners, 1834 / Vestry Minutes - SROL / Rate Books - SROL / Dumbarton Central Library / Lomond School, Helensburgh

Whately, Richard *Rector and Archbishop* 1787-1863

Rector of Halesworth from 1822-31, Richard Whately was the fourth son of the Rev. Joseph Whately, of Nonsuch Park, Surrey, and his wife Jane. The Rev. Joseph had inherited the Little Park at Nonsuch from his uncle, on condition that he should take Holy Orders. Jane was a daughter of **William Plumer** of Ware Park, Hertfordshire, who held the Manor of Halesworth from 1767 to 1822.

Richard therefore had a good start in life, though he was a frail child in infancy. He was born in Cavendish Square, London, on 1st February 1787, though his father held the living of Widford, Herts. As the family moved away from the London area when the Rev. Joseph became Prebendary of Bristol in 1793, Richard started his education in that city, going on to Oxford where he followed his father's example and entered Oriel College, becoming BA, Fellow and MA in 1812. While at Oxford his fellow students included John Keble, John Newman and Edmund Pusey, all later leaders of the Oxford Movement, and Thomas Arnold, who became the well-known headmaster of Rugby School. All these men were Richard's intimate friends and admirers - he was considered one of the great men at Oxford in his day. Indeed he earned the admiration of Charles Darwin who quotes Whately's opinions on language and civilisation in *The Descent of Man*, published in 1871 after Richard's death.

On 18th July 1821 he married Elizabeth Pope of Hillingdon Hall, Middlesex, and not long afterwards, on 18th February 1822, he was instituted to the living of Halesworth through the patronage of his grandmother **Jane Plumer**. This did not sever him from his Oxford connections, as in 1822 he gave the Bampton Lectures there, and in 1823 published his sermons given in Oxford. Their only son, Edward William, was born in 1823, and in 1826 a daughter, Henrietta; both were baptised in Halesworth, all their other children being baptised elsewhere.

Meanwhile, in 1825, Richard became a Doctor of Divinity and was appointed Principal of St Alban Hall, Oxford - an adjunct to Merton College. His Vice-Principal was John Newman (later Cardinal Newman); in 1829 Richard became Drummond Professor of Political Economy - all this while taking care of the running of Halesworth parish affairs, heading the Coal Subscription List, and overseeing several publications. The travelling between Halesworth and Oxford must have been wearisome, though he may have resided at Oxford at times. An entry in John Barber Scott's Diary counteracts this, though:-

"6.10.1830. To Halesworth & fix at Mr Crabtree. Dined there with Mr & Mrs Meadows White and Miss Revans who is staying here, and Dr Whately. At 7 to church and Whately lectures on the Catechism. Afterwards a long talk with him on Political Economy".

Frederick C. Lambert's *Records of Halesworth* notes a visit to the town by John Keble, Richard's Oxford contemporary, and gives us a delightful cameo of Richard in middle age that illustrates his lighter side: the Rector of Halesworth is described scaring boys scrumping in his orchard by pretending to be a ghost in his white surplice.

Nevertheless Richard Whately was a man of high principles and a fertile brain: he spoke out against slavery and transportation, and moreover conceived

Portrait photograph of Richard Whately

the idea of a universal currency.

In 1831 he made an extraordinary leap in his career in the Church, being consecrated Archbishop of Dublin - surely a most unusual step up from a modest Suffolk parish - a move that caused a stir in ecclesiastical circles. Charles Linnell's book *Some East Anglian Clergy* (1961) tells how the Bishop of Norwich, Dr Bathurst, was offered the Dublin appointment but declined because of his age (he was approaching his 90th year). He suggested his son instead, who was then Archdeacon of Norwich. However, in spite of considerable lobbying, the appointment went to Richard Whately by the influence of Earl Grey, and the Archdeacon stayed in Norwich.

Perhaps the younger Bathurst was happy to be passed over, as during Richard's time in Ireland the disastrous potato famine struck. Blight had appeared before, but never on the scale of 1845. In spite of famine relief and soup kitchens, by 1851 over a million had died and another million fled overseas. The clergy could not collect their tithes and became greatly impoverished and many died of fever caught by helping the suffering. Although in 1848 potato blight struck again, it did not seem unsuitable for Queen Victoria to visit Dublin in 1849 and to be entertained in grand style, presumably meeting Dr Whately amongst others.

One effect of the famine was to greatly reduce the status of the Church of Ireland. Though Elizabeth Whately helped establish Ragged Schools, and Richard tried to combine Protestant and Catholic teaching in the schools, this made him unpopular with both denominations. Pursuing his academic bent, he founded the Statistical Society of Dublin and endowed the Whately Professorship of Political Economy at Trinity College, Dublin.

On a lighter note, Richard was an enthusiastic gardener - perhaps inheriting the skill from his uncle Thomas Whately, a politician and horticulturist who was MP for Castle Rising, Norfolk, a "rotten borough", from 1768-72, and held office under Lord North.

Richard and Elizabeth's son Edward William went to Rugby School, then to Oxford, taking Holy Orders. He too went to Ireland, becoming Archdeacon of Glendalough, then Chancellor of St Patrick's Cathedral, Dublin. He married, and settled in England later, as Rector of Littleton, Middlesex, not far from his mother's old home at Hillingdon. His son, Arnold Robert, also went into the Church and became Rector of Gunton, Suffolk, in 1912.

Elizabeth died in 1860, and Richard on 1st October 1863; he is interred in St Patrick's Cathedral, Dublin. Of their several daughters, one E.J. inherited her father's literary talents and edited some of the later editions of his very extensive list of works and wrote his *Life and Correspondence* in 1866.

Oriel College Library, Oxford, holds a collection of Whately's letters, many describing his private life and concerns, voyages abroad and life in Ireland, including the Queen's visit.

Sources

DNB / Alumni Oxon. / Oriel College Library / Halesworth Parish records / S.R.O. / *Gentleman's Magazine* / Percival, J. *The Great Famine* (1995)

Appleton, Robert *Architect* 1790-1859

The only practising architect we have found in Halesworth. He was born at Prescot, Lancashire, now an outer suburb of Liverpool. His parents were Peter Appleton and Sarah Ogden, married at Manchester in 1781, and he married Susan Gooch (1794-1861) daughter of Edward and Susan of Bury St Edmund's.

It is not known how he came to move to Suffolk, but by 1821 Robert and Susan were living at Thorington, where twins Catherine and Betsy were baptised, their father being described as "carpenter and joiner". Three more daughters and two sons followed over the next sixteen years. He was also a farmer, and by 1841 was occupying the farm now known as Stone House and 301 acres - rented from Henry Bence Bence of Thorington Hall, who owned the entire parish. By the 1851 census this had increased to 399 acres and he employed eighteen labourers and four boys, while living in the house with the Appletons were their son Thomas Gooch Appleton (employed on the farm), two servants, a groom and a farm servant. This was a substantial enterprise, and one wonders how Robert was able at the same time to work up from carpenter to architect and to run a busy practice.

Although he lived at Thorington Robert kept an office at Halesworth, where *White* in 1855 has him as Architect and Surveyor in Pound Street, and the *Post Office Directory* of 1858 has him in the Market Place. His known works tend to be public commissions, for which records have survived, but one suspects he was also responsible for many of the private houses built in and around the town in the period 1820-60.

He started early, in 1823, on the first of many restorations of Halesworth church which were to leave it by the 1870's looking more Victorian than medieval. In 1827 a plum commission came along in the shape of the new St James's church at Dunwich to replace All Saints which was beginning to tumble over the cliff. Here however triumph led to disaster: he produced a stylish neo-classical design but by the time the church was dedicated in 1832 the Gothic Revival was in full swing. D.E.Davy visited on the 24th October 1839 - "Dunwich, to see the new church, a neat modern chapel, but Mr Barne threatens to convert it into an ancient church by new windows and flint walls. It is hardly finished yet, tho' it has been built 8 or 9 years".

The story is confirmed by two tablets in the chancel - Michael Barne (1759-1837) "by the aid of his liberal contribution this church was erected in the year 1830" and Frederick Barne (1801-86) "built the tower and chancel and restored the remainder of this church". In its present form it is a flint and stone neo-Gothic church, but it is possible that the Gothicisation started earlier, for *White* in 1844 describes it as "a neat structure of white brick in the Gothic style with a circular tower". Could it be that while the church was being built some Gothic elements crept in? The present East window has wooden tracery - totally unlike the correct stone tracery of the other windows - and a drawing in Dunwich Museum shows the church basically as the 1827 design but with what appears to be Gothic tracery in the windows, so it is likely that the East window was re-used from Appleton's church.

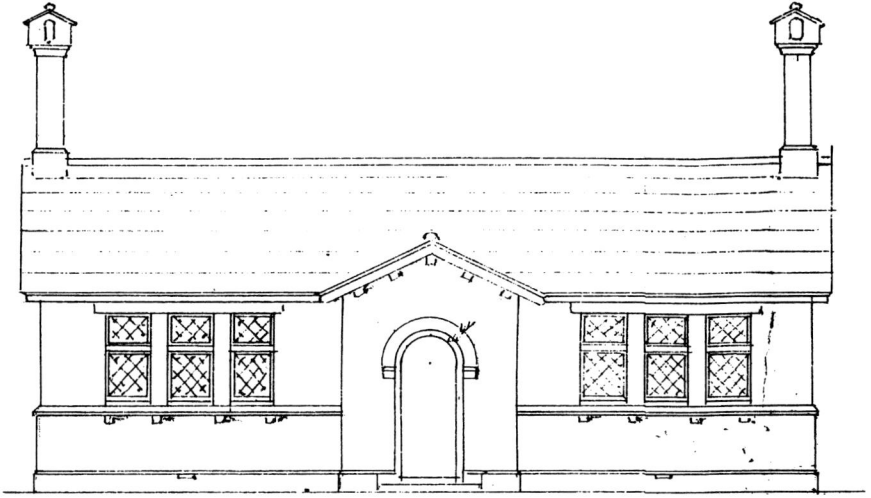

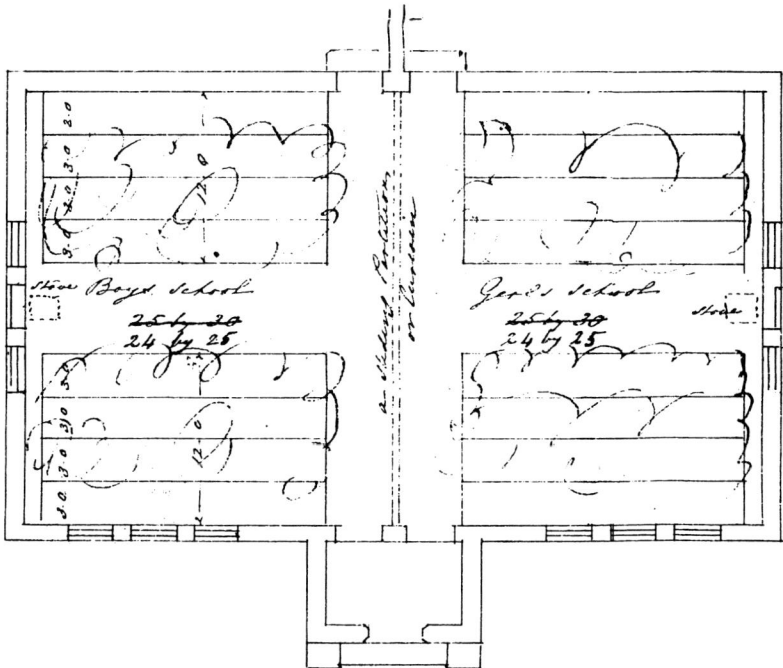

Drawing of Westleton National School, plan and elevation, by Robert Appleton, 1842

His next major design has fared better. This is Saxmundham Corn Exchange and Market Hall, for which he prepared designs in 1836, presented at the old Bell Inn, when "plans and estimates were submitted by that eminent architect Mr Appleton, which met with general approbation" and which still looks externally as he designed it though internally much altered except in the entrance hall. The adjoining Bell Hotel was rebuilt at the same time to Robert's design. The whole project was largely financed by William Long of Hurt's Hall, and the facade of the Market Hall bears his arms and motto.

In 1842 came Westleton National School, now the village hall. This is one of his most attractive designs, in a simple classical style in brick and flint, still hardly altered [see illustration]. Other schools were to follow at Leiston, Westhall and Holton, while at Halesworth he built the new Police Station in Quay Street in 1846. The Halesworth Vestry found it useful having an architect in town and he frequently gave advice, as in 1854 when he tried to improve the line of the new railway bridge over the Holton Road - "the plan by Mr Appleton the County Surveyor has not been carried out... even with the proposed alteration it is very objectionable as being at the turn of the road at the entrance to a large town, under which considerable traffic passes". A delegation met Sir Morton Peto, but cannot have been successful as the present (rebuilt) bridge still causes an awkward traffic dog-leg.

Appleton was still active in his last years as in 1858 the church was again drastically altered, with galleries and pews removed, new benches and new East window, but for this the Vestry decided he would need an outside adviser to get his Gothic details correct, so the "design was by Mr Jekyll of Norwich and superintendance by Mr Appleton of Halesworth". Mr Jekyll was Thomas Jekyll, the well-known decorative designer, responsible among other things for the Norwich Gates at Sandringham House.

The Appletons lie beneath two headstones in Thorington churchyard, he dying on 3rd August 1859 and she on 12th June 1861.

Sources

Brown, Haward, Kindred / Thorington parish registers / Thorington Census returns / Thorington tithe map (SROI) / Drawings at SROI (1D1/1/40 and 87 and B.108/1/61) / Halesworth Vestry minutes: SROL (124/A1/1-7) / Halesworth Times / Ipswich Journal.

Pedgrift Family 1790 to 1896

Sometimes called Pedgrave, this family of medical men lived and practised in Halesworth and Wissett from the early 19th century.

The first known was William Henchman Pedgrift, born about 1790 according to the 1851 Census, in Aldeburgh. This could be a mistaken version of Alburgh in Norfolk, near Harleston. There were several Pedgrifts in that area and in

Redenhall churchyard (the burial ground for Harleston residents) is a stone to Samuel Pedgrift, who died 9th January 1830 in the 70th year of his age. No trace has so far been found of Pedgrifts in Aldeburgh; a stone to John Pedgrift, born 1764 and died 1844, farmer, and his wife Elizabeth, is reputed to be in Alburgh churchyard. A Sarah Pedgrift married at Alburgh in 1806. The will of a Samuel Pedgrift of Westhall was proved in 1781; in it he bequeathed all his household goods to John Pedgrift; it also mentions George Pedgrift, a cordwainer of St Margaret's Ilketshall.

In 1812 a Mr Henchman, surgeon, was changing his residence in Halesworth, and an advertisement for the sale of "elegant modern household furniture and other effects" appeared in the *Ipswich Journal* on 13th June 1812. It seems likely that there is a connection with such an unusual name and the same profession. In 1805 a Dr William Henchman Crowfoot (1780-1841) was practising - together with an uncle - in Beccles, with great distinction, and was the second of four generations of Beccles surgeons similarly named.

William Henchman Pedgrift married Lucy Pedgrift in Great Yarmouth on 16th September 1813, and by 1815 he was established in Halesworth - their son, named after his father, was baptised in December 1815 in Halesworth. William Henchman junior was followed by Henry Edward in 1817, Robert Augustus in 1820, Elizabeth Lucy in 1821, Cornelius Shrofield in 1823, Eliza Ellen in 1824, Emma in 1826, Frederic Woodcock in 1828, Harry in 1830, Martha Anne in 1832, Eleanor in 1836. Of this large family Robert Augustus, Cornelius Shrofield and Frederic Woodcock all followed their father into branches of the medical profession.

William Henchman Pedgrift senior features frequently in the Halesworth Manor Court Rolls from 1825 until 1836. In 1825 he was a tenant of premises in the Market Place, next door to **Robert Gostlin White**, attorney. In the 1841 Census he does not appear, probably having moved to Wissett Place, his residence in the 1844 *White's Directory of Suffolk*; moreover his will, drawn up in 1841, leaves Wissett and Westhall properties to his wife, and after her to his eight surviving children. This will was proved at Halesworth on October 11th 1851.

Of his medical sons Robert Augustus Pedgrift was apprenticed to his father, and later lived in Bungay Road, Halesworth. Aged thirty-one he is described as a medical practitioner at the time of the 1851 Census. His wife was Frances, then aged twenty-five, and there was a stable boy but no children. Robert's will is dated 1857.

Cornelius Shrofield Pedgrift appears to have preferred Wissett and could afford to buy 46 acres of land between 1864 and 1884, now forming part of the Tyneholme estate; in 1874 he owned a house in Mill Hill Street, Halesworth.

Frederic Woodcock Pedgrift married Emma Swan of Halesworth at Wissett in 1850 - he was described as "surgeon", Emma's father was "a gentleman". The Court Roll of November 1859 shows Frederic Pedgrift, surgeon, occupying premises in the Thoroughfare, near the bridge, owned by the daughter of **Thomas Easterson**, the ironfounder. The *Halesworth Times* of November 1st 1859 records the meeting of the Petty Sessions of Wednesday, October 26th, chairman Thomas Rant Esq, magistrates Reverend H. Owens and **Andrew Johnston** Esq. The case they heard was brought by a Dr B. Chevalier, acting for the Medical

Association, who claimed that Frederic Woodcock Pedgrift was "wilfully pretending to be a general practitioner" and had not registered under the new Medical Act requiring all doctors to register with the Association. Frederic Woodcock was stated to have been assistant to Robert Augustus, his elder brother, and later to a Dr Irwin, but in spite of his defence he was fined £10 for each of two cases plus costs.

This case caused great consternation in the town, as people felt they were being forced to use only registered doctors, rather than exercising their freedom of choice. Feeling ran high, a meeting was held and donations were made to finance an Appeal. This was made and succeeded, and by June 1860 the magistrates' conviction had been quashed.

In spite of this drama, or perhaps because of it, the 1861 Census shows Frederic Woodcock still in the Thoroughfare. He is described as "surgeon dentist" and his wife Emma and family are listed. He died at the early age of thirty-three years.

In Wissett churchyard stand a fine collection of memorial stones to the Pedgrift family: "William Henchman Pedgrift died August 17th 1851 aged 61, also Lucy his wife died March 10th 1903"; "Cornelius Shrofield Pedgrift died November 2nd 1896 Charlotte his wife died March 10th 1903"; "Frederic Woodcock Pedgrift died June 5th 1861. Emma his wife died February 3rd 1882" and also three of their children - "Frederic Shrofield aged 2, Fanny Louisa aged 6 months, Emma aged 1 year 8 months".

Sources

The Pedgrift family / H.P.R. / H.M.C.R. / S.R.O.I. Will: 1c/AAI/271/94 / Goodwyn, E.A. *A Century of a Suffolk Town*

Canova, Peter *Jeweller* 1796-1882

Halesworth had an Italian connection through most of the 19th century. As early as 1830, in *Pigot's Directory*, there was "Molinari, Antonio, barometer and thermometer maker and dealer in jewellery", and the 1839 Pigot has "Antonio and Dominic Molinari, jewellers, travelling, Queen Street" (for a few years, presumably after Victoria's coronation, Chediston Street was known as Queen Street, but the name never caught on). Then in 1842 James Maggs records in his diary that "Anthony Molinari died on his way to Italy. Travelled with jewellery. Lived in Halesworth for some years". In the *Ipswich Journal* for 3rd February 1844 comes the last appearance of Dominic, presumably son of Antonio, when Crabtree and Cross, solicitors, announce a creditors' meeting at the King's Arms at which the Trustees hope to pay a dividend. At least six Molinari barometers are known to survive, and are reputedly of high quality [see illustration].

Meanwhile the **George Suggates**, father and son, had dominated this trade in Halesworth for nearly a century, but in 1844 George junior died. The field was wide open, and in came another Italian.

Peter Canova was a native of Como in North Italy, and claimed relationship to Antonio Canova the sculptor (1757-1822). The first record of him in Halesworth is his marriage in 1838 to Susanna Evans, daughter of John Evans, miller, of Halesworth, Peter's father being described as John, a farmer. By 1844, in *White's Directory* he was trading as a jeweller and tea dealer in the Thoroughfare. Peter and Susanna had six children: Emma (1839) who died in infancy, John Manzia (1844), Peter (1848) who also died in infancy, Peter Manzia (1850), Robert Walker (1852) and another Emma in 1854. In the 1841 Census, living in the Thoroughfare were Peter aged 40, Susan 25 and Emma 2. In 1851 Peter, 53, born Italy, Susanna, 35, born St John's, John, 7, and Peter, 1. In 1881 Peter, 85 (whose stated age finally seems to tally with the strict chronology of his life), is retired and notes his origin as "Como, British subject"; Susanna is 65, and Peter is unmarried and working as a printer employing three people.

Meanwhile next door John had taken over the business and was living there with Betsy, two daughters and two servants. John had joined the business "after several years experience with some of the best firms in London" and been made a partner in 1864. In 1870 he took on a new line and advertised "sewing machines from £6.6.0: instruction gratis". In the 1891 Census John was still in the Thoroughfare, but Peter had moved over the river to Bridge Street, where he traded as a stationer and printer, married to Emma from Barnstaple and with one daughter. Kelly, in 1904, lists John Canova, watchmaker, at 49 Thoroughfare. Peter died in 1882, aged 87, and Susanna in 1887 aged 72. Peter Manzia died at only 42 in 1892, and John Manzia in 1906, aged 62. All are buried at Holton Road cemetery.

Sources

Maggs, J. ed Bottomley *Southwold Diary* (1983-4) / Haggar and Miller *Suffolk Clocks and Clockmakers* (1974) / Burial registers SROL / Halesworth Times

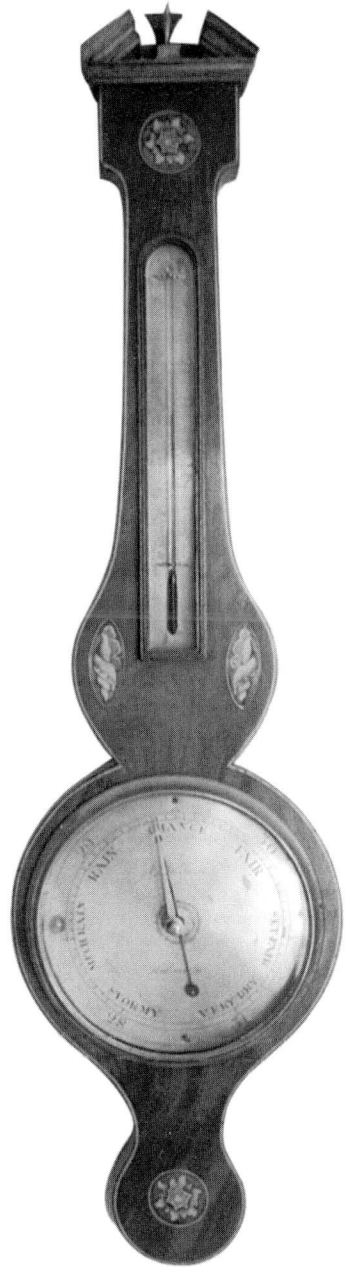

PRIVATE COLLECTION

Barometer, signed Molinari, Halesworth

Harvey, Joseph *Schoolmaster* 1797-1861

Page 335, Volume II of Suckling's *History and Antiquities of the County of Suffolk*, 1847, shows a pretty engraving of the front porch of Gothic House, Halesworth, opposite the church, then embellished with a Georgian sashed bay window and a panel bearing the inscription "Harvey's Academy".

The previous owners of the school in Gothic House were the **Rev. Thomas Tanqueray** and Mrs Parker. Joseph Harvey had taken over by 1816 - in the Parish Records his was a new Rate Assessment for that year. At this time Gothic House and its lands were owned by **John Dresser** of Blyford.

Joseph Harvey was born at Ufford, near Woodbridge, in 1797 or thereabouts, the grandson of Joseph I and Sarah, whose tombstone is in Ufford churchyard. Joseph I died in March 1808 aged 61 years, his wife Sarah died January 1799 aged 57; Joseph II, their son, was born in 1778. Joseph III - the principal subject of this profile - married Mary Pipe Knights on 19th June 1817 at St Mary's, Woodbridge, after he had started the school in Halesworth. Three children were born and baptised in Halesworth - Sarah, Caroline (1822) and Joseph Benjamin Pipe (1825). In 1830 Mary died at the early age of 38 years, and is buried in Halesworth churchyard beneath the ilex tree. On 16th June 1831, Joseph married again, to Harriet Rogers, a single lady of Halesworth, and by the 1851 Census they had had six children: Mary (1840), Frederick (1842), Clare (1843), Julius (1845), Rosa (1847) and Alexander (1850).

The school flourished, as both a day and boarding establishment, for many years. In 1817, not long after it had opened, Joseph Harvey advertised in the *Ipswich Journal* of 20th September for an articled assistant "not under 14 years of age... a Dissenter will be preferred. Apply, if by letter, post paid..." According to lists of pupils and census returns the numbers fluctuated, but still boarders came from as far away as London.

Amongst Joseph Harvey's pupils in 1817 were two boys from Saxmundham, Henry and Samuel Bright, sons of Jerome Bright, watch and clock maker. Henry Bright started his working life as a chemist in London Lane, Norwich, but soon became influenced by the thriving school of Norwich artists and changed his indentures to work for Alfred Stannard, the well-known painter. He moved to London by 1836 and made a good living painting and teaching, writing books of instruction and using his chemist's experience to manufacture coloured crayons. He returned to Suffolk and died in 1873 at Ipswich. Among his pupils was Miss Crabtree of Halesworth (Fanny, sister of **John Crabtree**, attorney) who executed the drawing of Gothic House for Suckling's book.

Harvey's Academy pupils made their names in businesses which still exist to this day, including the Jarrold boys from Woodbridge - Samuel, William and Thomas - who founded a bookshop that would develop into the large Norwich department store and printing firm, and the Copemans - John and Jonathan - of Norwich, whose descendants still figure in some of the city's leading businesses.

As well as being headmaster and instructing his pupils, Joseph was keenly involved with the Independent church in the town. James Newby in his *History of Independency* records the growth of the congregation during the **Rev. John**

Dennant's time, culminating with the building of the new chapel in Quay Street. Joseph Harvey was one of the committee formed to carry the project through, and on the completion of the work in 1836 he made a donation of £10 to help clear outstanding debts; this was not finally achieved until 1842, when a tea meeting was held on 2nd July to celebrate the final settling of accounts.

Joseph diversified into other fields of activity in the town - perhaps the school did not generate enough income to support his large family and maintain such extensive premises. *Pigot's Directory* of 1839 lists him as a coal and timber merchant with an address in the Thoroughfare, and as a specialist in Ryan's patented treatment against timber rot and decay. Roy Clark's book *Black Sailed Traders* records Joseph Harvey as owner of the ship *Iron Duke*, reputed to be of 40 tons and built of iron at Southwold, presumably for carrying merchandise up the New River. There is some doubt about the ship's size and origin, but it was eventually renamed the *James and Jessie* and lay at Great Yarmouth.

It is quite possible that Joseph over-reached himself, as in 1846 he was in financial trouble. A subscription list of his 'old boys' was compiled by **Benjamin Hugman** and John Lincolne (son of William Lincolne, draper in the Market Place and a deacon at the chapel). A printed appeal of 12th January 1848 was signed by several ex-pupils and named John Copeman junior and William Jarrold as treasurers. The aim was "to assist Mr Harvey in an endeavour to re-establish his school". The appeal was followed up by a list of subscribers on 18th May in the hope of generating more donations. £100 was the target but only £56.13.0 had arrived at Jarrold's booksellers premises.

Harvey had moved out of Gothic House by 1848, as the house, an acre of land, and other premises, had been bought at a sale held on 14th June 1848 by **Thompson George**, brewer and farmer. In 1850 Harvey was on his feet again and had opened the school in new premises at "The Folly or Castle" (now Castle House, Holton Road). The 1851 Census lists him, aged 54, "teacher of classics and mathematics and author of works on English Grammar", but no boarders. Castle House was built about 1813 by Robert Hinsby, builder and architect, as one grand house, later divided into three. In 1815 the main house was tenanted by Miss Thompson and Mr Stebbing Revans, Surgeon. A sale notice of 1817 describes Mr Hinsby the propietor as occupier and clearly states "the premises were first erected for one genteel residence... especial care was taken when the additions and divisions were made, not to destroy the original plan". By 1841 Robert Reeve, the brewer, was living there, and in 1850 the Court Roll states that Thomas Higham, maltster, owned the house "with schoolroom" now occupied by Joseph Harvey.

Joseph Benjamin Pipe Harvey (Joseph IV) had taken over the Academy from his father by 1855; Joseph, having retired, was eventually to move to Hadleigh, Suffolk, where he died in 1861. Joseph IV managed to buy Castle House from Thomas Higham in 1860 for £400. Although in smaller premises than Gothic House, by the 1871 Census there were 21 boarders, as well as family, staff and servants. His family, too, was extensive: his wife Caroline Cook of Wissett was three years his senior, and in 1861 her mother was living with them. There were two teachers (one male, one female) and five children. Grace (1851) and Caroline (1853) were both born at Woodbridge - presumably before Joseph III's retirement. Sarah (1855), Joseph V (1858) and Selina (1861) were all born in Halesworth. Like his father, and perhaps for the same financial reasons, Joseph IV was an agent for the General Life and Fire Association.

An announcement in the *Halesworth Times* in 1864 advertised his intention of adding "A preparatory school for young gentlemen of 6 - 9 years of age" and in later advertisements in 1873 and 1883 he proudly claimed "established 1817". During this time he continued his father's adherence to the Independent Chapel, becoming a deacon in 1857. Nine years later, when he was also organist, a disagreement arose as to the use of the Gloria in services. Such a disruption resulted that several members of the chapel resigned, including Joseph Harvey, and formed a Free Independent Church, meeting first at Castle House and afterwards in the Corn Hall behind the Angel Inn. It was not until 1877 that the two factions buried the hatchet and met jointly at the Quay Street Chapel again. Joseph Harvey was re-elected deacon.

The Academy changed hands in October 1883; Joseph retired and Professor Anthony Augustus Eisenhofer PhD, Professor of Languages, succeeded, announcing that pupils would be prepared for Oxford, Cambridge or the College of Preceptors (of which Joseph IV was a member). Eisenhofer only stayed five years, when Mr W.S.Frost took over in 1888. By 1891 the Census shows Mr W.H.Ives as resident. The school had finally closed.

Note: A Mr Richard Harvey kept a school in Bungay where George Crabbe, the future poet, attended from 1762 to 1776/7. We have found no connection with the Halesworth Harveys.

Sources

H.P.R. / Catalogue *Henry Bright*, Norwich Castle Museum (1973) / H.R.M.C.R. / Jarrold Archives / Chapel Minute Book - SROL 230/1/15

Hankinson, Robert Edwards *Rector* 1798-1868

Robert Edwards Hankinson was Rector of Halesworth from 1850 to 1863. He came from a family of clerics, but two generations back his grandfather is reputed to have been a wealthy cork-cutter in King's Lynn, flourishing about 1730. His son Robert Hankinson entered Trinity College, Cambridge, in 1786 and made his career in the Church. He became curate at St Margaret's, King's Lynn, in 1792 and in 1808 moved to Walpole St Andrew as Vicar, where he stayed for the rest of his long life. He became an honorary Canon of Norwich Cathedral, and was wealthy enough to endow a wing of the West Norfolk Hospital. He married Ann Edwards, who bore him three sons: Robert Edwards, Thomas Edwards and Edward Francis Edwards.

Thomas Edwards Hankinson, the second son, was born in 1805 and became a priest, having entered Corpus Christi College, Cambridge, where he became

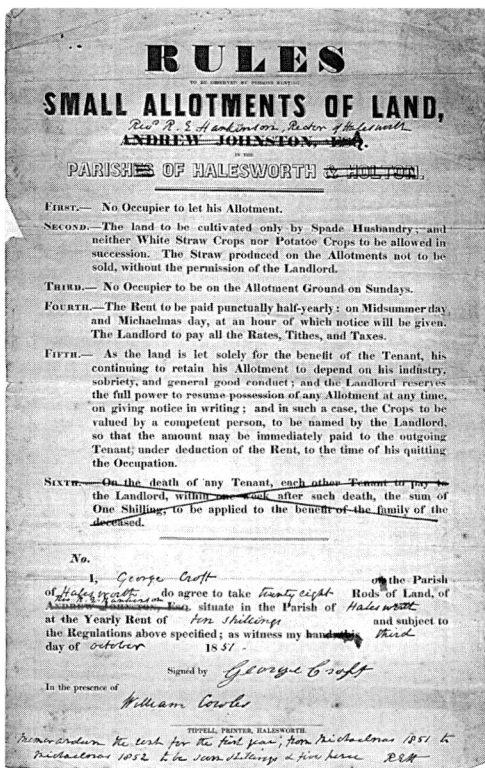

MA in 1831. He was a brilliant
scholar, winning the Seatonian
Prize for English verse at
Cambridge a record nine times.
After a curacy at St Nicholas,
King's Lynn, he moved to
London, to St Matthew's church,
Denmark Hill, where he published an address to the children
of the church school in 1839. He
married Caroline Peacock in
1831. His early promise was not
fulfilled, as he died at the com-
paratively early age of thirty-
eight while at Stainley Hall, near
Ripon, Yorkshire. In an obituary
in the *Gentleman's Magazine* for
1843 it states that in 1841 his
work was highly praised by Mr
Wordsworth. His brothers published a book of his sacred poems
after his death.

BY PERMISSION OF SUFFOLK RECORD OFFICE

Edward Francis Edwards
was the youngest son of Robert. He too entered the Church after Trinity College,
Cambridge, and became in turn curate of St John's and St Margaret's in King's
Lynn, then became Rector of Bircham Newton and Tofts, Norfolk, from 1870 to
1883. He married Catherine Hoare, daughter of Samuel Hoare the banker.

Robert Edwards Hankinson, the eldest son of Robert, was born in 1798 in
King's Lynn. He too went to Trinity College but transferred to Corpus Christi in
1817, becoming MA in 1824. He was ordained priest at Norwich in 1821, when he
became curate to his father at Walpole St Andrew. He seems to have held various
curacies including West Bilney, Norfolk, from 1817 to 1836, then St Lawrence,
Norwich, in 1836. For some reason he moved to London and became Minister of
Well Walk Chapel, Hampstead, a chapel of ease to the parish church. He was
there from 1841 to 1847, under the Rev. Dr Thomas Ainger who had been his contemporary at Cambridge and went on to become the Prebendary of St Paul's
Cathedral. Robert Edwards moved back to Norfolk, to become Rector of St
Margaret's and St Nicholas, King's Lynn, from 1847 to 1850. Duringthis period he
had married Susannah Mary Ann before 1824; she was born in West Bilney about
1802 and presumably met him while he was curate there. In 1824 a son, Robert
Chatfield, was born and christened at Walpole St Andrew by his grandfather
Robert; a daughter, Susanna Felicia (1825), and two more daughters - Marian
(1827) and Eugenia (1828) - followed, all baptised at Walpole St Andrew.

In 1850 a good living presented itself: the Rectorship of Halesworth, then in the patronage of Mrs Elizabeth Badeley, the mother of the **Rev J.C.Badeley**, the previous incumbent. Hankinson was inducted on 24th July 1850. The 1851 Census records the Rectory family consisting of Robert Edwards, aged 53, born in King's Lynn; Susanna Mary Ann his wife aged 49; Marian aged 24 and Eugenia aged 22. Robert Chatfield was making his way in other parts, and Susanna Felicia had presumably died. There were three servants.

Not long after this the Rector had the pleasant duty of officiating at the marriages of his daughters, both to very acceptable suitors. Marian married the **Rev. Samuel Blois Turner**, recently a widower, and Eugenia married Francis Hoare, a merchant of Hampstead, son of Samuel Hoare the banker and brother to Eugenia's aunt Catherine, who had married Edward Francis Edwards Hankinson. 1857 brought promotion within the Church to Archdeacon of Norwich, thus conferring responsibility on Robert Edwards for a large part of the Diocese. This must have gratified his father, by then an old gentleman of 87 years and himself an honorary Canon.

During his years in Halesworth Robert Edwards was responsible for several "improvements" and alterations to the parish church. At a Vestry meeting on February 11th 1858 a proposal was mooted "to take down the chief of the galleries in the church, removing the present pews and re-seating upon a uniform plan by which an increase of accomodation will be obtained". Their proposal was approved and the Churchwardens instructed to apply to the Bishop for a Faculty. The Halesworth architect **Robert Appleton** carried out the work, and by April 1859 the Victorian transformation was complete; the Rector thanked **Mr Andrew Johnston** for working out the re-allocation of sittings, doubtless a commission requiring a great deal of tact and ingenuity.

The Rector interested himself in the activities of his parishioners, organising the allocation and tenancy of allotments [see illustration] and proposing in 1851 that "the gravel pit" be made into a recreation ground - this possibly refers to what is now known as Bird's Folly. In 1854 a major decision was taken that would affect the appearance of the town: burials were to cease in the churchyard, which had been enclosed in railings erected by public subscription in 1812. The Independent Burial Ground was also closed. A Burial Board was appointed and an area of two acres allocated as the Burial Ground, still in use as the cemetery. It is thanks to this decision that Halesworth enjoys such an attractive setting for the parish church.

Further alterations were made to the church in 1862: the outer aisle was built and re-seated as a memorial to the late Andrew Johnston who had served for many years as a churchwarden as well as being a major benefactor to the town. A plaque commemorating this event is still to be seen on the North aisle wall.

Another major local event occurred during Robert Hankinson's time - the coming of the railway in 1854, initially to Old Station Road, when on the occasion of the opening of the line "Halesworth Station was very gaily decorated with flags, and during the day the bells of St Mary rang a merry peal". The line was extended into the town to the present station in 1859. Connected with this event, it is interesting to record that the Rev Hankinson baptised **George Lansbury**, the son of a railway timekeeper, on 13th March 1859. The Rector would have been very surprised to know that this infant would go on become such a well-known political figure.

After a full and active time in Halesworth, and the death of his father in January 1863 aged 93 years, Robert Edwards left the town and became Rector of North Creake. This was the wealthiest living in the personal gift of the Bishop of Norwich. He lived there until his death on 27th March 1868, aged 70 years. His will, proved in June 1868 by his son Robert Chatfield of Southampton, indicates that he was very comfortably situated. His first concern was that his father's collection of antique seals should go to his brother Edward, then to Robert Chatfield. These seals could well have finally come to rest in the hands of the Rev. Samuel Blois Turner, his son-in-law, who had a similar collection at his death - now in Ipswich Museum.

Robert Chatfield was also to inherit all the"plate which shall have been presented to me or my ancestors". His real estate, left between his son and Francis Hoare his son-in-law, is described as being "in England and Wales"; we have found no Welsh connections. His wife was left £3,000 and "jewels, ornaments, wine and other liquors, household effects, plate, books, pictures, engravings, carriage horse harness..."

A final interesting sidelight on this man of many interests is shown by a letter written by Robert Edwards from Bilney Lodge, Norfolk, to Lord Melbourne, then Home Secretary, on 31st August 1831. It refers to "incendiary letters" sent to him as a magistrate by a farmer of Walpole St Peter. What the threats were is not specified, although it was linked to troubles with agricultural labourers, at the height of the harvest and in the year of great unrest that would lead to the deportation of the Tolpuddle Martyrs. A request was made for financial help from the government to suppress this "dreadful spirit". As can be guessed, Lord Melbourne's reply - written on the back of the letter - expresses regrets at the threats but could not offer any financial help.

Sources

Alumni Cantab. / Diocesan Register / H.P.R. / Walpole St Andrew Parish Register / Halesworth Museum / Halesworth Vestry minutes / Halesworth Times

Johnston, Andrew *Banker* 1798-1862

Andrew Johnston came from a long line bearing the same names at the tiny burgh of Kilrenny in the East Neuk of Fife. Andrew I (1700-65) purchased Rennyhill House there and was followed by Andrew II (died 1796), Andrew III (1753-1836) and finally our Andrew IV. Rennyhill is a substantial stone structure with a three-storeyed main block and two-storeyed West wing - it would look much more impressive if its balancing East wing had not been demolished [see illustration]. Its date is confirmed by a stone inscribed "A.I. - E.C. - 1773", com-

Portrait photograph of Andrew Johnston

memorating Andrew II and his wife Euphemia Cléphane, though the house probably contains earlier work. It is however a middle-ranking laird's house rather than a mansion, and its quite small walled garden is surrounded by farm buildings. Our Andrew was to be the last Johnston Laird of Rennyhill, as the property was sold in his lifetime.

We have found no record of Andrew IV's education, despite enquiring of all the then existing universities in the British Isles, but by 1826 he was married and living in Edinburgh. His bride was Barbara Pearson, and daughters Charlotte and Margaret were born in Edinburgh in the next three years. Both died infants and were buried at Kilrenny. Finally on 20th January 1830 Barbara died and was buried in the Rennyhill tomb, North of the church at Kilrenny, where a tablet was erected "by the only survivor of the marriage".

After this harrowing experience a dramatic change occurred in Andrew's life

- in 1831 he was elected Whig MP for the five burghs of East Fife. This came about almost by chance as Kilrenny, which was never a Royal Burgh, was included "inadvertently" in the Act of Union of 1707 as one of the five burghs of East Fife electing an MP to Westminster. The electorate consisted of the Councils of each burgh, which were self-perpetuating oligarchies, so it did not need many votes to elect Andrew.

On arriving in Parliament he soon made the acquaintance of Thomas Fowell Buxton, and became his ally in the campaign to abolish slavery. Buxton (1786-1845) had strong Norfolk connections through his marriage to Hannah Gurney of the Norwich Quaker family, and through the family brewing firm of Truman, Hanbury and Buxton. Though of Essex origins he moved with his family in 1827 to Northrepps Hall, near Cromer, a Gurney property, and when in London lived at 54 Devonshire Street, which for a time was also Johnston's address. Buxton was William Wilberforce's chosen successor in the anti-slavery movement, and after Wilberforce's death in 1833 he piloted the Emancipation Bill through its final stages - it eventually became law in 1834. In the same year Andrew Johnston married Buxton's eldest daughter Priscilla (1808-52), and the wedding reception was also a celebration of the success of the campaign. The Johnstons lived in the Buxtons' house in Devonshire Street, a highly fashionable address near Regent's Park. However the two reformers were undermined by the great Reform Act of 1832 and in the first general election of Queen Victoria's reign Buxton lost Weymouth and Johnston lost Fife Burghs.

Andrew must have been at a loss to know what to do next, but Buxton soon found a job for him, through his family connections, in the Halesworth Bank. The local director, David Lloyd, had died in 1839, leaving a vacancy which Andrew filled. The Bank had been opened in 1782 as "Gurney and **Turner**", and was a kind of local head office with most of the Suffolk branches subordinate to it.

The 1841 Census saw the Johnstons installed in Bank House in the Thoroughfare, with Andrew aged 40, Priscilla 30, Andrew 6, Euphemia 4, Fowell 2 and Sarah 3 months (this first census only gave approximate ages for adults), plus a governess, a nursemaid and five female servants. Two more daughters were to appear later - Priscilla in 1843 and Catherine in 1844. At this date the bank was in the Market Place and separate from Bank House. It was not until 1855 that the Bank moved to the plot adjoining Bank House, when the *Halesworth Times* on 17th July praised "the very handsome facade now in process of completion at the Bank of Messrs Gurney".

Andrew was soon immersed in local affairs, being a regular attender at Vestry meetings, and in 1844 appointed Rector's Warden. The Rector at this time was **Joseph Badeley** and in 1844 he baptised the Johnstons' youngest child, Catherine Isabel. The next year he baptised "Rachel, daughter of Samuel Gurney of West Ham, bill-broker, and his wife Elizabeth" - another Buxton relation. Also in 1844 Andrew was appointed Treasurer of the Blything Union, and two years later purchased Highfield from Hartwell Corbyn for £2,300. This is the large villa at the top of Soaphouse Hill, later the home of **Frederick Cross**, but it appears the Johnstons never lived there.

In 1852 came a heavy blow when Andrew's wife Priscilla died at an early age. She was buried in Overstrand church, near Cromer, next to the seat of the

Buxtons. A tablet records "Within the adjoining ruins lie the remains of Priscilla, wife of Andrew Johnston of Halesworth Esq. and eldest daughter of Sir Thomas Fowell Buxton Bart. Of a kindred spirit with her father and gifted with like energy of mind, she largely shared his labours and his sympathies in the cause of the negro. She died the 18th June 1852 in the 45th year of her age". The reference to ruins arises from the fact that the church was largely unroofed from the 18th century till it was restored in 1914. Andrew decided to commemorate her in Halesworth by building and endowing a school in what is now School Lane, and a public subscription was raised in 1853. The subscription list survives at Lowestoft Record Office and apart fromHalesworth people includes large donations from the extended Buxton family, including Barclays, Birkbecks, Brightwens, Gurneys and Hoares, and even two pounds from the Buxton family servants. The school still survives and bears the inscription "These schools have been erected by the contributions of neighbours and friends as a tribute of respect and affection to the memory of Priscilla the wife of Andrew Johnston Esq. A.D.1853".

At about this date Andrew purchased the advowson of Halesworth apparently, as appears from his will, to ensure the presentation of "an efficient clergyman" at the next vacancy. This passed from Andrew to his executor Sir Thomas Fowell Buxton, the third Baronet, who presented in 1863. Meanwhile the living had gone to **R.E.Hankinson**, who was related by marriage to the Hoares, and who in 1854 married his own daughter Eugenia to Francis Hoare. In 1855 came another move when Andrew purchased Holton Hall, barely two miles from the town, from the **Rev. J.B.Wilkinson**, and that summer he entertained the children of the village in its spacious grounds. On a lighter note, the Sailors' Reading Room at Southwold has an excellent model of the beach punt "Rapid", built by James Critten in 1850 for Andrew Johnston Esq; the family used to spend much of the summer in lodgings at Southwold. Andrew did not, however, neglect Halesworth, and in 1856 the *Halesworth Times* reported that "our institute [full title 'Halesworth Institute for Moral and Intellectual Improvement'] has been enriched with a hundred volumes of miscellaneous works given by Andrew Johnston", while in 1860, at the age of sixty-two, he was "appointed Captain of the Rifle Corps. The brass band has been much improved".

Andrew Johnston died on 24th August 1862 - rather surprisingly at Sydenham, Kent. He must have been staying with his son Andrew, who reported the death and gave his residence as Welbeck House, West Hill, Sydenham. He was buried beside Priscilla in the roofless church at Overstrand, where a simple tablet beneath his wife's says "In memory of Andrew Johnston of Holton and Halesworth, died August 24th 1862 aged 64". There are two prominent monuments to him in Halesworth. One is the outer North Aisle of the church, where a brass tablet says "This North Aisle and Chapel were built and enlarged in the year 1863... as a memorial to the late Andrew Johnston Esq. of this town and of Holton Hall. Born 1798, Died 1862". The other is the Rifle Hall on Norwich Road, originally a theatre and used as such by the Fisher Company until about 1850 [see **Dennant, John**]. This was remodelled as the Volunteers' drill hall at the time of the Napoleon III invasion scares, and a tablet inside used to read "This Hall was placed in trust in the year 1862 by the children of Andrew Johnston of

Rennyhill House, Kilrenny, Fife. Birthplace of Andrew Johnston

Holton in memory of their father for the benefit of the town of Halesworth and especially of the 7th Suffolk Rifles whom for the last two years of his life he commanded".

Andrew's will was written in December 1852, a few months after Priscilla's death, when their children were still minors, so it is not surprising that by 1862 five codicils had been added. His executors were to be three of the formidable Buxton family - Sir Edward North, second Baronet, and his son Thomas Fowell, Charles Buxton, and Thomas Brightwen of the Bank. Codicil 2 nominated Andrew junior as executor in the place of Sir Edward, deceased. The bequest of the advowson, which we have already mentioned, takes pride of place, but broadly speaking each child gets one sixth share of the residuary estate while the two sons get additional cash bequests - £4,000 to Andrew and £1,500 to Fowell, but the latter only at age thirty, though the trustees may use capital to buy him a commission in the army at their discretion. By codicil 4 the wayward Fowell had made good - "now of H.M. 100th Regiment of Foot" - and would get his money without delay. The will was proved on 31st October 1862 by oath of T.F.Buxton of Brick Lane, Spitalfields and Andrew Johnston of Dowgate Dock in the City of London - "effects under £20,000".

The six children were Andrew, born 1835, Euphemia 1837, Fowell Buxton 1839, Sarah Maria 1841, Priscilla Hannah 1843 and Catherine Isabel 1844. Andrew attended Rugby School and University College, Oxford, though no degree is recorded. He inherited Holton Hall and in 1872 held a dinner for his

tenants at the King's Arms, but announced that the estate had been sold to C.Easton Esq., and in March the contents were auctioned by Lenny and Smith of Halesworth. Andrew was already living at Woodford, Essex, as a neighbour to his cousin Sir Thomas Buxton of Warlies. Andrew married Charlotte, daughter of the Rev. G.Trevelyan of Malden, Surrey, and in 1868 followed his father into Parliament as Liberal MP for South Essex. His tenure was, however, even shorter than his father's and after 1874 he devoted himself to local government, becoming the first Chairman of Essex County Council and holding the post for twenty-seven years. He was involved, with the Buxtons, in the fight to save Epping Forest from development and became a Verderer in 1878 [see illustration]. He and Charlotte were largely responsible for building the Wilfred Lawson Temperance Hotel, "erected in a commanding position on Woodford Green in 1883", with the laudable aim of providing non-alcoholic refreshment for the hordes of East-enders who now tramped the forest every weekend. It was demolished in 1974.

Euphemia Johnston married Miles MacInnes, a banker of Carlisle, and Fowell Johnston continued his army career. He was buried at Halesworth, where a tablet in his father's aisle says "Captain Fowell Buxton Johnston, born 5th January 1839, died 22 May 1914". Beside it is another tablet - "Sacred to the memory of Andrew Johnston, Lieut. R.F.A. attached R.F.C., youngest son of Fowell Buxton Johnston, born 18 May 1897, killed in Flanders 30 October 1917". Below this is a wooden propeller inscribed "Lieut. A.Johnston 30.10.17 R.I.P. 21 Squad. R.F.C.".

Sources

Wood, W. *The East Neuk of Fife* (1887) / Society of Genealogists "J" box / D.N.B. / Mottram, R.H. *Buxton the Liberator* (1945) / Anderson, V. *The Northrepps Grandchildren* (1968) / Bidwell, W. *Annals of an East Anglian Bank* (1900) / H.P.R. / H.M.C.R. / Halesworth Times / Vestry minutes - SROL (124/A1/1-7) / Subscription list - SROL (124/F1/1&2) / Gooch, M. *The Halesworth Theatre - Suffolk Review* (1995) / Alumni Oxon. / Addison, W. *Essex Worthies* (1973) / Smith, M. *Village to Suburb* - Woodford Historical Society (1982) / V.C.H. Essex vol VI p344

Part Three

19th Century

Turner, Samuel Blois *Cleric and Antiquary* 1805-82

The Reverend Samuel Blois Turner was a country parson cum antiquary who chose to spend most of his life in or near Halesworth. His father was Thomas Turner (1773-1865), an eminent medical man in London, and his mother was Lucretia Grace, daughter of Sir John Blois of Cockfield Hall.

Thomas Turner was the son of Samuel "an opulent West India merchant" of London. Thomas had three sons - Samuel Blois was the eldest, then Henry Blois (1808-97) who became a General in India, and Thomas Metcalfe Blois (1809-47) who died young, also in India. All three boys attended Charterhouse School, where their father had also been a pupil.

Thomas senior was admitted to Trinity College, Cambridge, in 1793, where he passed MB in 1799 and MD in 1804. He was admitted to the College of Physicians and was its Treasurer from 1823 to 1845. As Treasurer he presided over the construction of the College's new building in Pall Mall and at its opening was presented with "a piece of plate". He was Physician Extraordinary to King William IV and Queen Adelaide. His obituary in the *Gentleman's Magazine* says that "when over ninety years old he was attacked and garotted by a gang of ruffians, which had the effect of dispersing a goitre which had long resisted more orthodox treatment". He survived, and died at his house in Curzon Street at the age of ninety-two.

His wife Lucretia Grace was the daughter of Lucretia Ottley of St Kitts in the West Indies, which suggests a connection with the elder Turner. Lucretia Ottley became in 1772 the second wife of Sir John Blois, fifth Baronet. Sir John was in constant financial trouble, having inherited heavy debts and made matters worse with constant gambling. He must have been glad of Lucretia's dowry, but as Copinger says, he "lost much money on gaming, especially to Mr Fitzgerald, a well known Irishman. His losses caused him to let the Hall and live abroad. His principal creditor Mr Fitzgerald having been hanged in Ireland for instigating a murder, he was able to return to England, where he died in 1810". Lucretia had died two years before, but not before seeing her daughter safely married, in 1805, to a reliable medical man. After bearing Thomas Turner three sons she died in 1826. Thomas remarried, to Dorothy, widow of Dr Hacket. She died in 1843, aged sixty-nine, and is buried in the tiny church of Linstead Parva, outside Halesworth, where Samuel Blois Turner was then perpetual curate.

After Charterhouse Samuel entered Pembroke College, Cambridge, in 1824 and graduated BA in 1828, was ordained deacon at Norwich in 1829 and priest in 1830, and was appointed perpetual curate of Linstead Parva in 1832 and of Magna in 1838. He had probably at Cambridge made the acquaintance of the Rev. Jeremy Day [see **Dresser and Day Families**] and married his niece Marian Day at some date before 1840.

By 1836 he was living at the large new house now called the Elms in Pound Street (London Road), and his landlord was **George Suggate;** the Vestry minutes record that the new street lighting would "commence at the house now occupied by the Rev. S.B.Turner near the Theatre". Their only child was Thomas Day, baptised at Halesworth on 11th August 1840, and by 1851 Marion was dead.

Meanwhile in 1844 the Turners had moved house. Jeremy Day had sold Samuel Blois four acres of land fronting the Bramfield Road but with a long driveway linking it to Soaphouse Hill. On this Turner built South Lodge, an elegant white-brick villa, still looking very Regency, in a miniature planted park. The Vestry meeting on 10th October rated this at an impressive £60, and the 1851 Census records Samuel, widower, living there with a groom and two female servants.

Samuel was not to stay single for long. In 1850 a new Rector had arrived in Halesworth - **Robert Edwards Hankinson** - and he came with two very eligible daughters. On 7th January 1852 the Rector celebrated the marriage of Samuel to his eldest daughter, another Marian, and two years later came another son for the Turners - Samuel Hankinson. The 1861 Census has Samuel, aged 54, Marian aged 34, born at Walpole (in the Fens), Samuel junior aged 7, born Halesworth, a groom and three servants. The following year came another move, as Samuel gave up the curacies of the two Linsteads to take on the Rectory of All Saints, South Elmham. This time he must have decided that six miles was too far to commute from Halesworth, but there was no acceptable parsonage house at All Saints. In 1862, after an exchange of glebe lands, he built an ambitious new Rectory there and this time it was in the latest Butterfieldian polychrome brick style. The architect was Ewan Christian, a church and parsonage specialist from London. To finance this he took a mortgage with Queen Anne's Bounty (intended "for the maintenance of poor clergy") for £900. The house still stands, within another mini-park, though no longer used as the Rectory.

Like so many Victorian parsons, Samuel was a keen antiquary, and in this worked closely with friends like Jeremy Day and Alfred Suckling. The latter, in his History of Suffolk, writes of what is now Gothic House in Halesworth: "The mansion of the Bedingfields is now the property of the Rev. J.Day of Hetherset in Norfolk, but the ancient fittings just described [carved panelling and chimneypiece] have lately been removed from the appartment in which they were falling prey to neglect and decay, to the library of the Rev. S.B.Turner of Halesworth and form an appropriate shrine for the varied and valuable collection of antiquities possessed by that gentleman". He goes on to describe other relics, such as a musket from the Spanish Armada and a portrait from a Dutch ship captured at Sole Bay, and one must assume that all these were installed, somewhat inappropriately, in the neat Regency villa on Bramfield Road. It seems likely that they were moved again to a more suitable setting at All Saints. In 1867 Turner became one of the joint honorary secretaries of the Suffolk Institute of Archaeology, and three years later had the pleasure of showing its members the remarkable **Browne** brass newly re-installed in Halesworth church. The inscription he added to this tells how it "fell into the hands of the Rev. Samuel Blois Turner", and it was not the only thing to fall into them. He had a fine collection of casts of seals and ivories which had been Robert Hankinson's and are now in the Ipswich Museum, and a Roman bronze Venus found at Wenhaston but now untraceable. During his incumbency of All Saints he carried out extensive restoration of the little round-towered church.

Samuel died on All Saints Day 1882 and is buried in the church he so lavishly refitted. His will, dated 1877, is brief and simple, leaving everything to Marian and appointing as executors her and the two sons. It is witnessed by his brother Henry, now a retired Lieut. General living in Harley Street, and his butler, of the same august address. The nett personal estate was £2,700 10s 7d when the will was proved at Ipswich in December 1882, so the bulk of his real estate must already have been disposed. Fortunately the sparseness of the will is made up for by some fascinating personal recollections by Charles Bird of All Saints (1865-1950) who was persuaded to reminisce by his then employer and owner of the Old Rectory, Philip Harrold. Charles tells us - "Mr Turner used to have two maids, a butler and a gardener... his son Thomas, of Flixton Rectory, was lame... Turner was a nice man... he was short and thick and had a short neck... in the dining room he had carved oak... when he died some of it went to Ipswich Museum... Mr Turner didn't pay for the house right down but used to pay by instalments... Mrs T. was tall and slender like. She was more stern, and you mustn't pass them without a bow or a curtsey. The women used to nearly sit down on the road!"

Thomas Day Turner (1840-1908) was admitted to Caius College, Cambridge (his uncle Jeremy's), in 1859, took BA in 1863 and MA in 1868, became curate of Denton in 1865 and Vicar of Flixton from 1877 to 1892, and died at Beccles in 1908. Samuel Hankinson Turner followed him to Caius in 1872, took BA 1876 and MA 1879. For some reason he moved South, was ordained at Rochester in 1877 and 1878. He was Curate of Eltham 1877 to 1889 and of Aldenham 1889 to 1898, and Vicar of Radlett from 1898 to 1905. He died in 1941 at Aldenham. It appears that neither son ever married.

Sources

Munk's Roll / Lawrence (1990) / Copinger II / Alumni Cantab. / G.E.C. *Complete Baronettage* / Parish *List of Carthusians* (1879) / H.P.R. / P.S.I.A. Vol XXXIX (1997) Plunkett, S. *Hamlet Watling* / Suckling II / Halesworth Vestry minutes - SROL (124/A1/1) / Harrold family

Gilbert, Wilkinson John *Artist* born 1805

Wilkinson Gilbert is the only artist based full time in Halesworth to be found in our researches. Henry Bright spent his schooldays here [see **Harvey, Joseph**], and Thomas Churchyard worked for four years in the town articled to a solicitor [see **Crabtree, Robert**], but neither were functioning professional artists at the time.

Few of Wilkinson Gilbert's pictures survive, but many Halesworth residents will have seen his *East View of Halesworth from Castle Hill*, [see back cover]. Though small in scale it accurately depicts many features of contemporary Halesworth. This is a delightful rustic scene - ladies chatting in the foreground and a passing horseman on the Holton Road, another figure carrying a fishing net over his shoulder. In the middle distance are Town meadow and Angel mead-

'Gaffer, a chestnut pony'. Oil painting by Wilkinson Gilbert, dated 1868

ow, bordering the New River, with grazing cows and sheep. Two boats - a wherry and a keel - are sailing upriver to the Quay near the maltings. Three figures are by the bridge over the Old River - newly rebuilt in 1846, as described in the Vestry minutes for 27th April 1846: "£10 towards rebuilding the bridge over the Old River near **Thompson George's** malt office, being in a delapidated and dangerous state". The new malt office, assessed at £6 for rates in January 1847, is visible across the field beyond the bridge - the "Osier ground of Martin George" on the tithe map of 1839. Trees on the opposite side of River Lane, which runs from the bridge to the town, show the edge of **John Crabtree's** kitchen garden. In the far distance, rising above the old roofs of the town, is the East wall of the chancel of the church; the tower beyond, with a cupola installed in 1826, features a ball and weathervane. On the left can just be seen the gable of Gothic House. Alas the scene is now very different, as the railway embankment cut across the foreground when constructed in 1858.

This little picture was engraved by D.Buckle and published by John Row in *Pawsey's Ladies Repository*. Frederick Pawsey was a printer and bookseller at Ipswich from 1834 to 1897.

Another of Wilkinson Gilbert's pictures is in the Southwold Museum. An oil painting in the Dutch style, it shows Southwold from Harbour Road with cows in the foreground and a distant view of the town, with the salt works between and a windmill on the common. Several sailing ships and one steamer are out at sea. It is a delightful scene. The painting is signed W.J.Gilbert 1851, and has a number on the reverse. This could identify it as one of several pictures exhibited by Wilkinson Gilbert in London in 1851, as listed in A. Graves's *A Dictionary of Artists who have exhibited works in the Principal London Exhibitions from 1760 to 1893.*

Wilkinson John Gilbert was baptised at Wrentham on 14th May 1805. His parents were George and Betsy Gilbert and he had at least one brother, Henry, and one sister, Maria Tuthill - one wonders if these names indicate links with the Halesworth families of **Tuthill** and **Wilkinson**, but nothing has so far come to light to connect them.

In the 1841 Census returns Wilkinson Gilbert is described as "artist", living in Pound Street next to Robert Peachey the rope and twine spinner [see **Dennington, Ernest**]. Wilkinson's wife Hannah was then twenty and he was thirty-five (approximately), both born in Suffolk, and they had a daughter - Ada - nine months old. *White's Directory* of 1844 has him listed as "portrait and animal painter" still living in Pound Street. A son, Charles Edwin, was born and baptised in Halesworth on 2nd March 1850. Ada was apparently baptised elsewhere.

The 1851 Census repeats this information, then another son was baptised on 12th February 1854 with the impressive names of Claude Angelo, presumably reflecting Wilkinson's favourite artists - a fashionable thing to do in artistic circles. The parish register of 1854 shows the family living in Chediston Street; in 1855 Wilkinson is listed again in *White's Directory*, and the 1861 Census shows him still in Chediston Street but as a boarder in William Woods household.

There was a Gilbert family in the town at an earlier date: William Gilbert was a "bookseller, bookbinder, stationer, cutler, ironmonger and brazier" and figures in a sale advertisement for his premises in the *Ipswich Journal* in 1804. We do not know if there was any connection between the two families, nor do we know the date and location of Wilkinson Gilbert's death.

Sources

H.P.R. / Wrentham P.R. / Courtauld Institute - Witt Library / Southwold Museum

Wilkinson John Gilbert - *List of Known Works*

1832 - *A Dark Bay Horse and Gig* Signed and dated 1832. 15 3/4" x 23 1/2" Black and white. Sold at Christies 1979.

1838 - *Equestrian Portrait of a Gentleman on his Dapple Grey Hunter* Signed and dated 1838. 24' x 29" Oil on canvas.

1841 - *John Parksey with his Son out Coursing* Signed and dated 1841. 20" x 25" Oil on canvas. Stradbroke sale, 1998.

1847? - *East View of Halesworth from Castle Hill* 3 1/2" x 2 1/4" Black and white. Engraving in *Pawsey's Ladies Repository*. [see back cover]

1851 - *View of Southwold* Oil on canvas. Exhibited London 1851? Southwold Museum.

1856 - *Shooting: coursing a pair* Signed and dated 1856. 12" x 16 1/4" Black and white . Sotheby sale, 1981.

1868 - *'Gaffer' a chestnut pony etc* Dated 1868. 25 1/8" x 30" Oil on canvas. Christies sale, 1988. [see illustration]

George, Thompson *Maltster* 1806-74

Thompson George was overshadowed by **Patrick Stead** but nevertheless became a prominent figure in the brewing and malting trade that led Halesworth's expansion in the early 19th century. His father was a farmer, Martin George (1771-1848), who tenanted Dairy Farm , London Road, from at least 1806, under **John Dresser** and **Jeremy Day**. In 1803 he married Elizabeth Thompson of Bury St Edmund's and they had three sons: Martin (1805), Thompson (1806) and William (1811), who died at the age of twenty-two. Martin senior was one of the largest farmers in the parish, and increased his holding dramatically in 1827 when he took on "Carman's Land" (the site of the Manor), again as tenant to Jeremy Day. He now farmed 235 acres, by far the largest in Halesworth. He was a leading citizen, regularly attending Vestry meetings, serving as Overseer of the Poor, and a member of the Blything Board of Guardians.

Meanwhile the family were dogged by ill-health. After William's early death Martin junior died in 1841, aged only thirty-six. He had set up as a maltster and coal merchant in Holton Road, and Thompson took over his business in 1843 as a basis for his own future expansion.

Thompson had married, in 1838 at Halesworth church, Margaret daughter of Richard Reeve, merchant of Frostenden, a member of the milling and malting family of Wangford and Halesworth. They never had any children. In addition to taking over Martin junior's business, in 1847 he opened a new "malt office" (malting) by the New River, now the Leisure Centre, and in 1848 was able to buy a house suitable for his new status. This was Gothic House, lately used as **Joseph Harvey's** Academy, but constituting half, with his father's Dairy Farm, of the old mansion of the **Nortons** and **Bedingfields**. He purchased this for £350 from Jeremy Day, and soon set about re-Gothicising it from its then Georgianised appearance.

In 1855 came another big chance when Thomas Cracknell decided to retire from his brewing business - formerly Reeve and Cracknell - and Thompson purchased the Three Tuns in the Market Place, with the Halesworth Brewery at the rear, and thirteen tied public houses as far afield as Beccles and Leiston, but including four Halesworth pubs: the White Hart, Hawk, Swan and Wherry. Four years later he increased his hold on Halesworth by buying the King's Head in Quay Street from Henry Dowson of Geldeston for £770. This expansion was

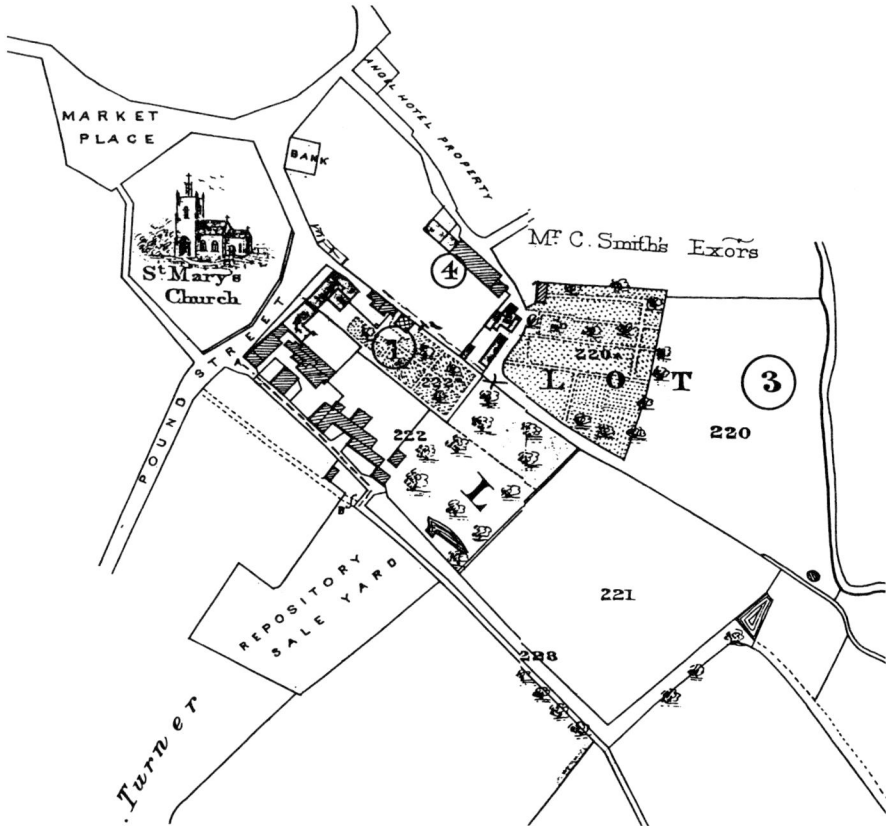

Thompson George's property at Gothic House, Halesworth, from sale particulars dated 1889

financed by a mortgage for £8,000 in 1862 from Henry Birkbeck and T.Brightwen, partners in Gurney's Bank.

Thompson had taken partners in the brewery, which by 1864 was known as George, Stanford and Holden, and by 1868 George, Stanford and Flick; after Thompson's death in 1874 becoming Croft and Flick until 1888, when it was sold to the Colchester Brewing Company. In the 1861 Census Thompson was described as a brewer and corn merchant, employing sixteen men, and he followed his father in public life, being a regular attender at Vestry meetings and a member of the Board of Guardians. However, as Rachel Lawrence says of the Georges, "their business was but a faint echo of Patrick Stead's".

The end is tersely stated in the *Halesworth Times* - "13 Oct. 1874: George Stanford and Flick have disposed of their business to George C. Croft and Richard W. Flick"; "10 Nov. 1874: 7th instant at Halesworth Mr Thompson George, brewer and maltster, an old and respected inhabitant of the town, aged 69 years" ; "17 Nov. 1874: The funeral of Mr Thompson George in the family vault, by permission of the Secretary of State. The Rifle Corps were present under

Lieut. Morris , and a dumb peal was rung". The special permission was necessary because Halesworth was by then a closed churchyard. Margaret George lived on at Gothic House for a further fifteen years. After her death in 1889 it was sold by auction to Mary Elizabeth, daughter of **Frederic Cross**.

Sources

M & S Gooch / Lawrence (1990) / H.P.R. / H.M.C.R. / Vestry minutes - SROL(124 / A1 / 1-7)

Phipps, Augustus Frederick *Rector* 1809-96

Probably the most socially elevated Rector of Halesworth was the Honourable and Reverend Augustus Phipps. He was the fourth son of Henry, first Earl of Mulgrave (1755-1831) who in turn was the son of Constantine Lord Mulgrave and his wife Lepel Hervey of Ickworth. The Mulgraves were landowners in Yorkshire, with their estate bordering the sea at Mulgrave, just North of Whitby. The cliffs there were found to be rich in alum, then a highly prized mineral, and this made their fortune. The estate is splendidly wooded, landscaped by Repton, and the Castle is a Georgian house castellated in the early 19th century.

Henry Phipps served in the army in America, succeeded his brother in 1792 to the Irish title of Baron Mulgrave, and two years later became Baron Mulgrave of Mulgrave. He served in the Napoleonic wars, was promoted General in 1809, then entered politics, becoming military adviser to William Pitt the Younger, then Foreign Secretary in 1805 and First Lord of the Admiralty in 1807. In 1812 he was created first Earl of Mulgrave. He was related by marriage to **Robert Plumer Ward**, which has a bearing on Augustus's future career.

Augustus entered Trinity College, Cambridge, in 1827, having been schooled at Harrow, took MA in 1831 and was ordained at Lincoln in 1834. He became Rector of Halesworth and Chediston in 1835, on the presentation of no other than Robert Plumer Ward, Lord of the Manor. He only stayed four years, during which he married, in 1837, Lady Mary Fitzroy, eldest daughter of the Duke of Grafton. In 1839 he moved to Boxford and in 1850 became Rector of Euston, Suffolk, on the Grafton estate, where he stayed till 1883. He was Chaplain to the Queen 1847-96 and Honorary Canon of Ely from 1875 to 1896, and died in London on the 27th January 1896.

Not much is known of his brief tenure of Halesworth, but the Vestry minutes give a glimpse of a rather daunting young man:-

"22 January 1836: Objections were reported by the Rector to the use of the Parish tenement known as the Committee Room for general purposes.

28 January: A deputation to meet the Rector, the Hon. and Rev. A.F.Phipps.

17 March: Rev. A.F.Phipps in the chair. The old Committee Room has been converted to an infant's school. The School agreed to the use of their room for committees, the Vestry being too small and the public houses too expensive".

So all was well.

Sources

D.N.B. / Alumni Cantab. / V.C.H. North Riding II / Pevsner *Yorkshire, North Riding* - Buildings of England (1966) / Vestry minutes: SROL (124/A1/1-7)

Burleigh, Robert William *Maltster* 1815-83

When **Patrick Stead** sold his maltings in 1849 to Truman Hanbury and Buxton, he leased them back for £1,200 per annum and continued to operate them. In 1851 however Trumans put in Robert Burleigh to assist Stead, and in 1854 he took over sole responsibility. Initially he appears to have been responsible to Truman's, but later to have operated fairly independently.

Burleigh was a native of Sible Hedingham in Essex, where he was born in 1815 to Robert Burleigh, maltster, and Mary nee Pearman, whose tombstones are in the churchyard at Castle Hedingham. He must have left Essex quite young, as he had been living at Woodbridge, where five children were born, before moving to Halesworth. His wife was Hannah, daughter of John Youngs the Norwich brewer (later Youngs, Crawshay & Youngs) so this suggests Robert senior must have been malting and brewing on a considerable scale.

After the Steads retired to Scotland the Burleighs moved into the brewery house, now known as Hooker House, and the 1861 Census records them living there in considerable state with their seven children, a governess, and five servants. By 1871 Robert was employing 39 men in the maltings, had only two children at home, but still kept a governess, cook and three maids.

There is an early reference to Robert in the Rectory Manor rolls on 13 October 1854 when he acted as agent for "Robert Hanbury of Brick Lane, Spitalfields [the location of Truman's brewery to this day]" for the purchase of Pond Field, at Halesworth "containing the bed of a reservoir of water". This was the Great Pond from which the brewery drew its water supply. In January 1855 he advertised in the new *Halesworth Times*: "Robert William Burleigh has always on hand manure, Peruvian guano, Truman Hanbury Buxton and Co's stout porter and ales, season-made malt and fine Kent hops". This suggests both considerable diversification and a more independent relationship with Truman's. By 1864 the new railway, opened in 1859, was beginning to move the focus of the trade away from the Navigation, as Burleigh advertises the sale of coal, lime, salt etc "at the railway station and on the Quay". However he still sat as a Navigation commissioner and in 1868 presided at the Annual General Meeting, but had to report tolls of only £47.10.6 for the previous year. At his death in 1883 he still owned three wherries and a ketch-barge. In 1868 he announced that he had taken his son into partnership as "Burleigh and Son, maltsters, corn, coal, cake, manure, lime and porter merchants. Sole agents for Truman Hanbury & Buxton's stout in barrels or kilderkins". In 1875, appropriately enough, Robert became one of the first Trustees of the Patrick Stead Hospital.

In November 1882 Robert suffered a road accident and died three months later. His will, dated November 1878, appoints as executors his brother Lawrence of Brick Lane Spitalfields, John Youngs of Norwich, brewer, Edmund Lovegrove Hickling of Frostenden, clerk, and John Lewis Marriott of Narborough, merchant. A gold watch presented to Robert when residing at Woodbridge goes to grandson Edmund Hickling, and another gold watch presented by the 3rd Battalion Suffolk Volunteers to grandson John Marriott. Yet another gold watch, once his father's, goes to nephew Sampson Burleigh of Spital Square "thinking he may like to keep it as a family relic". His executors are instructed to sell all properties within two years and pay the interest from this to his widow and his unmarried daughter Helen. After Hannah's death the residue to be shared by "all my children". The will was proved at Ipswich on the 27th April 1883, the gross personal estate amounting to £16,907 16s 1d.

Hannah outlived Robert by ten years, and they are both buried in Holton churchyard. Meanwhile their youngest daughter Helen had married Dr Percy Warwick, and the organ in Halesworth church bears the inscription "Presented by Helen Warwick in memory of her parents Robert and Hannah Burleigh, 10 September 1893". The business was purchased by James Parry (1842-1918), born at Wangford, who by 1891 was living in the brewery house, a widower, with his mother-in-law Jane Allen, four children and three servants. James expanded the business by building the massive new maltings adjoining the railway station sidings, which still stand.

Sources

Lawrence (1986) / Lawrence (1990) / Halesworth Times / H.R.M.C.R.

Cross, Frederick *Solicitor* 1818-92

The long-established firm of Halesworth solicitors known as Cross, Ram owes half its name to Frederick Cross. He joined **John Crabtree** as a partner in 1842, but his association with the town went back further, as his grandfather William was briefly Rector in the 1820's.

William Cross was born at Malton, Yorkshire, and admitted to Pembroke College, Cambridge, in 1787, passed BA in 1791 and MA in 1794. He was ordained at Ely in 1791 and the same year became Curate of Swaffham Bulbeck. In 1799 he became Vicar of Amwell, Hertfordshire, and in 1820 Rector of Halesworth cum Chediston. He died, however, the following year, aged fifty-six, and is commemorated by a tablet in the vestry.

The next generation is a blank, but Frederick gave his place of birth as Essex, and probably moved to Halesworth in 1842. He promptly cemented his position in the Crabtree firm by marrying Maria, the late Robert's spinster daughter, nine years his senior. At the 1851 Census he was living in Quay Street with Maria, daughter Mary Elizabeth aged one, and son Frederick William aged five months, and four female servants. Their Quay Street house is pinpointed by a report in the *Halesworth Times* of July 1856 of the Holton Road railway bridge being constructed "near the residence of F.Cross Esq". Perhaps this is why, by 1861, they had moved to Highfield, a massive white brick villa at the top of Soaphouse Hill, now London Road. In 1871 there, Frederick describes himself as "attorney, solicitor and landowner" and they have a gardener, cook, and two housemaids living in. After the death of John Crabtree in 1870 Frederick became the senior partner and soon took Willett Ram into partnership, giving the firm its present name in 1873.

In 1881 Frederick must have been away on Census night, but both children were present, with Frederick junior still living at home at the age of thirty and his employment entered as "none". The explanation must be his health, as he died three years later and was buried in the new cemetery. His father followed in 1892, having died at Edinburgh, but his mother lived on till the age of ninety-six. They are commemorated by the reredos in the parish church - "In loving memory of Frederick Cross 1818-1892 and Maria Cross 1809-1906". Nearby on the South wall is a tablet to "Mary Elizabeth Cross, daughter of Frederick and Maria Cross of Highfield, who died at Tunbridge Wells 27 May 1920 aged 70".

Willett Ram (1838-1921) was the son of a Yarmouth lawyer. He and his wife Lucy lived at The Limes on London Road, where they had eight children, all baptised at Halesworth between 1874 and 1885. Willett was joined in the practice by his eldest son, also named Willett.

Sources

Newby (1964) / Alumni Cantab. / Halesworth Times

Babington, Francis Evans *Banker* 1830-1920

One of the more modest members of a remarkable family, he took over from **Andrew Johnston** as local director of Gurney's, later Barclay's, Bank in 1863.

The Babingtons had been established at Rothley Temple, Leicestershire, since at least the early 16th century, though Anthony, the conspirator against Queen Elizabeth, belonged to a parallel branch in Derbyshire. In the early 19th century the family blossomed and Francis had three notable relations. His half brother was Churchill Babington (1821-89) who combined the rectory of Cockfield, near Lavenham, with being Disney Professor of Archaeology at Cambridge, and publishing *The Birds of Suffolk*. His second cousin was another Cambridge professor - Charles Cardale Babington - who was a fellow-student with Charles Darwin under Professor Henslow, and familiarly known as "Beetles Babington". He succeeded Henslow as Professor of Botany. His great uncle, though only thirty years older, was Thomas Babington Macaulay, the historian, whose aunt was married to Thomas Babington of Rothley, and who was born there in 1800.

Francis, born at Rothley in 1830, was educated at Eton and Trinity College, Cambridge. It is not known how he came to move to Suffolk, but there is a possible connection in the ubiquitous Buxton family, with whom Andrew Johnston was closely allied, and the anti-slavery movement, of which Macaulay's father was a leading member. Whatever the reason he presumably took a share in Gurney's Bank and arrived at Halesworth, which was then their local head office for a large area of Suffolk, in 1863. Three years later he married Susan Dunbar, who was one of the Ordes, another banking family. Meanwhile he had purchased South Lodge on the Bramfield Road, a "neat villa" in white brick built in 1844 by the Rev **Samuel Blois Turner**.

South Lodge, with its mini-park facing South over what was then open country, had a long tree-lined drive connecting it to the London Road. This drive still survives in part, but most has been built over by a modern housing estate, of which one of the roads has been named 'Babington Drive'. By the 1871 Census Francis, 41, and Susan, 27, lived there with a cook-housemaid and a parlourmaid. By 1881 a daughter, Catherine, was eight years old but Susan was dead. A governess, maid, and cook completed the household. Francis remarried in 1893, his bride being Mademoiselle Anet, from Brussels, but no more children appeared.

Meanwhile Francis seems to have busied himself in local affairs, regularly attending Vestry meetings, sitting as a Justice of the Peace, a Trustee of the Blyth Navigation, chairman of the Mechanics' Institute, a director of the Southwold Railway Company and - after the 1896 merger - a local director of Barclay's Bank, but never appearing on the national stage like his more famous relations.

Sources

D.N.B. / Alumni Cantab. / Halesworth Times / Bidwell W.H: *Annals of an East Anglian Bank*

Upcher, Abbot Roland *Rector* 1849-1929

Probably the most muscular of Halesworth Rectors, Abbot Roland Upcher was grandson of Abbot Upcher of Great Yarmouth, who purchased the Sheringham estate in North Norfolk and in 1812-17 built a new hall and landscaped the park and grounds. The work was carried out by Humphrey Repton for the landscape and by his son John Adey Repton for the design of the house. Humphrey Repton is supposed to have considered this his favourite project, and the house and park survive today under the care of the National Trust. Abbot died in 1819, and was succeeded by his elder son Henry Ramey, whose younger brother was another Abbot (1813-93), who attended Trinity College, Cambridge, and entered the

Church, becoming Rector of Kirby Cane, near Beccles, from 1851 to 1893. He married Mary Day of Earsham and they had a son baptised Abbot Roland on 19th October, 1849.

Abbot Roland followed his father to Trinity College on 1868, having been schooled at Rossall. He took BA in 1872, MA in 1875 and was ordained in 1874. While at Cambridge he also had time to become an athletics Blue, and Walter Rye refers to him as "the great Cambridge quarter-miler" who went on to win the national amateur championship three years in succession. A keen angler also, he is still remembered for the invention of "Upcher's Fly". After ordination he held curacies at Broughton, Cheshire, and St Pancras, London, and was Vicar of St Mary's Sheffield from 1877 to 1889. He was inducted as Rector of Halesworth with Chediston in the latter year. His presentation was by the Bishop of Norwich, but may be related to the fact that his brother-in-law was Henry Edmund, the son of Sir Edward Buxton the previous patron [see **Johnston, Andrew**].

While at Sheffield Abbot had married Alice Winstanley, a native of Briston, not far from Sheringham, and they produced four daughters - Marianne in 1879, Margery de B. in 1883, Alice in 1884 and Victoria in 1888 - all born at Sheffield. With the move to Halesworth came two sons: Lionel, baptised on 15th September 1890, and Peter on 11th October 1892. Abbot stayed at Halesworth twenty-four years, was appointed Rural Dean of Dunwich in 1890 and Diocesan Surrogate in 1894. In 1913 he moved on to the Rectory of Stradbroke and was appointed an Honorary Canon of the new diocese of St Edmundsbury and Ipswich.

In 1923 Alice died at Stradbroke. Abbot then remarried - for the last two years of his life - Dorothy Ibbetson of Sheffield, and died on 25th October 1929.

While Abbot was at Halesworth, yet more works were carried out to the church. In preparation for the installation of a new organ in the former **Argentein** chantry chapel [see **Burleigh, Robert**], a fine piscina was discovered and "the Rev. A.R.Upcher had it removed and placed on the North wall of the chancel". The piscina could be seen again, though the history of the church had been thereby falsified - the chancel now has both South and North piscinas.

Sources

Alumni Cantab. / Pevsner *Norfolk North-East* The Buildings of England (1962) / Rye, W. *Norfolk Families* (1913) / Census 1891 / E.A. Notes and Queries (N.S.) III p283

Lansbury, George *Politician* 1859-1940

Lansbury, one of the founding fathers of the Labour Party, is often considered Halesworth's most famous son - there is a road named after him and a plaque in the Thoroughfare. However our researches show that he was not born in the parish, although he only missed it by two hundred yards and later spent part of his first year in the town.

Photograph dated about 1935 of George Lansbury [left], the then leader of the Labour Party, at an Election meeting with Edwin Gooch MP, father of Michael Gooch

In his autobiography *My Life* Lansbury says "My mother said I first saw the light of day in a toll-house somewhere on what was then the Turnpike Road between Halesworth and Lowestoft... my natal day was 21st February 1859' and this is confirmed by his son-in-law Raymond Postgate in *The Life of George Lansbury*. The confusion arises from his birth certificate which records his birth as the 22nd February at Thoroughfare, Halesworth, but the birth was not registered until the 10th March. Three days later George was baptised at Halesworth church by the **Rev R.E.Hankinson**, stating the parents' abode as Halesworth.

However on the 10th October of the previous year George's elder brother James, who must by then have been a few months old, was also baptised at Halesworth with his parents described as of Wenhaston. It seems clear that the family had moved into Halesworth some time between the 21st February and 10th March, and that Mrs Lansbury decided not to confuse matters by telling the Registrar about this.

His parents were George and Mary Ann (née Ferris) and the reason for their being in Suffolk was that George worked as a timekeeper for Thomas Brassey the railway contractor, who was then engaged on building the East Suffolk Railway from Woodbridge, already connected to the South, to Halesworth, already connected to the North. Lansbury recalls in *My Life* the primitive hutted camps in which the navvies lived a few years later than this, and it is quite credible that his mother had moved into more salubrious quarters for George's birth. This is confirmed by a family tradition quoted by Mrs Heather Philips of Wenhaston whose great grandfather Robert Clarke is believed to have taken pity on the heavily pregnant Mary Ann and moved the family into his toll-house, which was only a matter of yards from the line of the new railway. The 1861 Census of Wenhaston-with-Mells shows Robert Clarke, 40, tollgate keeper living at 106 Halesworth Road, Mells, with his wife and three children. Nothing now remains of the toll-house ,which was demolished when the Turnpike Trust was wound up in 1872, but it stood on the South side of the Halesworth to Bramfield road about two hundred yards from the bridge over the Blyth which forms the boundary with Halesworth. It would therefore be much nearer to Halesworth church for baptisms than to Wenhaston church.

The East Suffolk Railway was formally opened on the 1st June 1859, and it is likely that by then Brassey's team had moved on to their next contract, with the Lansburys living - in a hutted camp again - at "Penge near Sydenham".

From these humble beginnings George was to go on to a remarkable career in politics: first in local government in the then Borough of Poplar, in London's dockland, then at national level as Poplar's MP (first elected for Labour in 1910), and as editor of the Daily Herald. He reached cabinet level as Minister of Works in the Labour government of 1929-31, and is best remembered for "Lansbury's Lido" in Hyde Park. After the disastrous split in the party and their electoral defeat in 1931, George Lansbury was the most senior member of the left, and was elected party leader. Always an ardent pacifist, he resigned over the issue of re-armament in 1935 and was succeeded by Clement Attlee. The outbreak of war in 1939 was the final blow and he died in 1940.

George writes in his autobiography that he only visited Halesworth once as an adult - in 1922. However, when in 1904 the Poplar Guardians decided to set up a colony for getting the unemployed "back to the land" the chosen location was Hollesley Bay. It is tempting to think that subconsciously Lansbury was returning to the county of his birth.

Sources

H.P.R. / Census 1861 / Lansbury, G. 1928. *My Life* / Postgate, R. 1951. *The Life of George Lansbury* / Tithe map - Wenhaston-with-Mells - SROL. / Birth certificate

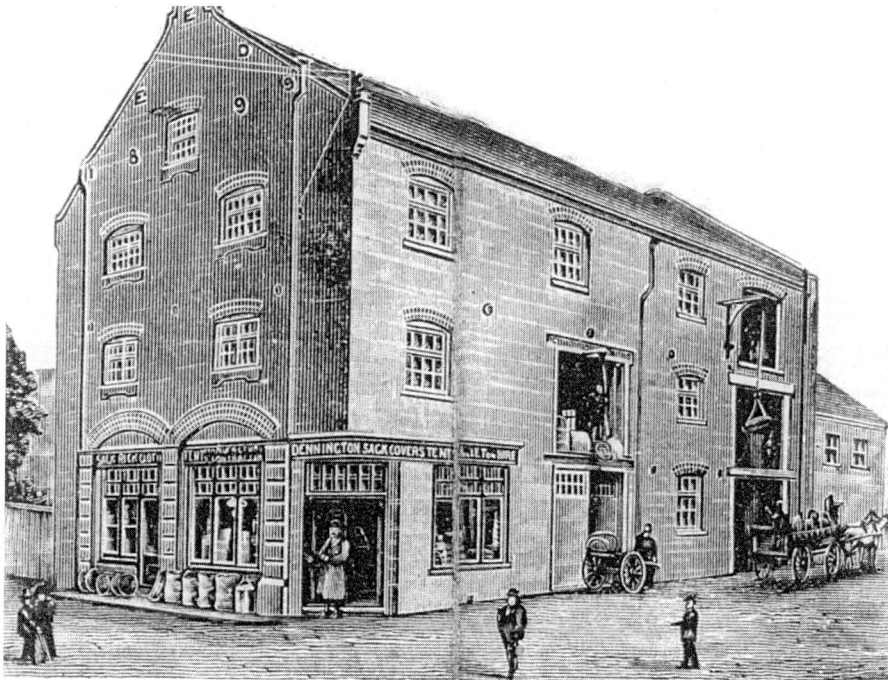

Engraving of Dennington's factory and warehouse as built in 1899

Dennington, Ernest *Manufacturer* 1862-1927

A length of brick wall between numbers 2 and 3 London Road, Halesworth, is all that is left of the Dennington sack factory. Many older local people will remember the devastating fire which destroyed a building which had once housed a thriving local industry.

Rope and sack making was an old-established trade in Halesworth; hemp was extensively grown and processed in the surrounding area until the early 19th century. As far back as 1654 there is a baptism in the parish registers - Anne, daughter of Thomas Curby, ropemaker; in 1659 John Kirby, roper, buried his wife. Later there were ropemakers and twine spinners living in Chediston Street, but the Peachey family in Pound Street (now London Road) were the founders of the business, later to become Dennington's, in the premises now a fish and chip shop.

David Peachey was a cordspinner in 1827. In *Whites Directory* of 1844, J.Peachey is listed as "shopkeeper, rope and sack manufacturer" in Pound Street. J.Peachey may in fact be Robert Peachey who in the 1841 Census was aged 35, ropemaker and head of the family, with his wife Sarah, son Robert aged 9, and three daughters, all in Pound Street. By 1851 Robert (noted as born in Beccles)

149

Dennington & Co.

(1910) Ltd.

Sack, Rick Cloth and Tent Makers,

HALESWORTH.

Advertisement for Dennington & Co., early 20th century

was a widower; his son Robert the younger was a "Journeyman Ropemaker", also born in Beccles. The ropewalk was presumably on the line of Swan Lane, then known as Honeypot Lane. An invoice, listing items dating from May to July 1852 shows Robert Peachey carrying out work on the bell ropes in the church tower for the churchwardens.

By 1871, Robert had died and his second wife Catherine, although a dressmaker by trade, had taken over the business and was still running it in 1881. Shortly after this the Dennington family took over.

In 1881 Robert Dennington had an outfitters business not far from Halesworth in Wrentham, where the present village store now stands. His son Ernest Edward, then aged 19 years and unmarried, was a shopman. By 1882 Ernest had moved into Halesworth to the late Peachey premises and was described as "waterproofer and dealer in rope and twine etc". Still in Pound Street in 1891 he is described as "sack and tent maker"; he had married Emily and had a family of two sons and two daughters. Ernest's business grew and diversified - "oil, colour and grease merchant", "sack and rick cover maker" - and eventually flag, tarpaulin, wagon cloth and tent making were added to the range of manufactures.

So well did the business prosper, that in 1899 a new commodious building was erected, opposite the church and on the site of a barn belonging to Dairy Farm [see illustration]. Designed by Arthur Pells, architect, of Beccles, and built by Woodyard Brothers of Halesworth, it cost £696 to build. A full report and description of the building appeared in the *North Suffolk Advertiser* of 6th April 1900. The ground floor was divided between offices at the front and heavy storage behind; the first floor displayed sacks, bales and tarpaulins and above this the sackmakers sat at "powerful Singer sewing machines" and names were stamped on the sacks and tarpaulins.Within the open roof space tents and marquees were dried off before being stored away, the process assisted by heating stoves. The different levels had a central trapdoor with a crane for hoisting heavy bundles, and the rooms all had speaking tubes to the offices and stores. Further diversification included the hire of flags and marquees to the Suffolk Agricultural Association, horticultural shows and Halesworth Horse Show amongst many others.

Regular advertisements appeared in the local papers [see illustration]. In 1901 machinery oil, leather, cotton and india rubber beltings had been added to the stock. 11th August 1903 carried an advertisement which stated at the foot "Factory Halesworth; Ropeworks Southwold; Branch at Wrentham". Southwold ropeworks were behind Station Road; the Wrentham branch was presumably in his father's shop.

On 13th June 1905 the Suffolk Show was held at Chediston Park, just outside Halesworth. Denningtons provided all the tents, canvas and marquees; their stock was "taxed to the utmost". The town of Halesworth was decorated, and Chediston Street was choked with traffic - not for the first or last time. Alas, the weather was unfavourable.

In 1910 the business became a Limited Company of which Ernest Dennington was the Managing Director. In addition to local contracts, goods were sent all over the country and exports went as far as South Africa. Two sons, Ernest Robert and Herbert, went into the business, cycling to markets for orders in the early days.

By 1900 the senior Denningtons had moved to a select residence - "The Laurels" in Rectory Lane, off Chediston Street, and by this time the family had been increased by the addition of two more sons. As well as being ardent supporters and regular worshippers at the Independent Chapel in Quay Street, Ernest the elder served on the Urban District Council. After his death in 1927, Ernest the younger donated "The Laurels" to the Chapel in memory of his parents.

The firm played its part in the 1939-45 war effort, making amongst other items camouflaged toilet tents. After the war times became increasingly difficult and in 1949 the business closed. Herbert Dennington told the *Halesworth Times* reporter on 28th September: "My chief reason is due to mechanisation of the farm. New corn sacks... are being replaced by hired sacks from the corn merchants. Binder twine is giving way to baler twine. The combines and balers are doing away with stack covers, and lorries have replaced waggons".

The late Mr Wilfred Ransby of Halesworth remembered the factory; he had worked for them while apprenticed in the late 1920's to Fred Wright, a local builder, whose yard was on Holton Road opposite the present Fire Station. In the winter they made tent and wall poles and floordecking panels - these were made in a large store and workshop in Chediston Street where Bouchain Court housing now stands. In the summer they helped erect the marquees; by this date no ropes were made at Dennington's, all were bought in. They helped to instal an extra attic floor for tent drying, also an electric hoist inside the outer doors to serve all three floors.

After closure, the premises were bought by Alston's Capacitors. The building burnt down on 28th October 1955; the cause of the fire was unknown.

Sources

Census returns / H.P.R. / I.R.O. / Mr D.Dennington / Newby (1936) / Brown, Haward & Kindred

Rugby, Lord *Colonial Governor* 1877-1969

For a few years in the mid-20th century Halesworth had a resident peer - probably the only one in the town's long history. The first Baron Rugby was John Loader Maffey, born in Rugby on 1st July 1877, son of Thomas Maffey (1842-1917) and his wife Penelope née Loader. He was educated at Rugby School and Christchurch College, Oxford, and entered the Indian Civil Service in 1899. In 1907 he married Dorothy Huggins of Buxted, Sussex.

Back in India he became Political Agent at the Khyber Pass from 1909 to 1912, Deputy Commissioner at Peshawar 1914 to 1915, Private Secretary to the Viceroy from 1916 to 1920, and Chief Commissioner, North West Frontier province from 1921 to 1924. Then came, presumably after some well-earned home leave, his highest colonial appointment as Governor-General of the Sudan from 1926 to 1933.

Having spent more than thirty years in various colonial hot-spots he returned home to spend four years as Permanent Under-Secretary of State in the Colonial Office. His last official appointment was as UK representative in Eire, where he was highly praised for his handling of the sensitive matter of Irish neutrality during the Second World War. He was awarded his peerage in 1947.

The Rugbys had one daughter - Penelope - who in 1938 married William Traven Aitken (1905-64), a nephew of Lord Beaverbrook. He served as a pilot in the Battle of Britain, became MP for Bury St Edmund's, and was knighted in 1963. The Aitkens lived at Magnolia House, then called The Firs, in Station Road, Halesworth, from 1947 to 1960, then moved to Playford Hall, near Ipswich, where Sir William died in 1964. They had two children, Jonathan and Maria.

Lord Rugby, having retired from his Dublin posting, moved with Lady Rugby to Halesworth, presumably to be near their only child, and lived at Quay House [see **Langslow, Richard**], the serpentine-fronted house adjoining the Quay, with a garden running down to the river and a private footbridge leading to a meadow opposite, now part of the Town Park. Lord Rugby died, aged ninety-two, on the 20th April 1969, and Lady Rugby in February 1973.

Sources

D.N.B. / *Who Was Who 1961-1970* / *Burke's Peerage* / Magnolia House deeds (Mrs H. Turner)

'Sir John Maffey, later Lord Rugby' Portrait by P.A. de Laszlo

Appendix 1. Lords of the Manor of Halesworth

Aluric ? - 1066
Earl Hugh Lupus c1086
Thomas de Halesworth c1130
?Richard de Argentein 1133
Reginald de Argentein 1197
Richard de Argentein 1223
Sir Giles de Argentein 1246
Reginald de Argentein 1283
John de Argentein 1307
Sir John de Argentein 1318
(Agnes Argentein and Adam Payn)
Sir John de Argentein 1375
Sir William de Argentein 1383
John Argentein 1418
Joan Allington and Elizabeth Allington 1423
John Allington 1459
John Allington 1480
William Allington 1485
Sir Giles Allington 1505
Sir Giles Allington 1586
Sir Giles Allington 1613
Sir William Allington 1638
William, Lord Allington 1642
Elizabeth, Lady Allington 1651
William Allington 1664
Diana, Lady Allington 1684
William Betts 1706
Dorothea Betts 1711
Thomas Betts 1736
Walter Plumer 1739
William Plumer 1745
William Plumer 1768
Jane Plumer 1822
Robert Plumer Ward 1831
John Cutts 1833
John Crabtree 1844
Miss Mary and Miss Fanny Crabtree 1870 to 1890

Sources

Suckling / C.S.P. / H.M.C.R. / Cross, Ram

Note: Dame Margery's Manor went with the main Manor. Rectory Manor was held by the Rector.

Appendix 2. The Argentein Manors and holdings

Listed in alphabetical order of Counties:

Bedfordshire:
- Chederton
- Elstow Priory
- Meppershall
- Ridgemont
- St Neot's Priory
- Sharnbrook Mill

Buckinghamshire:
- Ashendon

Cambridgeshire:
- Chishull Magna and Parva
- Melbourne
- Meldreth
- St Benet's church, Cambridge (advowson)
- Sutton

Essex:
- Bergholt Sakeville
- Fordham
- St Osyth
- Steeple Bumstead
- Wethermundeforde

Hertfordshire:
- Graveley
- Mentmore
- Royston - Chapel of Sts John and James
  - Leper hospital of St Nicholas
- Throkking
- Wandlington
- Weston
- Wymondley, Great and Little and Priory

Huntingdonshire:
- Colne
- Pidley

Norfolk:
- Ketteringham
- Little Melton
- Wiveton

Oxfordshire:
- Chalgrove

Suffolk:
- Acton
- Cratfield
- Gisleham

Halesworth
Kessingland
Newmarket
Rumburgh
Sotterley
Spexhall
Wissett

Surrey: Copthorne
                             Leatherhead

Sussex: Mundham

Wiltshire: Cheldrington

Appendix 3. List of Rectors of Halesworth

Rector	Date	Patron
Ulf the Priest	1086	
Roger de Halewrda	1273	
Richard Pyrot	1306	
Adam de Stanham	1308	John de Argentein
John de Ashton	1334	Edm. de Berford rac. cus
William de Trollesbury	1338	John fil et her John de Argentein
John Skencard	1371	John de Argentein
William Bachelor	1393	William Argentein miles
John Bredford	1400	id
William Hardy	1408	John de Heveningham miles
John Clement		
Walter Annable	1463	
Edward Lohton	1465	John Alyngton, arm.
Henry Boleyn	1471	id
James Hutton	1479	id
Radulphus Hyde	1490	William Chene, arm et Eliz. ux.
William Woderowe	1505	
Leonard Middleton		
Richard Henrison	1519	

Robert Woode	1532	Egidius Alyngton, miles
Robert Sturgis	(1559)	
Lucas Taylor	1564	id
John Argall	1580	id
Abdias Ashton	1606	id
James Ashton	1616	id
John Swayne		
Samuel Jones	1671	William Compton miles
Thomas Shortrudge	1690	Diana, Lady Allington
		Baroness Wymondley
John Beck	1722	Dorothea Betts
Thomas Anguish	1723	ead.
Isaac Collman	1736	Thomas Betts Esq.
Thomas Forster	1746/7	W. Plumer Esq.
Isaac Avarne	1786	id
William Cross	1820	id
Richard Whately	1822	Jane Plumer, widow
Joseph Badeley	1831	Robert Plumer Ward Esq.
Augustus Fred. Phipps	1835	id
Joseph Charles Badeley	1839	Elizabeth Badeley
R.E. Hankinson	1850	Sir T. Fowell Buxton Bart.
Vincent J. Stanton	1863	id.
Abbot Roland Upcher	1889	The Bishop of Norwich
Arthur Crompton Moore	1913	id.

Sources

Suckling / Lambert, F.C. (Records of Halesworth) / Lists of Suffolk Clergy S.R.O.I. S.283.

Index of Names

Bold numerals indicate main biographies

Allington Family 12
8, 19, 22, 27, 31, 37

Appleton, Robert 116
70, 126

Anguish, Thomas 48
38, 41, 51

Argall, John 21
12, 29

Annable, Walter 18
13, 14

Argentein Family 8
10, 12, 31, 37, 146

Assheton, James 25

Baas, Robert 95
40, 90

Babington, Francis 144

Badeley Family 45
54, 61, 62, 82, 107, 126, 129

Bedingfield Family 34
31, 33, 139

Betts, William 37
13, 40, 48, 57

Browne, John 23
135

Burleigh, Robert 142
112, 146

Canova, Peter 120
61, 96

Cary, William 32

Clement, Thomas 14
19

Crabtree, Robert and John 84
50, 51, 57, 58, 73, 78, 79,
101, 122, 137, 143

Cross, Frederick 143
50, 85, 129

Cufaude, John 73

Dennant, John 74
81, 96, 123, 130

Dennington, Ernest 149
138

Dresser and Day Families 58
50, 72, 122, 134, 139

D'Urban, Sir Benjamin 88
40, 55, 62, 66

Easterson, Thomas 93

Everard, John 19

Fawether, Samuel 31

Feltham, Thomas 24
29

Forster, Thomas 53
46, 52, 101

Garveys, Robert 11

George, Thompson 139
59, 123, 137

Gilbert, Wilkinson John 136

Hankinson, Robert 124
130, 135, 147

Harvey, Joseph 122
72, 76, 136, 139

Hooker, Sir W. J. and Sir J.D. 101
44, 54, 62, 108, 111

Hugman, John 80
76, 97, 105, 123

Ingham Family 27
79

Jermyn Family 49
41, 54, 55, 58, 76, 77,
78, 82, 85, 92, 98,105

Johnston, Andrew 127
105, 109, 126, 146

Kirby, John 41

Langslow, Richard 65
60, 71,

Lansbury, George...............................146
126

Lone, Roger 39

Moore, Philip..23

Norford, William 55
40, 90

Norton Family 15
20, 24, 34, 73 139

Packard, Harrison 98
71, 87

Payn, Adam...10

Pedgrift Family....................................118

Phipps, Augustus.............................141
46, 57

Plumer Family 57
28, 95, 113, 141

Popson, Thomas.................................20

Pullyn, Peter 39
50, 55, 90

Robinson, Francis 69
64, 76

Rugby, Lord 152
70

Saltonstall and Base Families 29
96

Stead, Patrick.....................................109
101, 108, 139, 142

Suggate, George 60
67, 120, 134

Tanqueray, Thomas 71
21, 65, 98, 122

Tippell, Thomas...................................96
76, 81

Turner, James 106
46, 62, 101, 111, 129

Turner, Samuel Blois.........................134
24, 59, 60, 106, 126, 145

Tuthill, Sir George Leman 82
46, 50, 77, 79, 85, 92, 138

Upcher, Abbot 145

Whately, Richard................................113
57

White, Robert Gostlin.........................77
40, 65, 73, 84, 87, 90, 95,
106, 119

Wilkinson, John 104
51, 72, 130, 138

Woodcock, John 61
40, 45, 61, 69, 79, 90,
101, 105, 107